The God of Mount Carmel:
Contending views about the deity associated with the Biblical Mount Carmel

If you can make one heap of all your winnings
And risk it on one turn of pitch-and-toss,
And lose, and start again at your beginnings,
And never breathe a word about your loss;
You'll be a Man my son! **Rudyard Kipling**

Dr. Samson N'Taadjèl **KAGMATCHÉ**, (Ph.D)

The God of Mount Carmel:
Contending views about the deity associated with
the
Biblical Mount Carmel

© Guérin Scholar's Press

Cover images
-Baal Shamin © Institut Suisse de Rome
-Baal Haddad © ULg
-Baal-Melqart © Aleppo Museum

For the same author

- *Étude comparative entre les Lamaasu et les chérubins bibliques,* © L'Harmattan, Paris, 2011.
- *The Lamassu and the Cherubim: Two Hybrid genii.* How did the Cherubim become Angels? © Guérin Scholar's Press, Montreal, 2017.

© **Guérin Scholar's Press**, 2017
435 rue St-Roch, CP: H3N 1K2; Montreal,
Canada
www.guerinscholarspress.com
info@guerinscholarspress.com
e- ISBN: 978-0-9958987-3-8

All rights reserved. No part of this book may be reprinted or reproduced or utilized in any from or by any electronic, mechanical, or other means without permission in writing from the publisher.

The God of Mount Carmel:
Contending views about the deity associated with the Biblical Mount Carmel

By

Dr. Samson N'Taadjèl KAGMATCHÉ

ACKOWLEDGEMENTS

Foremost, I would like to express my sincere gratitude to my supervisor Professor Dr William Domeris for the continuous support for my Ph.D. study and research, for his patience and motivation. His guidance helped me in all the time of research and writing this thesis. I cannot imagine having had a better supervisor and mentor for my Ph.D. study.
Besides my supervisor, I would like to thank Dr Janvier Rugira for his encouragement and for everything. Many thanks to Mrs Leschenne Rebuli and the rest of the committee of South African Theological Seminary.
My sincere thanks also go to my son Mikhaël Woumbor-Lidjome KAGMATCHÉ for the important role you played in saving my Ph.D. manuscript. May our Lord Jesus Bless you.
I would like to express my special and thanks to my principal reader Ms. Jennifer De Bruyn for suggestions, corrections, and comments. I thank my friend Dr Ionut Aurelian Marinescu of the University of Strasbourg (France) for his help and encouragement during my Ph.D. study. My thanks also go to my friend Daniel Joaquim, professor at United Seminary of Ricatla, Maputo, Mozambique. I would like to express my thanks to my professor of Old Testament of University of Strasbourg Dr Régine Hunziker-Rodewald. My thanks go to my professors of Akkadian, and Near Easten History and Civilizations, Dr Alice Mouton and Dr Daniel Bodi, of University of Strasbourg, France. Special thanks to my family. Words cannot express how grateful I am to my

father, brothers Woumborati, Josué N'Mani, Jacob, and my younger sister Esther (KAGMATCHÉ) for all of your sacrifices, encouragement and prayers that you've made on my behalf.

Special thanks also go to my friend Étienne Mponabor Djalodo and Benjamin Cerutti for supporting me. I would like to express my thanks to my friends' pastors: Napoli Damigou, Nanlièbe Gédéon Kolani, Odah Gaston Fatotcha, Émile Namessi Nakordja Kombaté and Émmanuel N'Kiboiré. Your prayers supported me during the writing, and encouraged me to strive towards my goal.

Finally, I would like to express my thanks to our and Saviour Lord Jesus for everything. Almighty God, you were always my support in the HARD moments of my life when there was no one to answer my queries and my distress.

Thank you very much Lord Jesus.

ABSTRACT

Baal is the second deity mentioned after YHWH in the Old Testament. This Semitic god has often been in conflict with YHWH in the Old Testament. Most of the time, the Hebrew Bible mentioned only Baal. Therefore, there are many kinds of Baal (Baal Hadad, Baal Melqart, Baal Shamin). In the contest on the Biblical Mount Carmel in 1 Kings 18, YHWH and Baal were invited to prove their power, and send fire which was to come to devour (holacaust) the pieces of bull placed on the altar. The loser in this contest would be the impostor deity. Which Baal among three (Baal Hadad, Baal Melqart, Baal Shamin) was the competitor of YHWH on Mount Carmel? There are many hypotheses from different fields of study (Archaeologists, Historians of Religious Studies, and Specialists of Biblical Studies, (Old Testament). Our motivation in this research is to establish exactly which Baal was in conflict with YHWH on Mount Carmel.

We undertake this work using the HB and the LXX (biblical data) to understand the text of 1Kings 18 and know the Baal invoked in this text. The extra-biblical data studies are: (iconographies, epigraphs, Akkadian, and Ugarit sources) and the research on the nature and functions of the deities (Baal Hadad, Baal Melqart, and Baal Shamin) associated with the Biblical Mount Carmel. All these deities in this research have points in common. They were agrarian deities. They were deities of the atmosphere bringing rain and fertility. These gods were worshipped by their devotees in the old Syro-Palestinian and Ancient Near Eastern societies, according to their role and functions. However, all assumptions and arguments regarding them in this research have their strengths and weaknesses. Let us summarize that finally some evidence of Baal Melqart and some details in 1Kings 18 make a case for the Master of Tyre (Baal Melqart).

CONTENTS

ACKOWLEDGEMENTS 9
ABSTRACT 11
CONTENTS 13
Abbreviations 17

CHAPTER 1: METHODOLOGY 19
   1.1. Design and methodology 19
   1.2. Background study 21
   1.3. Research problem 25
   1.4. Research objectives 25
   1.5. Purpose 26
   1.6. Delimitations 27
   1.7. Methodology 27
   1.8. Overview 30

CHAPTER 2 33
MOUNT CARMEL 33
   2.1. Mount כַּרְמֶל and the etymology of its name 33
   2.2. The Carmel of Judah 35
   2.3. Mount Carmel of the territory of Israel 37
   2.4. Mount Carmel: political control 39
   2.5. Mount Carmel: Elijah's place of choice for confrontation 42
   2.6. Mount Carmel, a mountain god or a deified mountain? 43
   2.7. The high places: בָּמוֹת 45

CHAPTER 3 49
BAAL SHAMEM/BAALSHAMIN 49
   3.1. Baal Shamin: A god with different spellings 49
   3.2. Origin of Baal Shamem/ Baal Shamin 51
      3.2.1. Complex origins 51
      3.2.2. The temple of Baal Shamin at Palmyra 52
      3.2.3. Brief description of the temple 53
   3.3. Epigraphic study of Baal Shamin 54
      3.3.1. The Baal Shamin in the inscriptions of the temple of
      Palmyra 54
      3.3.2. The epigraphic inscriptions of Baal Shamin 57
         3.3.2.a. Egypt 58
         3.3.2.b. Gönze 58
      3.3.3. Aramaic inscriptions of Hatra 59
      3.3.4. Baal Shamêm in other epigraphic inscriptions 59
         3.3.4.a. Byblos 60

3.3.4.b. Karatepe..60
3.3.4.c. Carthage..61
3.3.4.d. Sardinia...61
3.4. Iconography testimonials of Baal Shamin 62
3.4.1. Baal Shamin: The Master of Heaven 62
3.4.2. Other iconography testimonials of Baal Shamin 65
3.4.3. Eagle symbol of Baal Shamin 65
3.4.4. Worship of Baal Shamin at Palmyra: worshipping a foreign God? 73
3.5. Dedication Monuments to Baal Shamin at Palmyra..................74
3.5.1. The cult of Baal Shamin 74
3.5.2. The staff of the cult of Baal Shamin 75
3.5.3. Functions of Baal Shamin 76
   3.5.3.a. Atmospheric, blessings and imprecations 76
   3.5.3.b. Baal Shamin god of security......................................79
   3.5.3.c. Baal Shamin guarantor of treaties..............................79

CHAPTER 4..81
THE BAAL OF MOUNT CARMEL: THE GOD OF STORM?..........81
4.1. The gods of storm: Haddad and Zeus on Mount Carmel..........87
4.2. A seasonal god 88
4.3. Baal a bellicose god..90
4.4. Baal and his weapons 90
4.4.1. The Bellicose character of Baal of storm: its origin in mythology..96
4.4.2. The Storm-God: god with political outlook.......................97
4.5. Death and resurrection of the Storm-god...............................98
4.5.1. Death and Resurrection: Myth worship or seasonality god? 99
   4.5.1.a. The first hypothesis focuses on the seasonality of the myth..100
   4.5.1.b. Second hypothesis: the ritual interpretation...............101
   4.5.1.c. The third view is a cosmogony 101
   4.5.1.d. The fourth view - life versus Death 102
   4.5.1.e. The fifth view - interpretation of Baal's kingship......102
4.5.2. Baal and Mot 106
4.5.3. The death of Baal: A limit of its glory 107
4.5.4. The mourning of Baal 109
4.6. Ritual and worship...110
4.6.1. Burial and funeral rites of Baal.....................................110
4.6.2. Royal Funeral Ceremony KTU 1.161 or RS. 34.126........111
4.6.3. Worship Staff of Baal and prophecy..............................116
4.6.4. Comparative table of mythic ritual and royal burial ritual 119
4.6.5. Resurrection of Baal 124

4.6.6. Iconographical representations of the Storm-god 125
4.6.7. Preliminary conclusion 142

CHAPTER 5 145
BAAL MELQART: GOD OF MOUNT CARMEL? 145
5.1. Brief study on the context of the pericope 147
5.2. The structure of the text 1 Kings 18:1-46 148
5.3. Questions and difficulties of the text 150
   5.3.1. The beginning of Elijah's mission 152
   5.3.2. Dialogue between Elijah and Obadiah 154
   5.3.3. The fear of Obadiah 156
   5.3.4. Observations and critical analysis 160
   5.3.5. Elijah the order giver 160
5.4. The courage of Elijah in front of Ahab, 1 Kings 18:17-20 163
   5.4.1. Table of comparison between MT and LXX 168
   5.4.2. The ordeal on Mount Carmel 171
   5.4.3. The healing of the altar (v. 30bMT) = (v. 32bLXX) 172
   5.4.4. Variants between the MT and the LXX of vv.31-39 177
   5.4.5. Context and theological implications 180
5.5. Irony of the Prophet Elijah or reality of the god? 184
   5.5.1. The sacred dance of the Baal prophets 184
   5.5.2. Baal worries, he is travelling 190
   5.5.3. Baal sleeps 192

CHAPTER 6 195
THE NATURE AND FUNCTIONS OF BAAL MELQART 195
6.1. Melqart: Religious ideology and geostrategy 195
6.2. Nature and iconography of Melqart 198
6.3. Melqart god of good fortune and guarantor of treaties 202
6.4. Melqart and the rite of egersis 204
   6.4.1. The date of the ceremony of Melqart's egersis 204
   6.4.2. The ceremony 209
   6.4.3. The material evidence of Melqart's resurrection 213
   6.4.4. The Ceremony of the egersis: A Palliative to the Weaknesses of Melqart 215
   6.4.5. The Resurrector of Melqart 216
6.5. The ritual of deity Baal Melqart 219
   6.5.1. The animals of the Melqart's ritual 219
   6.5.2. A Substitute in Melqart's Place 220
   6.5.3. The God of the Fire 221

SYNTHESIS 223
Synthesis 1 227
The strengths and weaknesses of the first hypothesis 227

Synthesis 2 231
The Strengths and weaknesses of the Second hypothesis 231
Synthesis 3 241
The Strengths and the Weaknesses of the third hypothesis 241

CHAPTER 7 249
CONCLUSION 249
    7.1. Baal: YHWH'S Competitor in the OT 250
    7.2. Which Baal in conflict with YHWH in the Ordeal of Mount
    Carmel? 251
        7.2.1. The historical context 252
        7.2.2. The Ordeal elements 253
        7.3. Final view 256
Index 257

TABLE OF ILLUSTRATIONS 261
    Chronological Division for the Ancient Near East 264

BIBLIOGRAPHY 265

Abbreviations

- **A A A** Annals of Archaeology and Anthropology, Liverpool University Press, 1908-
- **A B D** Anchor Bible Dictionary (6 volumes; ed. D.N. Freedman et al.), Doubleday, New-York, 1992
- **Ant.** Jewish Antiquities by Josephus
- **Apn.** Against Apion
- **ANEP** Ancient Near Eastern Pictures Relating to the Old Testament, (ed. James Pritchard), Princeton
- **ANET** Ancient Near Eastern Texts Relating to Old Testament,(ed. James Pritchard),Princeton
- **AOAT** Alter Orient und Altes Testament, Neukirchener Verlag/Neukirchen-Vluyn
- **BASOR** Bulletin of the American Schools of Oriental Research
- **B M B** Bulletin du Musée de Beyrouth
- **BWL** Babaylonian Wisdom Literature, (ed.) by Wilfred G. Lambert,Eisenbrauns, Indiana, 1996
- **C H** Codex Hammurabi
- **C I S** Corpus Inscriptionum Semiticarum, Paris
- **CRAIBL** Comptes Rendus de l'Académie des Inscriptions et Belles Lettres, Paris
- **D D D** Dictionary of Deities and Demons in the Bible, E.J. Brill, Leiden.New-York.Köln
- **EA** Tell el Amarna Tablets
- **I E J** Israel Exploration Journal, Jerusalem
- **IG** G. Kaibel (ed), Inscription Graecae, XIV, Berlin, 1890.
- **Illus.** Illustration
- **IRAQ** British School of Archaeology
- **JBL** Journal of Biblical Literature
- **JCS** Journal of Cuneiform Studies
- **JHS** Journalof Hebrew Studies
- **JNES** Journal of Near Eastem Studies
- **JPOS** Journal of Palestine Oriental Society
- **JRAS** Journal of the Royal Asiatic Society
- **JSOT** Journal for the Study of the Old Testament
- **JTL** Journal Theological Literature
- **K A I** Kanaaäische und Aramäsche Inschriften. Mit einem Beitrag von O.Rössler Band I : Texts, Band II, Kommentar, Band III : Glossare (ed. Donner

	Herbert, Röllig Wolfgang), Indizen, Tafeln, Zweite, durchgesehence und ervweiterte Auflage, O. Horrassowitz, Wiesbaden
KTU	*The Cuneiform Alphabetic Texts from Ugaritic, Ras Ibn Hani and Other Places (KTU)*
LXX	*Septante*
LXX ᴬ	*Codex Alexandrinus*
LXX ᴮ	*Codex Vaticanus*
LXX ᴸ	*Text antiochien*
LXX ˢ	*Codex Sinaiticus*
OABA	*The Oxford Annoted Bible with the Apocrypha*
OBO	*Obis Biblicus et Orientalis*
RA	*Revue d'Assyriologie et d'Archéologie Orientale*
RAI	*Rencontre Assyriologique Internationale*, A. Finet (éd.)
RIM	*Royal Inscriptions of Mesopotamia*
SAA	*State Archives of Assyria*
SJOT	*Scandinavian Journal of Old Testament*, University of Aarbus
SPUMB	J. C. de Moor, *The Seasonal Patern in the Ugaritic Myth of Ba'lu*, AOAT 16, 1971
Studies Robins on	*Studies in Old Testament Prophecy, Presented by T.H Robinson*
SVT	*Suplements Vetus Testamentum*
SYRIA	*Revue d'art oriental et d'archéologie*, Paris
UF	*Ugarit Forschungen* Neukirchener Verlag/Neukirchen-Vluyn
UGARITICA	*Ugaritica*, Librairie Orientaliste de Paul Geuthier, Paris
VT	*Vetus Testamentum*
NA	*Neo-Assyrian*
OB	*Old Babylonian*
ZAW	*Zeitschrift für die alttestamentliche Wissenschaft*

CHAPTER 1: METHODOLOGY

1.1. Design and methodology

The biblical text (1 Kings 18:1-46) tells us the story of the confrontation that took place on Mount Carmel between Elijah, the prophet of YHWH and the prophets of Baal. On the same mountain, the Israelite archeologist, Avi-Yonah discovered in 1952 a Greek inscription dating from the IInd - IIIrd century AD dedicated to Zeus.[1] Tacitus argues that Vespasian, in 69 AD, before his appointment as the emperor, climbed up Mount Carmel in order to offer sacrifices to the god found there. In his statement Vespasian says:

> Est Iudaeam inter Syriamque Carmelus: ita vocant montem deumque. Nec simulacrum deo aut templum sic traditere maiores: ara tantum et reuerentia. Illic sacrificanti Vespasiano, cum spes occultas uersaret animo, Basilides sacerdos.[2]

A translation reads:

> „Between Judea and Syria there is a mountain called Carmel, which is also the mountain of a god, there is no statue or temple to be found there,... just an altar and a cult... officiated by the priest Basilides".

In view of this evidence, we are obliged to believe that Mount Carmel has been the scene of a large number of religious episodes throughout history. Moreover, this makes us wonder about the identity, the nature, and the function of the true god of Mount Carmel. Moreover, this leads us to ask the following question, was Mount Carmel the place of worship for more than one divinity?

---

[1] AVI-YONAH, 1952, pp. 118-124.
[2] TACITUS, Hist. II, 78:3.

Furthermore, it is important to note that there are two Carmels. One is located in the south of Judah territory. This Carmel has the same name as the city situated at its base (Josh 12:22; 15:55; 1 Sam 15:12; 27: 3; 2 Sam 2:2), (Pritchard, 1990: 118). Miller and Hayes[3], state that the Mount Carmel of Judah reaches a height of 803 m. The other Carmel is a mountain found in the northern part of Israel and has formed a frontier between the Phoenician Kingdom and the territory of Israel. This northern Mount Carmel marks the Israelite border and overlooks the Mediterranean Sea. It pinpoints the north-western part of the triangular mountain chain measuring 20 km long and reaching a peak of 550 m.[4] According to Giordano[5], the Carmel in the Holy Land, was 25 km long and had a width of 6 km. The mountain was full of caves, and could retain water, thereby guaranteeing long-lasting access to water. In the Bible, Mount Carmel is mostly evoked for its luxurious vegetation and fertility (Isa 35:2) and for its pastures (Jer 50:9). The Mount Carmel stands as the most visible point in the region[6]. It rises from above Haifa Bay.[7] According to Vischer, it refers to "Carmel" meaning "orchard", defined by the richness of its fruit trees.[8] Today we can contemplate the stark summit of Mount Carmel against a deep blue sky, an image of fearsome solitude. It seems, however, that in ancient times Mount Carmel was completely covered by magnificent foliage. This is the mountain which is of interest to us in our research because it is here that the confrontation between Elijah and the prophets of Baal took place in 1 Kings 18.

---

[3] MILLER and HAYES, 1934, pp. 138; 165.
[4] BEAUDRY, 1987, p. 235.
[5] GIORDANO, 1995, p. 13.
[6] VISCHER, 1951, p. 421.
[7] BREUIL, 1945, p. 75.
[8] VISCHER, 1951, p. 421.

1.2. Background study

Considering the fact that the biblical text seems to be silent on the topic, we wonder who the divinity was that was worshipped on Mount Carmel. The God Baal for certain, but which one? We are not sure about the actual divinity worshipped on Mount Carmel. There are many hypotheses. Is it Baal Melqart the patron of Tyre? Or maybe it is Baal Adad, the Storm-god? Or even Baal Shamin, the master of the skies?

Is Mount Carmel simply a mountain god or a deified mountain?

According to the first hypothesis[9] the god that dwells on Mount Carmel is the master of the skies, namely, Baal Shamin.

Katzenstein[10] has demonstrated the diplomatic relationship between the Phoenician and Israelite empires which yielded the introduction of the Phoenician gods in Israel. These diplomatic relationships were strengthened by the dynastic-diplomatic marriage of King Ahab and Jezebel, the daughter of the Phoenician king Ethobaal. He suggests that Baal, whose altar was established in Samaria (1 Kings 16:32-33), is in fact Melqart, and that 1 Kings 18 evokes Baal Shamin. For him, the use of בְּעָלִים (v. 18) explains the existence of these two different divinities. Baal Melqart was worshipped in Samaria and Baal Shamin on Mount Carmel[11].

Keel and Uehlinger,[12] explain that the Baal with whom Elijah had a contest in 1 Kings 18 was Baal

---

[9] KATZENSTEIN, 1991, pp. 187-191; KEEL and UEHLINGER, 2001, p. 257.
[10] KATZENSTEIN, 1991, pp. 87-191.
[11] KATZENSTEIN, 1991, p. 188.
[12] KEEL AND UEHLINGER, 2001, p. 257.

Shamin or Baal Shamem. During the ninth and eighth centuries, discussions were held about "the lord of the sky" attested to for the first time in Byblos during the tenth century[13]. He was responsible for the rain, but his greatness and sovereignty were best reflected by his solar and celestial powers. A similar episode of the same context (1 Kgs 18) took place during a one-year drought when Ethobaal was the king of Tyre and Sidon. Ethobaal was a contemporary of, and father-in-law to, King Ahab of Israel[14]. During the period of great droughts, Phoenicians used to reach towards the sky entreatingly calling for the sovereign of the sky by the name of Beelsamen, which is the Greek Zeus, (Eusebius of Caesarea)[15]. So, these are different reasons put forward by these authors in order to support their own positions about the real description of the god of Mount Carmel (Melqart or the Storm-god or Baal Shamin).

The second hypothesis is supported by three authors[16], who believe that the god of Mount Carmel is Adad. According to Briquel-Chatonnet[17] the presentation of the "pyre" is not as in the "pyre" of Melqart. In the Carmel ordeal, the sacrifice is a holocaust and the entire bull must be consumed. If the ritual was performed to stop the drought, then this means that the ceremony of Mount Carmel cannot be the ceremony of *egersis* of Melqart. The "fire" which must fall from heaven and the sacrifice on Mount Carmel were performed in order to cause it to rain and bring fertility. The choice of place (Mount Carmel) is the traditional location of the cult of the Storm-

---

[13] EISSFELDT, 1939, pp. 1-3.
[14] ANT. J. VIII: 324.
[15] P.Ev. 1:6-8.
[16] AVI-YONAH, 1952, pp. 118-124; BRIQUEL-CHATONNET, 1992, pp. 303-313; LIPINSKI, 1995B, pp. 284-288.
[17] BRIQUEL-CHATONNET, 1992, pp. 308-309.

god[18]. Lipinski[19] based his interpretation of the series of coins of Akko-Ptomais produced during the reign of Antiochus IV Epiphanes (175-164 BC).[20] On these coins, the Hellenic god Zeus was represented. He was represented as a god who tends the crown, and was symbolized by the eagle standing on lightning, holding on his shoulder an ear of wheat. This is the symbol of the Storm-god or sky-god (the god Adad) worshipped on Mount Carmel. This god was associated or identified with Jupiter Heliopolis, Zeus of Baalbeck[21]. A Greek inscription discovered in 1952 by Avi-Yonah[22], dating from the second to third century AD, dedicated to Zeus, confirms that the Baal worship at Mount Carmel was of the storm-god. The theophany of Zeus, a storm-god known as "Lord of rain and thunder, was located on prominent mountains"[23]. He says:

> "For without the evidence of our inscription, there are many indications that the Ba'al of the Carmel was Adad: the sacrifice of bull, the invocation WnnEë[] l[;B;äh; with the article, i.e. addressed to the Ba'al par excellence; the fact that the whole proceedings were arranged on a mountain; the purpose, i.e. prayer for rain, which was to restore the fertility of the barren land; the fire (lightning), which fell from heaven... We have therefore to deal with a god of fertility, bulls, mountain, rain and lightning in short, with Adad. We conclude therefore that the Ba'al of the Carmel was identical with Adad, the 'Lord of Heaven', the great god of the Syrian and the Phoenicians, whose all-embracing worship was in the ninth century BC. a serious menace to the God of Israel".[24]

---

[18] BRIQUEL-CHATONNET, 1992, pp. 311-312.
[19] LIPINSKI, 1995b, pp. 286-287.
[20] SEYRIG, 1962, pp. 194-195.
[21] LIPINSKI, 1995b, pp. 286-287.
[22] AVI-YONAH, 1952, pp. 118-124.
[23] AVI-YONAH, 1952, pp. 121.
[24] AVI-YONAH, 1952, p. 124.

The third hypothesis is supported by a number of authors[25]. The latter author, the scholar Ribichini[26], did not put forward his position, but only presented the hypotheses of the first two. They identify Baal of Mount Carmel with Melqart, the patron of Tyre. There are many reasons behind this hypothesis. The first reason is the diplomatic marriage between Ahab and Jezebel the daughter of the Sidonian king Ethobaal, (1 Kgs 16:31).[27] It is by Jezebel that the cult of Baal of Melqart was introduced in Israel. Her husband Ahab adopted this divinity and built its temple.[28] According to Bonnet,[29] the ritual dance of the prophets of Baal (1 Kings 18:26) was linked to the dance of the devotees of Melqart, and the mockery of Elijah saying that "Surely he is a god! Perhaps he is deep in thought, busy, or travelling. Maybe he is sleeping and must be awakened" (1 Kgs 18:27) referred to Melqart as the deity of the Phoenician merchants and sailors, ensuring their protection in crossing the seas (thus the busy activity or travelling of Baal); that 'he must be awakened' was referring to the rising of Melqart.

Epigraphic, archaeological and classical records prove also that Melqart had a remarkable role in the religious ideology of the commercial expansion of Tyrians westward throughout the Mediterranean world, and that his cult was very popular in all Phoenician colonies, from Cyprus to Malta, from Carthage to the whole of North Africa, from Sardinia to Iberia.[30] Dussaud[31] added that the 'fire' in the

---

[25] BONNET, 1988, pp.136-144; DUSSAUD, 1948, pp. 205-230; De VAUX, 1941, pp. 7-20; RIBICHINI, 1999, pp. 563-565.
[26] RIBICHINI, 1999, pp. 563-565.
[27] BONNET, 1988, p.137; De VAUX, 1941, p. 8.
[28] DUSSAUD, 1948, p. 209; BONNET, 1988, p. 137.
[29] BONNET, 1988, p. 141.
[30] RIBICHINI, 1999, p. 564.
[31] DUSSAUD, 1948, p. 209.

biblical text was compared to the "fire" in the ceremony of the *egersis* of Melqart. The "fire" in 1Kings 18:23-25 which must come to devour the pieces of bull placed on the altar was compared to the burning at the pyre of Melqart. De Vaux[32] points out "the Tyrians had given to their god some features of their own character. They had imagined this god industrious and a trader like themselves, and that is enough to explain the word of Elijah" (1 Kgs 18:27).

1.3. Research problem

Given these three hypotheses about the god of Mount Carmel, it is important to explore why many scholars have not come to an agreement concerning the Baal of Mount Carmel. What elements are highlighted by each author in relation to the biblical text of 1 Kings 18:1-46? What are the reasons for and elements of their various studies that have proven the god of Mount Carmel to be this or that Baal? The works of many scholars who have identified Mount Carmel with various Baals, set the reader on a path of contradictory assumptions rather than setting out a solution to the identity and nature of the god of Mount Carmel. Instead of getting lost in all these assumptions, we hope our research has provided viable solutions to the identity, nature, and function of the god of Mount Carmel: among the Baals, which Baal?

1.4. Research objectives

The aim of our research is to identify the god of Mount Carmel, its nature and its functions. To achieve this goal, we are obliged to examine all three

---

[32] De VAUX, 1941, p. 15.

hypotheses. We must also study the identity, nature and function of each god Baal mentioned in each case as the god of Mount Carmel. Since all this research is related to the biblical text 1 Kings 18, we will analyse this text exegetically in order to better understand the factors that have led previous scholars to work with their particular assumptions. Our aim is to make explicit in the same work all the assumptions of the previous studies, and to present a new study of the god of Mount Carmel which includes contending views about the deity associated with the biblical Mount Carmel. Another objective is to contribute to the enrichment of various disciplines, such as Old Testament History, Ancient Israel Religions and Near Eastern Religions and Archaeology, as well as the scholars who work within these disciplines.

1.5. Purpose

The fact that several points of view from archaeology, history of the Ancient Near East, and the study of the Old Testament diverge in regard to the biblical text of 1 Kings 18:1-46 has aroused in us the desire to make a single search in which all existing interpretations are included. This research will distil all the previous studies of or interpretations about the god of Mount Carmel. It will help scholars of biblical studies, particularly of the Old Testament, Near Eastern studies, as well as pastors, to understand the biblical text of 1 Kings 18:1-46 with the new views. Thus, we will present all the various views of the previous studies, so that the readers of our work can better understand the confrontation between Elijah and the prophets of Baal on Mount Carmel, and why Elijah used irony, mocking the prophets of Baal in 1 Kings 18:26-27.

1.6. Delimitations

We will limit the geographical region of our work. Since several deities, coming from several and different regions, are all referred to as Baal of Mount Carmel, we need to specify the regions which the research will cover. These regions are natural choices given the cities or kingdoms from which Baal Melqart, Baal Adad or Baal Shamin came. Baal Melqart came from Phoenicia, Baal Adad from Syria and Baal Shamin from Pamyra, an 'oasis in the Syrian desert passage between the Phoenician coast and the Euphrates.[33] Above all, the focus of all the interpretations of the identity of this Baal is centred on Mount Carmel, which is located in the northern part of Israel, and forms the coastal border between the Kingdoms of Israel and Phoenicia. The geographical delimitation brings us to the delimitation of the period covered by this research from 1000 BC to AD 300. Epigraphic inscriptions, archaeological evidence, and biblical texts used will all come from this time range.

We will make a critical analysis of the entire chapter of 1 Kings 18 to understand the whole message of this biblical text. Finally, the verses 1Kings 18:20-46 of this chapter will be carefully analysed, because they represent the focal point for all interpretations, and the three hypotheses are mostly based on these verses, especially verses 1Kings 18: 26-27.

1.7. Methodology

This research falls into the category of literary research, but given the hybrid nature of the data from various disciplines (history, archaeology of the ancient

---

[33] GAWLKOWSKI, 1992, p. 136.

Near East and Old Testament), we are required to use the various research methods of these disciplines. With regard to the Old Testament, our research will be based on textual criticism and the appropriate exegetical methods for 1 Kings 18. Concerning the exegesis of this text, we will aim to bring out elements pertinent to the solution of the problem of this study. We will verify whether the text of the LXX (Septuagint) and BHS (Biblica Hebraica Stuttgartensia) show some differences concerning 1 Kings 18. We will also do a structural analysis based on these two sources. Perhaps the variation can provide a better understanding and interpretation of this text. In terms of the exegetical method, firstly we will focus on the historical criticism of the text to explore the historical dimensions of the text. Secondly, we will focus on redaction criticism to explore the theological message of 1 Kings 18:20-46. All interpretations of Baal of Mount Carmel focus particularly on this passage (1 Kings 18:26-27).

The fragments of Hebrew Bible text from Qumran (Attride A. et al., 1996) can provide as a contribution some information about the history of 1 Kings 18, enriching the understanding of the attitude or quality of some of the characters of some of the persons mentioned in the text.

We have other resources for this research in other languages, namely Greek[34] and Akkadian.[35] We also have epigraphic inscriptions in Aramaic,[36] and twenty epigraphic inscriptions of Baal Shamin in Palmyra (n° 1A; 1B; 3; 7; 10; 11; 12; 13; 14; 18; 19; 20; 21; 23; 24; 35; 40; 41; 44A 44B; 45A and 25B).[37]

---

[34] AVI-YONAH, 1952, pp. 118-124.
[35] DUNAND, 1993, pp. 44-45; 2002, pp. 14-15.
[36] DONNER and WOLFANG, 1966; 1968 et 1969.
[37] DUNANT, 1971, pp.1ff.

All these sources have a connection with the three deities of our dissertation. The study of these sources can help us to know more about their (deities) nature, characters and functions. We will compare this epigraphic study to the biblical text of 1 Kings 18:1-46. All of this will be done in light of the other contending views about the deity of Mount Carmel.

For this research, it would have been helpful to have some knowledge of the Ugaritic language, but because of the importance of our dissertation proposal we have not given up on the project. Not having this ability, we have decided to rely on some translated works about Baal Adad in English and French from Ugaritic sources. Akkadian is another source that will be important in this research. Two tablets in cuneiform (Akkadian) will also be studied. For most word-definitions and grammar in this language, we will use:

✓ Bodi (2001), *Petite grammaire de l'akkadien à l'usage des débutants.*

✓ Black, George and Postgate (2000), *A Concise Dictionary of Akkadian.*

✓ Labat and Malbran-Labat (1994), *Manuel d'Epigraphie Akkadienne.*

✓ Oppenheim, (1964-2006). *The Assyrian Dictionaries.*

In archaeology, we will rely on iconographical study of the different forms of representations of the gods Baal Shamin, Baal Adad, and Baal Melqart. Each iconographic representation hides the exact nature, attribute, or character of the deity. This study may help us to identify the function of each deity. Epigraphic studies will be conducted to determine the nature and functions of the three gods of our dissertation. It will play an important role in our research because of the inscriptions on stones, buildings, or monuments mentioned, for example, of the god Baal Shamin. It will also help us to discover the historical, religious, and especially political context of these epigraphic inscriptions and the roles played by the deity, or provide any other information about the god mentioned.

1.8. Overview

Since we have three deities as the possible hypotheses for the god of Mount Carmel, we will organize our research into three parts with five chapters. In the first part of the dissertation, the focus will be on the initial hypothesis, supporting the belief that the deity of Mount Carmel is Baal Melqart. The second part will look at the possibility that the divinity is in fact the Storm-god, the master of fertility and rain. Our research aims to analyse the characteristics of each divinity together with the cultic elements surrounding his worship. In the third and last part we will work on the hypothesis supporting the conviction that the Baal of Carmel was after all בַּעֲלְשָׁמַיִם Baal Shamin „the master of the skies". A study of twenty epigraphic texts coming from the temple of Palmyra, and some other twelve epigraphic texts extracted from the work of Donner and Wolfgang[38] (1966; 1968; 1969) will help us understand what the other functions undertaken by the divinity Baal Shamin were.

Afterwards we will refer to the temple of Baal Shamin in Palmyra. We will see how he (Baal Shamin) managed to cross Phoenicia in order to get to Syria. We will study the elements that constituted the cult of the divinity in order to understand his role for his worshippers. Our research will take into consideration both extra-biblical (archaeological,

---

[38] DONNER and WOLFGANG, 1966; 1968; 1969.

historical, epigraphic) and biblical data. As a result of the consideration given to all these hypotheses, we will be able to deliver a synthesis which will eventually lead us to a conclusion containing our personal point of view concerning the identity of the divinity worshipped on Mount Carmel. At the end of our research, we will present our position. We have in this PhD theisis several illutrations (39), all of them have their sources cited but all the 5 diagrams are mine. We made diagrams to compare original languages (MT and LXX,). In another case, we have Ugaritic source and its translation.

CHAPTER 2

MOUNT CARMEL

2.1. Mount כַּרְמֶל and the etymology of its name

Before we begin our research about the meaning of Carmel, it is important to note that we have two Carmels. The word *Carmel* appears in many texts of the Old Testament and it has different meanings. The word Carmel means "orchard", "cultivated field", or "garden of fruit trees" and "vine" (Isa 10:18; 16:10; Jer 4:26; 48:33; 2 Chr 26:10): וּכְבוֹד יַעְרוֹ וְכַרְמִלּוֹ "and the splendour of its forest and fertile fields" (Isa. 10:18); מִן־הַכַּרְמֶל וּבַכְּרָמִים "from orchard and in the vineyards' (Isa 16:10); רָאִיתִי וְהִנֵּה הַכַּרְמֶל הַמִּדְבָּר 'I looked and the fruitful land was a desert" (Jer 4:26); מְכַרְמֶל וּמֵאֶרֶץ "from orchards and fields" (Jer 48:33). This last text is not in the LXX. It can also mean plantation of trees, or fruitful land in general: יַעַר כַּרְמִלּוֹ "its forests" (2 Kings 19:23 and Isa 37:24); אֶרֶץ הַכַּרְמֶל "the land of garden" (Jer 2:7). Carmel also means "new grain" גֶּרֶשׂ כַּרְמֶל or the "Fresh ears" (of cereal), "The fresh ears from a garden" (Lev 2:14; 23:14; 2 Kgs 4:42). It is also a place (Josh 12:22; 19:16; Isa 33:9; 35:2; Amos 1:2; 9:3): הַר הַכַּרְמֶל 'the mountain of *Carmel*' (1 Kgs 18:19, 20; 2 Kgs 2:25; 4:25); רֹאשׁ הַכַּרְמֶל "head" or "the top of *Carmel*" (1 Kgs 18:42; Amos 1:2 and 9:3); הֲדַר הַכַּרְמֶל

"the glory" or "the splendour" of Mount Carmel (Isa 35:2).

We can conclude that sometimes "Carmel" can refer to a "mountain" or an "orchard". We must be careful when we read the biblical text to determine which meaning is in use. In Isaiah 29:17; 32:15-16 the word is mentioned twice. The LXX sometimes speaks clearly of Mount Carmel: τὸ ὄρος τὸ Χερμελ (1 Sam 29:17). However, Jeremiah 2:7, 4:26, and 48:33 also refer to Mount Carmel. אֶרֶץ הַכַּרְמֶל is usually translated "fruitful land". Although the context mentions the fruits and good things of the land of Israel, and the semantic nuance of 'orchard' would be quite appropriate, it is not entirely out of the question that Carmel stands as a synecdoche for all Israel. The verse would then allude to the fertility of the Mount Carmel region in particular, and to the land in general. A similar usage appears in Jeremiah 4:26: וְכָל־עָרָיו נִתְּצוּ הַכַּרְמֶל הַמִּדְבָּר, "the fruitful land/orchard was a desert and all its cities were laid in ruins…" Orchards can turn into deserts; this meaning agrees with the visions of chaos.[39] The word כַּרְמֶל does not share a root with any Semitic languages. We only have *karānu* in Akkadian which means "vine" (CAD/k: 203, *karānu* 1a), "grape vine" or "grapes": GIŠ.GEŠTIN[40] *in panātūa ṣaḫat* "the grapes were pressed in my presence."[41] In the tablet 149 of ARMT, 13 (149: 3-5) one servant *la-wi-llâ* writes to his lord about a *karānu* "vine."
umma la-wi-llâ {ma} Said la-wi-llâ
warka-ka-a-ma aš-šum ka-ra-nim Your servant. About the vine
ša Na-ga-bi-ni-ya (ki) Of Nagabiteans.

---

[39] MUDLER, 1995, 330.
[40] GIŠ.GEŠTIN is the Sumerian synonym of *karānu*.
[41] CT 22 38, p. 39; CAD/ K, *karānu* 2a and 3, pp. 205-206.

2.2. The Carmel of Judah

The toponym *Carmel* appears in: Josh 15: 55; 1 Sam 15: 12; 27:3; 2 Sam 2:2; 25:2. It is a city in the tribe of Caleb located about 12 kilometres southeast of Hebron between Negev and Gilgal. Carmel is a city in the territory of Judah.[42] This city was called by the name of Mount Carmel on which it was built. Among the kings defeated by Joshua in the conquest of Canaan there appeared Johanan the king of the city of Carmel (Josh 12:22). Saul erected a monument or victory stele to mark his triumph over the Amalekites at Carmel of Judah, claiming his authority over the city of Carmel and the surrounding areas (see 1 Sam 15:12). David found refuge in Carmel with his band of men to escape the wrath of king Saul (1 Sam 25). Nabal lived in Maon and sheared his sheep in Carmel (1 Sam 25:2-8). At the altitude of this Mount Carmel (803 m) barley is sown in the spring, but still harvested all year.[43]

---

[42] PRITCHARD, 1990, p. 118.
[43] HEIDET, 1912, p. 228.

Illus.1. Geographical position of Carmel of Judah which belongs to the tribe of Caleb (Aharoni and Avi-Yonah, 1991:50, fig. 68).

Aharoni and Avi-Yonah,[44] write Carmel of Judah with "K" to make difference between Carmel and the Carmel of Judah. Other scholars do not use this orthography.

---

[44] AHARONI and AVI-YONAH, 1990, p. 50, fig. 68.

2.3. Mount Carmel of the territory of Israel

This mountain ridge has an altitude of about 550 m.[45] This Mount Carmel is smaller than the one in Judah. Mount Carmel has been on a shifting border, sometimes belonging to Israel, and sometimes to Phoenicia. The Mount Carmel has been conventionally attributed to Phoenicia and the Phoenicians around the first millennium BC. Mulder acknowledges that Mount Carmel was a fluctuating borderland, but this idea differs from one author to another according to the periods.[46]

The borders of Phoenicia underwent changes over the centuries, but in general, its southern border would be limited to Carmel.[47] In 677 BC, at the time of Sennacherib, the kingdom of Tyre extended to Akko, including its traditional boundary of Carmel. [48] During the reign of David (1040-970 BC), the Israelites took possession of Mount Carmel and established worship to the Lord (1 Kgs 18:30). From the coast of Joppa to Mount Carmel was under the control of King David.[49] In the tenth century BC, king Hiram of Tyre had very good relations with David and Solomon, kings of Israel. We have 20 cities given by Solomon to Hiram king of Tyre (1 Kgs 9:11 b-14; 2 Chr 8:2). Then, Mount Carmel was under the control of the Phoenician kingdom after the reign of David.[50]

---

[45] MUDLER, 1995, 330.
[46] BONNET, 1988, p. 4; LIPINSKI, 1995, p. 23; BRIQUEL-CHATONNET, 1992, p. 201.
[47] LIPINSKI, 1995, p. 23.
[48] BRIQUEL-CHATONNET, 1992, p. 201.
[49] RHYMER, 1985, p. 74.
[50] ALT, 1935, pp. 137; 147; NOCQUET, 2004, p. 138.

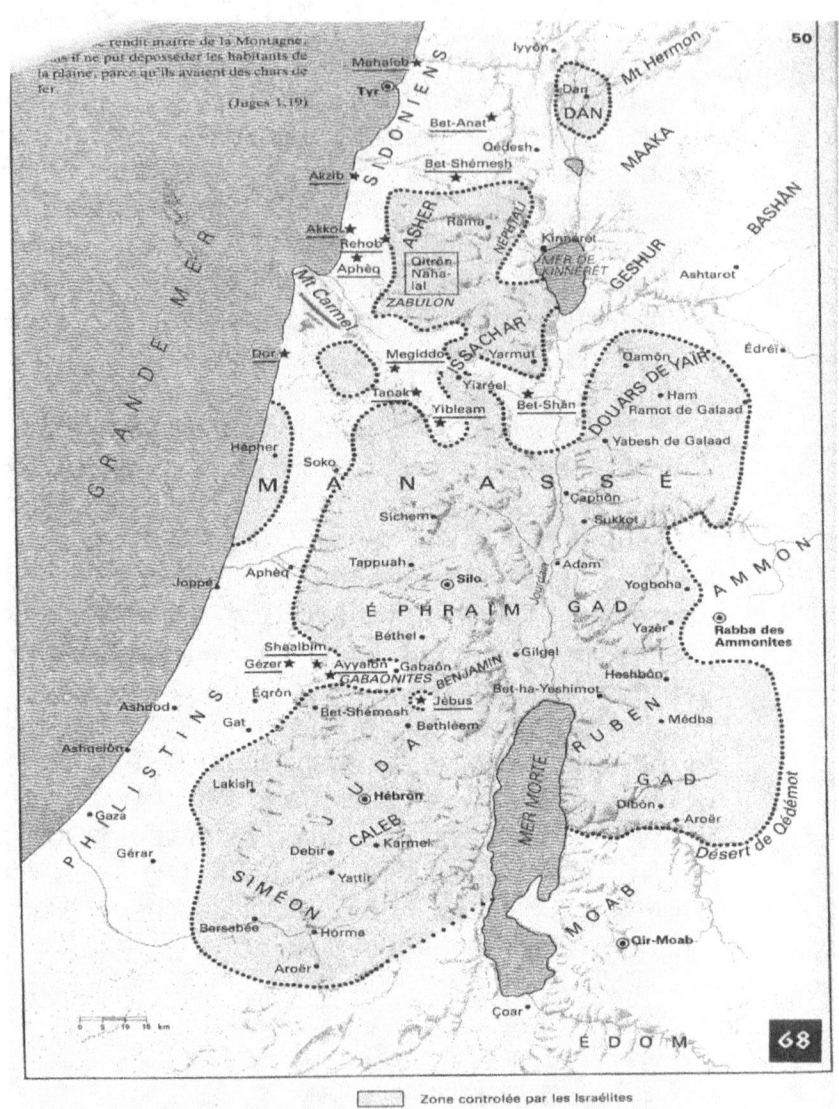

Illus. 2. Geographical position of Mount Carmel in the 12th century BC. At this time Mount Carmel belonged to Phoenicia (Aharoni and Avi-Yonah, 1991:50, fig. 68).

2.4. Mount Carmel: political control

This mountain is among the list of cities conquered by Thutmose III in 1468 BC, and had the label of a sacred mountain, or the name *"Rash-Qadesh"* meaning *"Holy Head, Sacred Cape."*[51] In 1270 BC, at the time of Pharaoh Ramses II, a track, called the road of Horus, that started from the south of Carmel was used by the armies of the king of Egypt to march on Syria and Palestine. In their campaigns, Assyrian-Babylonian kings and Syrians would naturally be interested in using it as well.[52] In the Papyrus Anastasi I from the reign of Rameses II (thirteenth century BC), some hills and rivers are mentioned. For example, Mount *w-š-r* in Egyptian, meaning "strong, mighty", could refer to Mount Carmel.[53] Mount Carmel was known by the Egyptian sailors from ancient times.[54] In 734 BC, Tiglath-Pilazer III, at the head of his army, was preparing an attack against Philistia. However, the essential road was Israel's coastal region, south of Mount Carmel.[55] The Biblical Mount Carmel was a strategic and economic crossroads. Agricultural products of the northern regions of Israel were exported by land and would pass along this road past Mount Carmel, as did products of the neighbouring countries.[56]

The Phoenicians and the Israelites had already competed over Mount Carmel. This conflict extended to the gods of these peoples. Mount Carmel would later be at the centre of a controversy between the two nations. On this mountain Elijah, the defender of *YHWH*, challenged the prophets of Baal.

---

[51] ANET, 1969, p. 243.
[52] AHLTROM, 1993, p. 68.
[53] AHARONI, 1962, p. 111.
[54] AHARONI, 1962, p. 99.
[55] WISEMAN, 1956, p. 126.
[56] RHYMER, 1985, p. 16.

The goal of this challenge was not to establish the property rights of Mount Carmel, but to determine which of the two gods was more powerful or authentic: YHWH or Baal? The result was a contest. The response of one of the two gods to his disciples proved that the opposite god was the impostor. Therefore, the two parties decisively separated.

This scene took place during the reign of King Ahab (874-853 BC) who was linked to Phoenicia by a diplomatic-dynastic marriage.[57] In his work Contenau,[58] underlines that Ithobaal, a zealot of his religion, married his daughter Jezebel to Ahab the monarch of Israel. It is here that the cult of Yahweh would be replaced by the cult of the Phoenician gods. The daughter of the first lady of the empire, Athalia, married Joram, king of Judah, and managed to introduce, like her mother, the religion of her country in Judah. Moret,[59] evokes this story of Ethobaal and Ahab, and gives the same information as Contenau, but he argues that Ethobaal had usurped the throne (887-856 BC) and that he was a priest of Astarte. The marriage with the daughter of Ethobaal, Jezebel, might have seemed ordinary and simple. As a result of the ill-fated liaison, according to the Bible, Baal became Israelite and Israel became profoundly attached to the divinity of Baal. The Bible mentions that the monarch Ahab built an altar in Samaria (1 Kgs 16:31-32). Josephus Flavius puts into perspective the perverse character of Jezebel, and ascribes to her the introduction of the cult of Baal in Samaria.[60] In order to win the appreciation of his stepfather, Ethobaal, the king of Tyre and Sidon created a sanctuary of Baal in

---

[57] BRIQUEL-CHATONNET, 1992, p. 297.
[58] CONTENAU, 1926, p. 73.
[59] MORET, 1929, p. 612.
[60] ANT. J. VIII: 316-318; RUSAK, 2008, p. 31.

Samaria and honoured it with a full cult.[61] According to this information, the first lady of the Israelite kingdom would, therefore, be responsible for having *'Baalised'* Samaria. Such an affirmation may be considered as somewhat categorical in the eyes of a historian who does not possess substantial facts regarding the exact role played by queen Jezebel in the introduction of Tyre Baal in the Samarian kingdom, and her deadly action against the prophets of YHWH (1 Kgs 18: 40). Even if the biblical author presents the portrait of the queen in a tendentious way, she should not be held solely responsible, as the author, himself, affirms: "through Jezebel Israel has sinned". King Ahab shared a part of the guilt in his position as a political authority. In the spirit of this shared responsibility, we can assume that the heart of king Ahab had religiously run off the rails because of the love he had for Queen Jezebel, as well as for diplomatic reasons.

The marriage took place in a context of troubled international relations. Israel felt threatened by its neighbors, Syria and Assyria. Omri, Ahab's father, regarded as undesirable the position of vassal to the Syrian power. In his plan of rebellion against Syria, he arranged the marriage of his son Ahab with Jezebel. This alliance would constitute a backbone of support, and aimed to secure the kingdom of Israel, not only against Damascus, but also against the Assyrian power led by King Assurbanipal (884-859 BC).[62] The relations between Israel and Sidon, (or Tyre), were sustained by economical interests dating from the Iron Age II (1000-800 BC). The Phoenicians had been industrially and economically prosperous. Therefore, they offered technical and artisanal competencies to

---

[61] ANT. J. IX: 138
[62] WISEMAN, 1980, pp. 126-145.

Israel, and in return Israel exported its agricultural goods to Phoenicia (1 Kgs 9:11-19; Ezek 37:17).[63] Rusak also explains that the dynasty of the Omrides had made Israel flourish through the alliances and relations established with its neighbours.[64] These relations ended up profoundly influencing the people of Israel. As a result, commercial exchanges were established between the two kingdoms.

2.5. Mount Carmel: Elijah's place of choice for confrontation

Mount Carmel, where the challenge of Elijah to the prophets of Baal was setting the stage for confrontation, was once covered with pines, oaks, myrtles, and laurels. Because of this vegetation, the place earned the name "Orchard". Carmel is also the most visible place in the country.[65] Before the drought, Mount Carmel offered great beauty. But at the time of the confrontation between Elijah and the prophets, after a dry period of three years, it inspired little more than apathy under the weight of the curse of drought. Apparently, the altars to Baal and Asherah stood in leafless bush. On one of the high points there was also an altar to *Yahweh,* albeit in ruins (1 Kings 18:30). It is obvious that Elijah chose instead to display the power of God and avenge the honour of his name אֵלִיָּהוּ "my God is YHWH". It is therefore no coincidence that Elijah chose Mount Carmel for this event.[66]

---

[63] RUSAK, 2008, p. 35.
[64] RUSAK, 2008, p. 36.
[65] VISCHER, 1951, p. 421.
[66] VISCHER, 1951, p. 421.

2.6. Mount Carmel, a mountain god or a deified mountain?

Given some of the information we have now established concerning Mount Carmel, we ask the following question: was Mount Carmel a deified mountain or would it be a mountain in which dwelt a god? The worship of mountains was widespread among the Semites; for example, Baal of Lebanon, Baal of Hermon, Zeus of Casios among others. The mountain, we might say, was the preference of some deities. Mount Carmel was a holy mountain already in the middle of the second millennium known as *Rosh Qadosh*, "Sacred Cape."[67] According to Shalmaneser III's annals, in 841 BC the king of Assyria erected a stele by the sea upon the mountain named in Akkadian *Ba'li-ra'ši*, "Baal of Cape", where he received tribute from Tyre and Sidon and from Jehu the Israelite.[68]

Many historians of the Ancient Near East and biblical scholars have identified the mountain of *Ba'li-ra'ši* with Mount Carmel.[69] Pseudo-Scylax of Caryanda, in the fourth century BC, called this Mount Carmel: Κάρμηλος ὄρος ἱερὸν Διός "the holy mountain of Zeus."[70] He described Mount Carmel as belonging to the Phoenician territory. Josephus Flavius qualified Mount Carmel as the "mountain of the Tyrians."[71] Iamblichus, the Neo-Platonic philosopher (ca AD 250-325) informs us about the solitary, meditative sojourn of Pythagoras on this Mount Carmel. He named it

---

[67] ANET, 1969, p. 243.
[68] RIMA III, Textt, AO. 102.10:54, L. 8-9.
[69] OLMSTEAD, 1921, pp. 355-382; AHARONI, 1967, p. 310; LIPINSKI, 2004, p. 2.
[70] PERIPLUS § 104; LIPINSKI, 2004, pp. 268-289.
[71] THE JEWISH WAR III, 3,1 § 36; LEEMING and LEEMING, 2003, pp. 332-333.

"the highest peak of the Carmel"; "the holiest of all mountains, regarded as inaccessible to common people."[72]

There was an oft-fluctuating border with respect to Mount Carmel. Sometimes the mountain belonged to the kingdom of Tyre, and at other times to the kingdom of Israel. From the extra-biblical data, it would be difficult to say with accuracy that this mountain was a deified mountain. We endorse the view that Mount Carmel is located among the high places worshipped by the Canaanites. Canaanites worshipped the mountains because their peaks were closer to the sky or because the peak of a mountain is nearest to the residence of the gods, but also because "mountains were traversed by divine energy."[73]

"The mountain itself imposes an image of power, greatness, strength, verticality, and physical domination, evoking a sense of moral domination. It seems immutable and eternal."[74] If Semites preferred to place their sanctuaries on the top of the mountains or hills, it is not that these places were conducive to contemplation, but that they believed in the tangible presence of gods or spirits there. This could explain why the servants of Ben-Adad, king of Aram, when they were defeated by the Israelite army, said to him: "Their God is a God of the mountains" (1 Kgs 20:23).

Mountains were places that had captivated, including the Canaanites; we could say that the worship of mountains was sacred and legendary to the peoples of West and East, North and South. Men have peopled the mountains with gods and demons for different reasons. Men always had a fascination for

---

[72] De Vita Pythagorae, III: 15.
[73] ROUX, 1999, p. 107.
[74] ROUX, 1999, p. 29.

the mountains. According to Theotokos "the notion of the sacred mountain is an idea which is found in all traditions."[75]

The most everyday language expresses unambiguously that what is higher is superior to what is lower. Social rising corresponded to spiritual elevation.[76] The Bible is full of examples that explain this trend. It is the idea of a walk or to approach the one who sits in the hills, who has a spiritual elevation or relief; "I lift up my eyes to the hills where does my help come from?" (Psa 121:1); Elijah went to the God of Mount Horeb (1 Kgs 19:8); "Come, let us go up to the mountain of the Lord" (Isa 2:3); "Who may ascend the hill of the Lord?" (Psa 24:2); The sacrifice of Isaac took place on the mountain (Gen 22:1-2); "Blow the trumpet in Zion; sound the alarm on my holy hill" (Joel 2:1); "To the Lord I cry aloud, and he answers me from his holy hill" (Psa 3:4); "Those who were perishing in Assyria and those who were exiled in Egypt will come and worship the Lord on the holy mountain in Jerusalem" (Isa 27:13); "Our Father in heaven" (Matt 6:9). The most remarkable phenomenon is to see a huge number of mountains, which became the places where various religions built their shrines and monasteries.[77]

2.7. The high places: בָּמוֹת

The "high place" is a translation of Heb. בָּמָה, sing., and pl. בָּמוֹת. Ugaritic is *bmh* singular, and plural *bmt*.[78] Usually this word, "high place, platform", refers to a site of worship, and also "hill or mountain", for

---

[75] THEOTOKOS, 1969, p. 8.
[76] ROUX, 1999, p. 27.
[77] ROUX, 1999, p. 30.
[78] HOFFIJZER and JONGELING, 1995, p. 167; KAI, 18:3.

example Numbers 21:28.⁷⁹ The word בָּמָה is a term primarily referring to an "ordinary place chosen as a holy place because it was considered to be closer to the gods."⁸⁰ It could be applied to "a knoll, a hill, a summit and so on…" It was usually a piece of higher land. We have another meaning of בָּמָה: The cognate word in Akkadian means "back", "centre of the body" of the animal, but also "ridge", "high place in territory."⁸¹ The word בָּמָה also refers to the back of a man (Deut 33:29).The texts that talk about בָּמוֹת (1 Kgs 11:7; 14:23; Jer 19:5; 2 Kgs 23:8) indicate that the high places were often mounds of ground artificially made higher for reasons of cult.⁸² There was always an altar (2 Kgs 21:3; 2 Chr 14:2; Ezek 6:6) and other elements of accessory as the מַצֵּבָה (Gen 28:18; 2 Kgs 3:2), or imposing rocks, in order to symbolize the presence of the divinity. There were also אֲשֵׁרָה or other sacred plants protecting the altar against direct sunlight (Deut 16:21; Jud 6:25-30).⁸³ The term אֲשֵׁרָה "could be a live tree (Mic 5:13-14)"⁸⁴ This high place had its priests or masters of worship, בַּעֲלֵי בָמוֹת "masters of high places", (Num 21:28), כֹּהֲנֵי הַבָּמוֹת "priests of high places" (1 Kgs 12:32; 2 Kgs 17:32). Therefore, the term בָּמוֹת could refer just as well to a Canaanite sanctuary or a sanctuary dedicated to Yahweh (1 Sam 9:12; 1 Kgs 3:4). We can cite the most common and known sanctuaries for the Hebrews in their conquest at Gilgal (Josh 9:6, 10:6-7; 1 Sam 10:1-8; Bethel: Judg 20:18; 1 Sam 10:1-4; Mitspa: Judg 20:1-2; Shilo: 1 Sam 1:1-3; Josh 18:1-3,

---

[79] DAVIES and ROGERSON, 1995, p. 184.
[80] LIPINSKI, 2002, p. 576.
[81] SCHUNK, 1975, 140.
[82] LIPINSKI, 2002, p. 576.
[83] LIPINSKI, 2002, p. 576.
[84] SCHUNK, 1975, p. 142.

19:51). After the conquest of Canaan, and when the cult was centralized in the temple as a legitimate cult of *Yahweh*, the high places were declared illegal. The prophet Hosea named "high places" בָּמוֹת אָוֶן "high places of iniquity", (Hos 10:8). But the new system of adoration centred only in one place did not stop the proliferation of בָּמוֹת in Israel (1 Kgs 3:1-3), "for centuries High places and foreign gods continued to champion the *Yahweh* religion."[85] After the schism, the Northern Kingdom would become influenced by unfaithful monarchs and priests. They shifted their religious practice to paganism with the cults of Baals and Asherahs even though Judah's kingdom had not spread. Once more we are forced to conclude that the high places were situated mostly on high lands, though later they would be built in valleys or inside cities (Jer 7:31, 32:35; 2 Kgs 17:9; Ezek 16:24).

---

[85] SCHUNK, 1975, p. 144.

CHAPTER 3

BAAL SHAMEM/BAALSHAMIN

This last chapter will not be another exhibition or excavation of the Palmyrene temple of Baal Shamin. The goal here is to show the different functions and nature of the deity Baal Shamin. We will focus in this chapter on the ritual, iconography and epigraphy surrounding the Baal Shamin. This last part of our research will help us to form the synthesis and conclusion.

3.1. Baal Shamin: A god with different spellings

Baal Shamem or Baal Shamin means the "master of heaven". There are several spellings referring to the god Baal Shamin, depending on the region where he was worshipped. In one of the Nabateans text, we have B'LŠN (Baal Shamin).[86] However, B'ŠMN, is another Nabatean spelling of Baal Shamin.[87] Stracky said that the habitual Nabatean pronunciation was: [Ba'aššemîn].[88] In the

---

[86] STRACKY, 1953, p. 44.
[87] CIS II, 176; STRACKY, 1953, p. 44.
[88] STRACKY, 1953, p. 44.

Palmyrean, we have B'LŠN.[89] In addition, a Phoenician epigraphic inscription was found at Sardegna (Sardinia) with: B'ŠMM.[90] which means Baal Shamem. The name Baal Samay is found in Safaitic references, (Rycmans, n.d: 355). In Aramaic the name is Baal shamyn, and in Akkadian, ^{d}Ba-sa-me-me. However, that name is far from being the name of one god, but rather the name that was applied in the second millennium to several supreme deities of the Syro-Palestinian pantheon, or Sumerian-Akkadian Anatolia. In the first millennium that name was imposed on a specific god. Given the multiplicity of spellings, we will use the spelling "Baal Shamin" throughout this text, except when discussing the thoughts of a particular author.

---

[89] CIS II, 3912; 3959; STRACKY, 1953, p. 44.
[90] CIS I, 139; STRACKY, 1953, p. 44; BONNET, 1992, p. 61.

3.2. Origin of Baal Shamem/ Baal Shamin

3.2.1. Complex origins

The origin of Baal Shamin remains rather controversial. For Lagrange, (1905:88) the Baal of heaven is both Canaanite and Aramaic. This dual nationality of the divinity complicates their study. At the time of Esarhaddon[91] King of Assyria (680-669 BC), the divinity Baal Shamin was considered Phoenician. In the inscriptions of Palmyra, this "Lord of Heaven" played the role of supreme god. The deity Baal Shamin is a foreign god. The tribe Benê-Ma'azîn, introduce Baal Shamin to the Palmyrians in the second century. This god was known to the Canaanites, and was "an avatar of the storm god Adad of the oldest Semitic populations."[92] The god Safaitic Baal Shamin is in the pantheon, and was probably borrowed from the sedentary Horan.[93] In the first millennium, the cult of Baal Shamin had a simplified name of "Baal of heaven" and its worship widespread in Aramaic regions, from the IXth century BC to the third century AD.[94] Acording to Du Mesnil,[95] this deity is known as: $Ζεὺς\ μέγιστος\ κεραύνις$ "Grand Zeus Thunderer" or for Bonnet[96]: $θεὸς\ ἅγιος\ οὐράνιος$ "Holy god heavenly", it is the name of temple in the Phoenician, town Qedeš/Kadasa.[97] Qedeš/Kadasa is located 24 km from the town of Homs (Syria).

---

[91] Esarhaddon: in Akkadian=Aššur-ahhe-iddina, means 'Aššur has given a brother.'
[92] GERARD, 2001, p. 216; STRACKY and GAWLKOWSKI, 1985, p. 97; TEIXIDOR, 1980, p. 278.
[93] RYCMANS, n.d., p. 354.
[94] LIPINSKI, 1985a, p.84.
[95] MESNIL, 1962, p. 313.
[96] BONNET, 1983, p. 61.
[97] RÔLLIG, 1999, p. 150.

The Baal Shamin has been known among the Phoenicians and the Palmyrenes and had a sanctuary at Carthage. The Nabataeans began to worship Baal Shamin when he was identified with their god Un-Tel, great god of heaven.[98] This god was also present in Safaitic, nomadic Arab tribes who had finally settled in Syria. The name of this god is thus either isolated or associated with the name of other deities in the invocations with which many Safaitic graffiti end.[99] In the light of this analysis, one might conclude that a deity Baal Shamin would be adopted after their installation in Syria.[100] How did these Safaitic people come to say that there was a Baal of heaven? The answer seems simple. Certainly, with their own eyes they saw water falling from sky. According to that, they did not hesitate to say that this residence (sky) had its own Baal. It was he who opened the gates of heaven and the rain fell.[101] (Lagrange, 1905:456).

3.2.2. The temple of Baal Shamin at Palmyra

Not only in Pamyra did the god Baal Shamin have a temple. He had temples, and was worshipped at Sia in the Hauran,[102] (south-west of Syria) and in Batanea,[103] or the Hellenized form Bashan (south of Syria), located at the east of Golan.

Temples were erected for the deity Baal Shamin throughout modern-day Turkey, Syria and Israel. One of the most impressive examples that remain can be found in Palmyra (Tadmor) in a northern district of the city. It consists of three courtyards, a sanctuary, a

---

[98] De VAUX, 1965, p. 259.
[99] RYCMANS, n.d., p.354.
[100] RYCMANS, n.d., p. 354.
[101] LAGRANGE, 1905, p. 456.
[102] COLLART and VICARI, 1969, p. 196.
[103] SEYRIG, 1934, p. 95.

banquet hall, and a mass grave.The monument of Palmyra would have preceded the construction of the temple. It dates from twenty-three (23) BC.[104] Its foundation dates back to around the year twenty (20) of our era. The building itself has followed the chronological stages according to many dedications carved on columns or barrel architraves.[105] A study based on this building will be useful to see if we can find some elements of the worship of Baal Shamin.

3.2.3. Brief description of the temple

The temple of Baal Shamin was discovered in Palmyra in the middle of the eighteenth century by Wood and Dawkins, who published their findings in 1753.[106] The shrine buildings of Baal Shamin at Palmyra have retained their original plan to the present day.[107] The oldest inscription (No. 10) of the temenos is dated November 23 AD; it is very possible that it was around AD 20 that the construction of the sanctuary of Baal Shamin was undertaken.[108] An altar was dedicated in AD 62-63 to Baal Shamin and Dourahloun god. The shrine was built step by step, and according to special gifts which followed. This explains the timeline in the construction of the temple. Many dedications carved on the columns reflected this reality. The work of beautifying of the temple was interrupted for a quarter century. It was begun in AD 90 and extended to the mid-second century.[109] The temple was completed between the receipt of the Emperor Hadrian in Palmyra, AD129 and the erection

---

[104] GERARD, 2001, p. 210; TEIXIDOR, 1980, p. 278.
[105] GERARD, 2001, p. 212.
[106] COLLART and VICARI, 1969, p. 11.
[107] COLLART and VICARI, 1969, p. 24.
[108] COLLART and VICARI, 1969, p. 45.
[109] COLLART and VICARI, 1969, pp. 212-213.

of the statue of Malé in AD130/131.[110] The temple is oriented (west-east), and has a rectangular shape (60 m x 160 m).[111] In September AD 67, four porticos in the north courtyard were completed, three of which were dedicated to Baal Shamin with the inscription "good and profitable."[112] The epigraphic and iconograpic studies will allow us to learn more about the nature and functions of this deity Baal Shamin.

3.3. Epigraphic study of Baal Shamin

3.3.1. The Baal Shamin in the inscriptions of the temple of Palmyra

Twenty inscriptions are found in the temple of Baal Shamin (No. 1A, 1B and 3, 7, 10, 11, 12, 13, 14, 18, 19, 20, 21, 23, 24, 35, 40, 41, 44A 44B, 45A, and 25B). In these writings, we will be attentive to their contents to see if they can provide us with additional information on the nature and functions of Baal Shamin.

No. 10 "In the month of Kanoun of the year (November 23), and Attai Shebhai, Shahra daughters, and Atta, daughter of Perdresh, offered two columns to Baal Shamin, good god, for their salvation and the salvation of their son and their brothers."[113]

This inscription is the oldest of the shrine; it would be the reference point for dating the sanctuary.

No. 11 "In the month Tebet of the year (January AD 52), this column has been provided by Amtallat, daughter of Bara, the son of Aténatan, of the children of Mita…., tribe of the Benê-Maziyân to Baal Shamin,

---

[110] COLLART and VICARI, 1969, p. 202.
[111] COLLART and VICARI, 1969, p. 190.
[112] COLLART and VICARI, 1969, p. 212.
[113] DUNANT, 1971, p. 24.

the good God and profitable for their salvation and the salvation of his children and his (or her) brother (s)". Here it is a woman whose husband was a descendant of the tribe of Benê-Maziyân.

No. 1A "This whole portico, columns, entablature and the roof have been donated by Yarka, son of Lishmash son of Raai, ... to Baal Shamin, the god of good and profitable for their salvation and the salvation of his sons and his or her brother (s) in the month of Elul ... September 67."[114] No. 13 "These five columns, their entablature and roof have been donated by the son of Zabadnédo, (son of) Qahzân, the children of Maziyân, to Baal Shamin, the god of good and profitable for their salvation and the salvation of his children and his (or her) brother (s) in the month of Elul ... September 67."[115]

No.14 "These three columns, entablature and their roof have been donated by the son of Alaisha son of Malkou, Asra son of Maziyân to god Baal Shamin and Dourahloun, good gods and paying for her salvation and salvation of his sons and his or her brother (s) in the month of Elul ... September 67." [116]

No. 3 "The whole portico, columns, entablature, and the roof have been donated by Alaisha son of Lish to Baal Shamin, the good god and profitable for his salvation and salvation..."[117]

This entry is incomplete or interrupted. The only information it provides us with are the parties to the dedications, dedicant name, and the name of the deity.

No. 7 "The median whole portico, columns, entablature and the roof have been donated by

---

[114] DUNANT, 1971, p. 14.
[115] DUNANT, 1971, p. 27.
[116] DUNANT, 1971, p. 27.
[117] DUNANT, 1971, p. 17.

Malkou son of Oga, son of Wahbi, son of Bêlhazai from the tribe of Benê-Maziyân to gods Dourahloun, and Baal Shamin good gods and profitable for his salvation and the salvation of his children and his (or her) brother (s) in the month of Elul ... September 90."[118]

No. 44 B "By decree of the senate and people, this statue (is that) of Malé, the son of Yarka, (son of) Lishamsh, (son of) Raai, who as Secretary for the second time when came our Lord the divine Hadrian, provided oil for citizens, foreigners who came with him, took care of everything in his camp, and made the temple, its vestibule and any ornamentation at their own expense for Baal Shamin and Dourahloun.... the of...at 130-131."[119]

In the inscription No. 44, Malé is called Agrippa.[120]

As we can see from the above inscriptions, they all tend to follow the same formula; they start with the party or parties to whom the inscription is dedicated, followed by the name and descent from the tribe or dedicant and divinity, and finally the date. The remaining entries are made in the same manner as those mentioned above. The bulk of dedications and inscriptions are dated the month of September, suggesting this month was meaningful in the worship of Baal Shamin. The repeated mention of the tribe of the children of Maziyân, suggests that this tribe held the highest positions in the administration of the shrine or as priests. A short epitaph, describing the god as one giving salvation, in other words, protector, benefactor, and one who rewards, typically follow the name of the deity. What were the dedicants referring

---

[118] DUNANT, 1971, p. 21.
[119] DUNANT, 1971, p. 56.
[120] DUNANT, 1971, p. 55.

to when they evoked Baal Shamin as the "Master of Heaven" for a "good and profitable" outcome? In all likelihood, they were recalling his cosmic importance, as Baal Shamin refers to an atmospheric and agricultural deity.

3.3.2. The epigraphic inscriptions of Baal Shamin

Inscriptions presented below are in chronological order. They mention the name of the same god in the form of Baal Shamin.

Inscription of Zakkur:[121]

The name of this god is mentioned in the Royal inscription of Zakkur, the king of Hamath and Lu'ath. This inscription is on the stele which was discovered at Afis, 45 km south of Aleppo, and is dated to the early VIIIth century.

> L 2-14: "I am Zakir king of Hamah and Lu'ath. A pious man was I, and Baal Shamin [delivered] me and stood with me; and Baal Shamin made me king in Hadrach. Then BarAdad son of Hazrael, king of Aram, organized against me an alliance of sixteen kings... But I lifted up my hands to Baal Shamin, and Baal Shamin answered me, and Baal Shamin [spoke] to me through seers and messengers; and Baal Shamin [said to me], fear not, because it was I who made you king, and I shall stand with you, and I shall deliver you from all these kings..."

In this inscription, the king Zakkur gives recognition to the god Baal Shamin which lifted the siege of the capital of Hizrak from the coalition of Aramean and Neo-Hittite kings. The brain of the coalition was Bar-Adad King, son of Hazael, king of Damascus. The inscription shows that this god Baal Shamin is a principal god and main patron of the King. Baal Shamin is responsible for protecting the king and the city.

---

[121] KAI 202; ANET, 1969, pp. 501-502.

3.3.2.a. Egypt

KAI 266:2: This inscription was found in Egypt and dated seventh to sixth century BC. There is a correspondence between a prince of the Middle East and the Pharaoh Neko II (609-594) in which Baal Shamin was mentioned asking for help against Babylonian threat.

> (L 1-3): "The Lord of kings, Pharaoh, your slave Adon, the king of ... May Astarte, the mistress of heaven and earth, and the god Baal Shamin always seek salvation for the Lord of kings, Pharaoh and they consolidate the throne of the Lord of kings, the pharaoh as long as heaven lasts! ..."

This letter is a wish to Pharaoh Neko II for a long reign. The gods responsible for bringing this vow are Astarte and Baal Shamin. On the one hand, we can deduce that the function of Baal Shamin here is the function of protection and support. These two deities have been cited as the divine couple in the same function of protection. On the other hand, is it plausible that they were independent deities, but worshipped in the kingdom of this vassal prince, having the same functions? However, nothing here hints at Baal Shamin being in the supreme position.

3.3.2.b. Gönze

KAI 259:3: There is an imprecation on point-Gönze border, 20 km north of Mersin port in Asia Minor and dated V-IV century BC. It is mentioned after the great god Baal Shamin, *SHR* and Shamas.

> L1-5: "far extends the territory of *DNL*. Whoever you are, which violates or breaks (the border), he (man who broke the border) will be broken, (he) and his descendants who he will have, by Baal Shamin, the Great, *SHR*, and Shamas".

The inscription shows that Baal Shamin played a protective role, and was the guarantor of territorial integrity, and over which he exercised his lordship.

3.3.3. Aramaic inscriptions of Hatra

Hatra is located in Mesopotamia, 100 km northwest of Aššur. On this site was found several entries mentioning the god Baal Shamin. They date from the I-II AD.

KAI 24: 1-2.
> L 1-2: "Memory and remembrance for *QWB*, magnificence of .., son of the king before *BDSLM* Baal Shamin. Memory and remembrance for *HBWS*, architect, son of *WBDW*, son *NNJ*, front of the king Baal Shamin".

The deity Baal Shamin has a royal function in this inscription.

KAI 244: 1-3
> L1-3: "Blessed be *NSRQ* son of *MRJNW* son of *JHB* by the god Baal Shamin and by all gods and may they think about him in a sympathetic manner. Anyone with good intentions ... Baal Shamin, creator of the earth..."

This inscription was found on the wall of the temple of Hathra. The contents of the inscription show it is an expression of blessing.

KAI 245: 1-2
> L1-2: "Surely, be recommended a *BRZQJQ* to our Lord and the great Baal Shamin ...venerates him so kindly.

This inscription is a recommendation".

KAI 247: 1-5.
> L1-5: "Prayer addressed to our master and to the son of our Master, and to Baal Shamin, *SHRW* and to Atargatis, for each person who travels from here to Mesene".

This prayer is to several deities including Baal Shamin

3.3.4. Baal Shamêm in other epigraphic inscriptions

The Baal manifested in the storm clouds, the Baal Shamêm or Baal of heaven is mentioned in the inscription of King of Byblos Yahimilku from the first millennium BC. In addition to this listing, we have others such as (KAI 4:3, 26, A III, 18, 78, 2, 64.1, 18,

1. 7, 202; 266 2, 259 3, 241 1. 2, 244, 1. 3, 245 1, 247, mentioning a god with two different spellings or with Baal Shamin or Baal Shamêm.

3.3.4.a. Byblos

Inscription of the king Yahimilku, from Byblos dated tenth century BC, KAI 4:3.

> L1-7: "Temple which Yehimilk king of Byblos (re) built; he it was who restored all the ruins of these temples. May Baal Shamêm, the Mistress of Bylos, and the assembly of holy gods of Byblos prolong the days and years of Yehimilk over Byblos! For he is a honest and rightful king in the sight of the holy gods of Byblos".

This inscription is a prayer in which Baal Shamêm is first mentioned alongside the 'Mistress of Byblos', the assembly of the gods of Byblos. We note that the purpose of this prayer is the protection of King Yahimilku. It seems that Baal Shamin is the chief god.

3.3.4.b. Karatepe

At Karatepe, an inscription dated 720 BC mentions several names which include the name Baal Shamêm:[122]

> (L12-18): "If a sovereign among sovereigns ... erases the name of Azitawadda, demolished the city Azitawadda ... or door made by Azitawadda ... as Baal and El Shamêm creator of the earth and the sun of eternity and the assembly of gods erase kingdom and this king...."

This inscription is a curse which aims to eliminate anyone who dared to erase the name of King Azitawadda or seek to destroy the city or the door made by the king. Baal Shamêm is again mentioned in the first position alongside the god El and other deities. The function denoted in this inscription is protector of the city.

---

[122] KAI 26 A III, 18; ANET, 1969, p. 499.

KAI 26: "This treaty imposed by the king Esarhaddon on King Baal of Tyre, is dated 676. Baal Shamêm tops the list of gods of Phoenician witnesses and guarantors of the alliance between the two sovereigns. Shamêm Baal of the city is mentioned, with other Baals, Baal Saphon and Malagê"[123].
> L: "May Baal Shamêm, Baal Malagê, and Baal Saphon raise a bad wind against your ships."

Baal Shamêm occupied a dominant position in the pantheon of Tyre.[124]

3.3.4.c. Carthage

KAI 78:2: In Carthage, on a stele from the third century BC, Baal Shamêm occupies the first place on a list containing the names of 'Mistress' and 'Tanit' in the face of Baal.
> (L1-2): "May they bless him and grant his appeal from the lord Baal Shamem, the Mistress of Tanit, and to the face of Baal..."

3.3.4.d. Sardinia

KAI 64:1

(L 1-2): This inscription is from the third century BC.
> "The lord, Baal Shamêm Island of hawks, here are two steles and two *hinwti* beloved B'lhn', the servant of *bdmqrt*, son of *hin'*."

This inscription is a dedication, to the god Baal Shamêm. It presents Baal Shamêm as a personal and family god.

KAI 18: 1.7 the inscription, discovered in the ancient city of Laodicea and dated 132 BC.
> (L1-2): "By the Lord, Baal Shamem, be praised bd 'lm, son of mtn..."

---

[123] KAI. 26; ANET, 1969, pp. 533-534.
[124] GRELOT, 1972, pp. 363-365.

This inscription shows Baal Shamêm is a personal god. The author speaks about the beginning of the work and the installation of the gates of the city. As the god Baal Shamêm is the only deity invoked in this inscription, we can conclude that he was worshipped as the principal deity, protecting the city.

3.4. Iconography testimonials of Baal Shamin

From the inscriptions found at the temple of Palmyra, we will now turn our attention to iconography testimony which will help us flesh out the nature and functions of Baal Shamin. The iconography that we will examine comes primarily from Israel, and shows significant Egyptian influence, as will be shown.

3.4.1. Baal Shamin: The Master of Heaven

In the northern kingdom of Israel, the representations of art and craft of deities, the illus.[125] 20, 21 and 22 are seals dating from the eighth century BC, belonging to worshippers of YHWH, and the owner is an officer of King Azariah, kingdom of Judah (773-735).[126] These three types of representation of the 'Lord of Heaven' reflect Egyptian influence. These seals portray a young sun god, beardless and kneeling on a flower, making the gesture of blessing. A showing of hands in a gesture of greeting and another placed on the chest is common on Phoenician seals.[127] This raised hand is a gesture of blessing, but these figures are more references to Baal Shamin.[128]

---

[125] Illus. means illustration.
[126] KEEL and UEHLINGER, 2001, p. 246.
[127] KEEL and UEHLINGER, 2001, p. 246.
[128] KEEL and UEHLINGER, 2001, p. 391; see pp. 196-197, figs.

According to Seyrig,[129] and Collart and Vicari,[130] the god Baal Shamin has many titles, including 'Master of Heaven'; "Master of the World", and is also known as "Supreme God,"[131] He rules the sun and moon, with which he was associated,[132] These titles show the cosmic character of Baal Shamin.[133]

The deity Baal Shamin holds the thunder in his hand (see illus. 6; 13). The thunder is not a threat, but is the symbol of the fertilizing rains.[134] The followers of this deity worshipped him because he protected them against drought. By his power, the rains fell and made the vegetation green, essential for the life of people and animals. According to this function, he was called, "*dieu bon et rénumérateur*," (good god and rewarder).[135] This god Baal Shamin was another aspect of the Storm-god Baal Hadad and worshipped by the Semitic populations.[136]

Illus. 3, Seal from Judah, Keel and Uehlinger, 2001:247, fig. 241a.

Illus. 4, Seal from Judah, Keel and Uehlinger, 2001: 274, fig.241b.

Illus. 5, Seal from Judah, Keel and Uehlinger, 2001: 247, fig. 241c.

241b-241c.
[129] SEYRIG, 1934, pp. 93 and 95.
[130] COLLART and VICARI, 1969, p. 203; CIS III, 3986.
[131] SEYRIG, 1934, p. 96; COLLART and VICARI, 1969, p. 203.
[132] COLLART and VICARI, 1969, p. 203.
[133] MICHALOWSKI and al., 1960, p. 447, note 33.
[134] SEYRIG, 1934, p. 96.
[135] COLLART and VICARI, 1969, p. 203.
[136] STRACKY and GAWLIKOWSKI, p. 97.

Illus. 6: the engraving from Gezer, Keel and Uehlinger, 2001:196, n°210.

Illus. 7: Ivory from Samaria, Keel and Uehlinger, 2001:197-198, n°212a.

Illus. 8: Seal from Carthage, Keel and Uehlinger, 2001:197-198, n°212b.

Illus. 9: Seal from Tell el-Fara, Keel and Uehlinger, 2001:198-199, n°213.

Illustration 6 is an engraving on bone from Gezer dating to the first half of the VIIIth century and is another aspect of Baal Hadad, the celestial divinity.[137] The group of illustrations 8, 9, and 10 found in the south of Syria Hazor dates from the first half of the VIIth century BC. These engravings show the juvenile god holding in his

---

[137] KEEL and UEHLINGER, 2001, pp. 96; 99.

hand a plant or flower. This representation of gods with wings and flowers in their hands exhibits clearly their Uranian aspects. These documents certify the evolution of Baal to a "Lord of heaven" (Baal Shamem). The illustration 10 engraving, represent an *égyptisée* and *solariséé* variant of the youthful god with two pairs of wings, topped by a disk and giving life with his two hands. It again suggests a relationship (it's simply interchangeable) between juvenile Baal with four wings and the sun god,[138] or solar god. The wings (illus. 7, 8, 9, 10) indicate that the god is a celestial god, and plants or flowers show that these gods are associated with vegetation.

3.4.2. Other iconography testimonials of Baal Shamin

In the following sections I will describe various portrayal of Baal Shamin found in the decorations in the Palmyrian temple and in Si'a. Baal Shamin had another Temple at Si'a in Syra. Here, we find dedications to Baal Shamin and the symbolism of the Eagle and the orientation of the sanctuary west-east on the diagonal.[139] Whether in the sanctuary of the Sia or in Palmyra dedications, Baal Shamin has been repeatedly named and represented by an eagle, the bird of heaven.[140]

3.4.3. Eagle symbol of Baal Shamin

The Eagles are "messengers of heaven", winged angels of Baal Shamin, the supreme god, they (Eagles) exalted the glory, and benefits assigned.[141]

---

[138] KEEL and UEHLINGER, 2001, p. 99.
[139] COLLART and VICARI, 1969, pp. 190; 209.
[140] COLLART and VICARI, 1969, p. 220.
[141] COLLART and VICARI, 1969, pp. 221-211.

The eagle is the symbol of this cosmic god.[142] On the tesserae or reliefs, the eagle unfurled indicates the symbolic evocation of Baal Shamin, in another essential function.

Illus. 10. The lintel of eagles, from the temple of Baal Shamin, Palmyra, Collart and Vicari, 1969: pl. XCVII, 1; Du Mesnil, 1962:317, fig. 185.

The lintel portrays eagles carrying branches (see illus. 10). Two eagles with wings parted laterally hold in their beaks a laurel branch turned to the supreme god (Baal Shamin-eagle), thus expressing invincible sovereignty. Also portrayed on the lintel are two young eagles standing with folded wings, which also hold in their beak a laurel branch. Two deities: Lunar god Aglibôl and solar god Malakbel are shown to the left and right, with the beardless face framed by curly hair. On their heads, unfolded discs, haloes, where the rays are modelled as beams.[143] It forms a triad of Baal Shamin, since this figure had the moon god Aglibôl respectively on his right and the sun god Malakbel on his left.

---

[142] COLLART and VICARI, 1969, pp. 221; 227.
[143] COLLART and VICARI, 1969, pp. 163-164; 209.

In a glypotheque (collection of statues) housed in Copenhagen, of which the original location is unkown, there is the tiara of Baal Shamin. On the motif of this tiara, can be seen a rectangle which supports a globe. On the globe, the eagle is shown with wings parted and flanked by two ears of wheat.

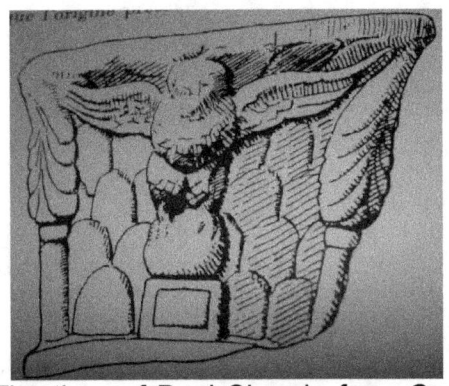

Illus.11. The tiara of Baal Shamin from Copenhagen Glypotheque, Seyrig, 1953:37, fig. 5.

On the Votive Stele Tell Sfir, from Northern Syria[144] we see the back of a bull, and above that the hand of a man holding the thunder or perhaps stalks of grain. At the top of the votive, the sun and moon are depicted side by side. Several things can be surmised from the iconography on this stele. We can surmise that the deity is being invoked as the ruler of both day and night, or the ruler of all the heavens. The stalks of wheat imply that the deity is also the god of fertility. The association in this same iconography of the bull, the sun, the moon, and the ear of grain, prove that this deity rules the two heavenly bodies. The bull and the ear of grain show the function of fertility and provider of rain.

---

[144] SEYRIG, 1946, p. 24.

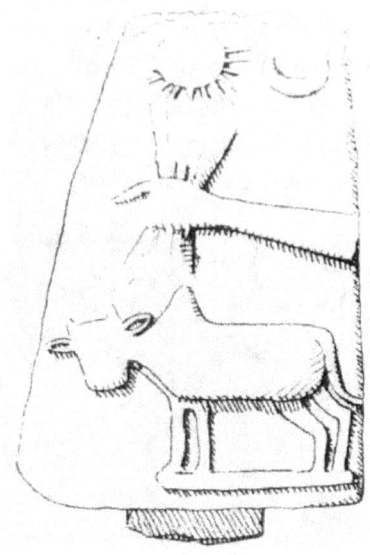

Illus. 12. The Bull carved on a stele of Tell Sfir, north of Syria. Seyrig, 1946:24, fig.12; Collart and Vicari, 1969: CIII 3; Du Mesnil, 1962:328, fig. 5.

On the monuments we see a man holding in his raised hand lightning or a bunch of spikes. In this picture, we see the bull standing, topped by a hand holding a thunderbolt and the image of the sun and the moon. If the hand holds the lightning, it should be noted that the bull would be a sacrificial animal rather than interpreting it [the thunderbolt] as an attribute of the particular God.[145]

"The lightning he brandished in his hand is not an image of terrifying power, but the recall of fertilizing rains that accompany the storms, which are greening the desert and prevent the drying up of sources."[146] Sometimes, the god Baal Shamin is represented in an anthropomorphic form.

---

[145] COLLART and VICARI, 1969, p. 211.
[146] SEYRIG, 1934, p. 34.

Illus. 13. Baal shamem represented in human form. See Collart and Vicari, 1969: pl. CIII 2; Du Mesnil, 1962:306, fig. 180.

On a bas-relief from Palmyra discovered at Dura-Europos, located in the south-east of Syria, dated 31/32 AD, Baal Shamin is represented in human form seated on his throne, with a beard and wearing a calathos and a large overcoat, the left hand pressed on a sceptre, the right holding a bunch of an ear of corn and fruit.[147] The fruit and ear of corn are things demonstating the atmospheric and agricultural

---

[147] COLLART and VICARI, 1969, p. 202; Du MESNIL, 1962, p. 307.

function of Baal Shamin. The sceptre in the hand is a mark or symbol of authority and power. Also, we have on this relief, someone standing near to Baal Shamin. Maybe the person could be the consort of Baal Shamin. In another iconograph or limestone relief[148] we can see the simple human hand representing the god Baal Shamin. The votive offering is from Palmyra and dedicated to Baal Shamin, the god holding in his hand three ears with this inscription.[149]

For the inscription, see pages 43-44 translated and edited by Stracky:

אחוהי לבעש   וענגן   ירחי   בר   מלכן   עבד 1
מן . ////ע   3 כ--   ע כ--   שנת   טבת   2בירש

Malkô fils de Iarkai et Annô son frère ont fait (cet ex-voto) pour Baal Shamin, au mois de Tebet de l'an 539 (janvier 228 après J.C).

Malkô son of Iarkai and Annô his brother made (this ex-voto) for Baal Shamin, in the month of Tebet in the year 539 (January AD 228).

---

[148] SEYRIG, 1934, pp. 36-37.
[149] SEYRIG, 1953, p. 36.

Illus. 14. The votive offering dedicated to Baal Shamin from Palmyra, Collart and Vicari, 1969: pl. CIII 4. H. 29 cm, W. 26 cm; Seyrig, 1953:36, note 1, pl. I.

The following iconography,[150] recalls the divine triad from Bir Wereb, near to Palmyra. All of them are standing and holding the sword in their left hand. Their right hand is raised but broken. Their legs also are broken at the height of the knees. The three gods wear belts. Each one has a chain around his neck. The two gods on the left and on the right of Baal Shamin have their heads surrounded by radiant haloes.

---

[150] SEYRG, 1934, pp. 32-33.

Illus. 15. The divine triad: this relief is from Bir Wereb. H. 60; W.72. Starcky, 1949:35-41; Collart and Vicari, 1969:pl. CV, 2; Dentzer-Freydy and Teixidor, 1993:144-145. See the Louvre Museum, AO 19801.

On this limestone relief from Palmyra, the deity Baal Shamin is bearded, standing between the lunar-deity Aglibol and the solar-deity Malakbel. The moon god Aglibôl is to the right and the god Malakbel to the left. These three gods are wearing Roman military dress. Baal Shamin governs the two heavenly bodies, the sun and the moon that are associated.[151] For the role of Aglibôl and Malakbel.[152] The name of Malakbel means "the messenger/ angel of Bel."[153] The name is made up of Malak (messenger or angel) and Bel (the god Bel).

---

[151] SEYRIG, 1934, p. 96.
[152] TEIXIDOR, 1980, pp. 281-283.
[153] STRACKY and GAWLIKOWSKI, 1985, p. 97; DENTZER-freydy, and TEIXIDOR, 1993, p. 5; TEIXIDOR, 1980, p. 283; Du MESNIL, 1962, pp. 313-314.

3.4.4. Worship of Baal Shamin at Palmyra: worshipping a foreign God?

The main sanctuary of Palmyra was dedicated to three deities namely Bel, Iarhibol and Aglibôl.[154] This proves that the temple of Baal Shamin was not the main sanctuary at Palmyra. Bel was known as the ancestral god of Palmyra[155] The god Baal Shamin came to Palmyra through contact with the Arabic and Aramaic nomadic tribes, and the Benê-Ma'azin tribe around the second century BC. The tribe of Benê-Ma'azin played an important role, and built for the deity the temple of Palmyra in the first century AD.[156] The name of the tribe appears in many inscriptions. All the Palmyrene monuments depicting the deity Baal Shamin are dated between 67 and 134.[157] If Bel was the supreme god of the city of Palmyra, the deity Baal Shamin retained his tribal characteristics while becoming one of the principal and supreme gods with Bel in the same city of Palmyra. Henceforth, the two gods, Bel and Baal Shamin, coexisted in the city[158] like two supreme deities of Palmyra.

Baal Shamin was a foreign god for the Palmyrenians, and the oldest monuments of this god are Phoenician. In the twelfth century BC, it seems he was in first place in the pantheon of Byblos. In Tyre, in the tenth century BC, a golden stele was dedicated to him by the King Hiram.[159] The worship of Baal Shamin is known in the area of central Syria, in the year 800 BC, where he was a protector, and the personal god

---

[154] SEYRIG, 1934, p. 88.
[155] SEYRIG, 1934, p. 89.
[156] STRACKY and GAWLIKOWSKI, 1985, p. 98; TEIXIDOR, 1980, p. 279.
[157] CIS II, 3911; 3959; SEYRIG, 1934, p. 96.
[158] De GEORGE, 2001, p. 150.
[159] COLLART and VICARI, 1969, p. 201.

of the king Zakkur of Hamath located in northern Syria.[160] Baal Shamin in Palmyra is revered not only under the epithet of "master of heaven" but also "master of the world,"[161] Seyrig[162] said that when Palmyra became an agricultural centre and received Aramaic civilization, then it was right at that moment for the farmers of Palmyra to send their wishes to the god Baal Shamin.

3.5. Dedication Monuments to Baal Shamin at Palmyra

3.5.1. The cult of Baal Shamin

Collart and Vacari state that they possess little information on the ceremonies of worship of this "master of the skies" of Palmyra. The only information available was provided by the structure of the building, monumental dedications, altars, the presence of a courtyard, a meeting of the faithful and through various manifestations of religion such as the divinity of sacrifices and ritual meals ...[163] Ceremonies were held in the southern courtyard of the temple of Palmyra, whose purpose was to safeguard secrecy. To achieve this, the court was surrounded by porticos and walls to prevent access and provide discretion.[164] His altar was 77 cm high, and clay pipes for water lines (hydraulic) suggest the use of blood sacrifices.[165] A burnt sacrifice was dedicated each year to Baal Shamin. At what time of year could this

---

[160] SEYRIG, 1934, p. 95.
[161] SEYRIG, 1934, p. 96.
[162] SEYRIG, 1934, pp. 93; 95.
[163] COLLART and VICARI, 1969, p. 235.
[164] COLLART and VICARI, 1969, p. 234.
[165] COLLART and VICARI, 1969, p. 236.

holocaust have taken place? Inscriptions on monuments were dedicated to Baal Shamin in the sanctuary, and were dedicated in September of each year. This feature is not without significance. As Collart and Vacari explained.[166] September was the beginning of the harvest and, in Palmyra, the harvest of dates. The agrarian character of Baal Shamin was depicted by his holding a bunch of stalks of grain and fruits or with vine.

3.5.2. The staff of the cult of Baal Shamin

A list dated June AD 49, mentions priests of the deity Baal Shamin.[167] Other people playing an important role in connection with the administration of the shrine of the 'Master of Heaven "were descended from the tribe Benê-Maziyân.[168] Durant[169] states that: "it seems quite likely that people who also hold high positions in the sanctuary, family, and tribal tradition built the monumental buildings certified by the dedications."[170] It could be that there was a priestly college which served the cult of Baal Shamin, suggested by the exhumation of effigies of priests discovered during the excavations. We know that the gods have always acted through their priests. Despite the fact that the information provided to us by research is scanty, it does not imply an organized structure of the priesthood through the priests who served **Baal Shamin** in his sanctuary. Even if we see that, there are several occasions in the dedications indicating that the persons making them were of the lineage of the sons of Benê- Maziyân, attached to the administration of the sanctuary.

---

[166] COLLART and VICARI, 1969, p. 210; 239.
[167] DUNANT, 1971, p. 51.
[168] DUNANT, 1971, p. 240.
[169] DUNANT, 1971, p. 15.
[170] COLLART and VICARI, 1969, p. 240.

3.5.3. Functions of Baal Shamin

3.5.3.a. Atmospheric, blessings and imprecations

The god was adored according to its climate functions. The devotees of the god of fertility refer to the vine and the tree. The votive monuments represent the god of Carthage surrounded by flowers and fruit clusters, symbols of its fertilising power.[171] The Safaitic followers of this god counted on his contribution of rain to fertilize the land, and protect their involvement in the fighting, in which the tribes were constantly engaged.[172] He was a deity invoked in several areas to seek salvation, peace, liberation, abundance, riches, not forgetting victory in battle, getting loot in the raids, getting revenge on their enemies, and so on.[173]

The Safaitic engraved on the rock walls around their camp; their names follow the genealogical list of their ancestors. Many graffiti end with reference to a deity followed by the invocation and imprecation against those who efface the inscription or drawings drawn close to it: "O Baal Shamin rest and blindness to that which would erase this inscription ... The rain will come with Baal Shamin and relaxation for those to whom the drought causes anxiety."[174] In the time of drought conditions, the Phoenicians implored Baal Shamin to bring rain. When droughts occured they considered him, the "lord of heaven," to be the only god and "called him Beelsamin which is Lord of heaven in Phoenician, Zeus in Geek."[175] Gerard concludes his study about Palmyra Baal Shamin, that it was qualified by its weather

---

[171] VIGOUROUX, Col. 1318.
[172] RYCMANS, n.d., p. 357.
[173] RYCMANS, n.d., p. 359.
[174] RYCMANS, n.d., p. 355.
[175] EUSEBIUS of CASAERA, P.E.I, 10:6-14.

function, and the eagle symbolized its iconography of the reigning king, unfurled the stars, and thus gave the master of the world his skills. He is the Storm-god and god of fertility; these features make him the cosmic god of farmers and ranchers of Palmyra. This deity Baal Shamin was worshipped by the West-Semitic as "Weather-God who manifests himself in the skies by his thunder and his lightnings."[176] We found in our research another Tarhunza, who is celestial Storm-god as Baal Shamem.[177] This god is known in the inscription of Karatepe "Celestial Tarhunza of the Luwian version is rendered by [Baal Shamem], example "Lord of Heaven" in the Phoenician version."[178]

---

[176] BUNNENS, 2006, p. 81; LIPINSKI, 1994, p. 196.
[177] HAAS, 1994, p. 325; BUNNENS, 2006, p. 81.
[178] BUNNENS, 2006, p. 81; KAI 26 III: 18.

Illus. 16. Stele from Jekke, Bunnens, 2006:119; 162, fig. 78; 1.62 m x 0.70 m. Cf. also (Dunand, 1940:85-92).

On the stele of Jekke, (42 km north of Aleppo) we can see the god with human form standing on the back of a bull. He holds in his right hand something like an axe. In his left hand, the deity holds the end of a stick with three branches like a thunderbolt or the trident-lightning. On the stele in the Adiyaman Museum (southeastern of Turkey) both these steles "portray a god to which are inscriptions calling Celestial Tarhunza, example: Storm-god of Heaven."[179] This god "Celestial Tarhunza" is another aspect of the deity [Baal Shamem], the Storm-god of heaven, the weather and fertility god. For the Adiyaman stele, see fig. 79.[180]

---

[179] BUNNENS, 2006, p. 56.
[180] BUNNENS, 2006, p. 119.

3.5.3.b. Baal Shamin god of security

The Baal Shamin played a protective role, a sort of guardian angel of his followers. For Safaitic people, [Baal Shamem] through the structure of priests forbade access to towns where we can assume that the temples were dedicated to him.[181]

3.5.3.c. Baal Shamin guarantor of treaties

[Baal Shamem] "Master of Heaven" was the guarantor of treaties in 676 BC; he was one of the gods, guarantors of the treaty imposed on the king of Tyre by Esarhaddon of Assyria (680-669 BC).[182]

> "If a sovereign among sovereigns ... erases the name of Azitawadda, demolished the city Azitawadda ... or door made by Azitawadda ... as Baal and El Shamem creator of the earth and the sun of eternity and the assembly of gods erase kingdom and this king... May Baal Shamêm, Baal Malagê, and Baal Saphon raise a bad wind against your ships."

[Baal Shamêm] occupied a dominant position in the pantheon of Tyre.
In this treaty, he was associated with two others, Baal Shaphon and Baal Malaga, (KAI, 26) [Baal Shamem] ranked first among the deities witnesses.

---

[181] RYCMANS, n.d., p. 357.
[182] KAI, 26 A III, 18, L.12-18; ANET, 1969:499; GRELOT, 1972, pp. 363-365.

CHAPTER 4

THE BAAL OF MOUNT CARMEL: THE GOD OF STORM?

Although some authors[183] agree that the Baal of Mount Carmel should be Baal Melqart, this hypothesis is not commonly accepted.[184] We can say with confidence that Melqart is Baal of the biblical text 1 Kings 18, and we can conclude that this interpretation is not out of doubt. According to Avi-Yonah's research on the inscription found on Mount Carmel, $Ζευς$ $Ἡλιοπολίτης$ the god talked about, is Adad, the Storm-god.[185] The divinity has an ideogram in Akkadian ᵈIM, read as: *dingir Im*, which is also a determining factor for divine names. The value of this sign is 399 (cf. Labat and Malbran-Labat).[186] In Akkadian, this sign IM has many meanings, *zunnu* "the rain"; *šāru* "the wind"; *imḫullu* "the devastating tempest."[187]

---

[183] BONNET, 1988, pp.136-144; DUSSAUD, 1948, pp. 205-230; De VAUX, 1941, pp. 7-20; RIBICHINI, 1999, pp. 563-565.
[184] AVI-YONAH, 1952, 118-124; BRIQUEL-CHATONNET, 1992, pp. 303-313 ; LIPINSPI, 1995b, pp. 284-288.
[185] AVI-YONAH, 1952, p. 124.
[186] LABAT and MALBRAN-LABAT, 1994, p. 185.
[187] DUSSAUD, 1931, p. 362, note n°1.

The Storm-god, Baal Adad was also known by ^{d}Iškur. Certain elements in 1 Kings 18:24-25, that is the fire and the flash of lightning, had to come down from the sky, evoking the god of the atmospheric phenomena.[188] The scholar Briquel-Chatonnet[189] affirms that: "a later identification of the god worshipped on this mountain with Zeus [was made], the god of the sky and the lightning, underlines the particular connections between Mount Carmel and the cult of the Storm-god." The Storm-god rules the clouds, the thunders and produces lightning flashes[190] Putting aside the fire, we can conclude that "the sacrifice on Carmel was intended for the Storm-god, who it was hoped would produce the returning of the rain" (1 Kings 18:25-26).[191] In this section, Elijah had also chosen to fight Baal on his terms, allowing him to use his most effective weapon, lightning. The "fire" and the "Bull" and "clouds" are references to the Storm-god, Baal.

Fire and Bull have been used in the royal writings during the reigns of Ramses II (1279-1212 BC) and Ramses III (1182-1151 BC), to compare the majestic power of the Pharaoh with Baal Storm-god. According to Gardiner,[192] the Pharaoh is compared to "Fire" and "Bull". Gardiner[193] continues his affirmation about Pharaoh and says: the Pharaoh is "like fire at its time of burning; firm of heart like a bull ready upon the battlefield." On the battle, among the enemy armies he is compared to the deity Baal:[194] "I (Pharaoh) was after them like Baal at the moment of his power," and about

---

[188] BRIQUEL-CHATONNET, 1992, p. 311.
[189] BRIQUEL-CHATONNET, 1992, p. 311.
[190] LIPINSKI, 1995a, p. 80.
[191] BRIQUEL-CHATONNET, 1992, p. 312.
[192] GARDINER, 1960, p. 7.
[193] GARDINER, 1960, p. 7.
[194] GARDINER, 1960, p. 12.

the work of (Edgerton and Wilson,[195] the Pharaoh had: "great strength like Baal" and was a warrior king like Baal:[196] "He (Pharaoh) appears upon the battlefield like Baal." This comparison of king Pharaoh with the powerful Baal is a testament to the popularity of the deity Baal who crosses boundaries and the usual areas of Mesopotamia and Syria.

In the Epic of Baal, other internal indications that the Baal's epithet, *rkt 'rpt,* "Cloud-Rider" and meteorological elements include Baal's KTU 1.3 IV: 6-11,[197] see also the fragment 3 AB of Ras Shamra;[198] *rkb 'rpt* in KTU 1.2IV.8, 29, and also: KTU.1.3 II:38-40;1.3 IV:1-5, 25 1.4 III:17-18;1.4V:55-60). In CTA 4. III: 10-20, we found that not only does this text talk about Baal as: "Cloud-Rider", but he (Baal) is also like a man using his feet:[199] [*'d*]. *ydd. 'wyqlṣn*= [Even-as] "he jumps, he storms." Baal's lightning is the sign of his power and also symbolizes the rain. Mann[200] in his work proposed and identified with the Ugaritic word *'nn* which means "cloud" translated as "clouds" or "cloud messengers". He made a connection between this Ugaritic word and Hebrew עָנָן meaning "cloud:"[201] This word עָנָן appears 87 times in the Old Testament. We can find other words meaning "clouds" or "cloudbank" like עָב (Exod 19:9; 1Kgs 18:44; 2 Sam. 22:12); עֲרָפֶל "thick clouds" (Exod 20:21; Deut 5 :22 ;1Kgs 8 :12); חֲזִיז "thundercloud/ thunderclap" (Zech 10:1; Job 28:26; 38:25).[202]

---

[195] EDGERTON and WILSON, 1936, p. 41, pls. 37-39.
[196] EDGERTON and WILSON, 1936, p. 9, pl. 17.
[197] SMITH, 1994, p. 97.
[198] OBERMANN, 1947, pp. 197-198; DAY, 2002, p. 91; BUNNENS, 2006, p. 62; GREEN, 2003, p. 195.
[199] MARGALT, 1980, pp. 37; 41.
[200] MANN, 1971, pp. 19-24.
[201] GOOD, 1978, p. 436.
[202] FREEDMAN, 2001, p. 254.

In this case, the word עָנָן should refer to the meteorological or to the atmospheric phenomenon, as for example in Genesis 9:13-16; Job 7:9; Isaiah 44:22 or "as water-carriers" (Eccl 11:3; Jer 10:13; Is. 5:6).[203] It can be associated 'with storms, tempests and the powerful forces of nature' to describe the theophany of YHWH, his anger against his enemies (Ezek 30:3, 18; 32:7; 34:12; Nah.1: 3). Mann,[204] says: "the term 'nn is used with the Storm deity." The עָנָן 'the cloud' also indicates the presence of YHWH and his appearance to Moses, Aaron and Miriam and the Israelites (Exod 14:19; 16; 24:15-18; 34:5; 40:34,38; Num. 9:15-22; 12:5; 14:14; Neh 9:12; Psa. 99:7).[205] Another meaning as "servant" can be found for 'nn in Ugaritic texts. In KTU 1.2, I:34-35 b'l w'nnh is translated as "Baal and his servants [messengers]." Mann[206] said that: the Ugaritic word 'nn "appears in the literary form of scenes where the gods are pictured as dispatching the messengers on mission" (see also KTU IV: 76), in this text we found 'nn ilm "whom Anat specifically dispatches back to Baal.[207] Therefore, in KTU 1.3, IV 32; 1.4, VIII, 1.5 we can read 'nn ilm, which means "servant of gods", (Fabry, 2001:253).

If we draw a parallel between some elements such as fire, the bull and clouds of the god Baal, and the biblical text of 1 Kings 18 : 1-46, we notice that the biblical text also mentions them as elements of paramount importance in the ordeal on Mount Carmel. We highlight the phrases as: הַפָּר; the 'bull' for sacrifice (v.23), הָאֱלֹהִים וַיַּעַן 'the god who will answer by אֵשׁ "a

---

[203] SCUTCLIFFE, 1953, pp. 99-103.
[204] MANN, 1971, p. 21, n° 31.
[205] FREEDMAN, 2001, p. 255.
[206] MANN, 1971, pp. 21; 22.
[207] MANN, 1971, p. 21.

fire" (v.24), and the "dark clouds" עָבִים at the end of this ordeal of Mount Carmel shows the return of the rain (v.44-45). The god Baal is to be considered as rain god as YHWH. He is the known God who "covers the sky by dark clouds" הַמְכַסֶּה שָׁמַיִם בְּעָבִים (Psa 147:8) and prepare the rain for the earth. The God YHWH gives מָטָר, 'the rain' on the earth עַל־פְּנֵי־אָרֶץ (Job 5:10); and He [YHWH וְנָתַתָּה מָטָר sends rain on the land (1Kgs 8:36); (see also Amos 4:6-13; 9:6). Baal fills the same roles as YHWH, or has the same function as an atmospheric god. הד

According to the fertilization of the land and the atmospheric functions retained by the god Baal, Parker[208] states that Baal (Adad): has been a Storm-god with no rain either on the field or on the earth, the vegetation dried up; the trees dried up; and would bring forth no fresh shoots. The pastures dried up, the springs dried up. In the land famine arose so that man and gods perished from hunger." It is important to add Dussaud's[209] concern, who gave his view about the Baal Haddad (=Baal Adad) according to the meaning of Haddad. Firstly he said that the *Hd* with the double "*d*" was an old-form name of the deity. But for Dhorme[210] there are two forms of the name Adad used: the complete form,הדד or its short form הד Secondly, he makes a connection between the name Haddad and the name *hadda* which means "to break, to smash" and the subtantifs *hâddu* and *hâddat* meaning respectively "rumble " and "thunder". These elements have a connection with the Storm-god Haddad (Adad). For us, Dussaud[211] does not define the period attributed to 'old form' and the connection of the meaning of Haddad with

---

[208] PARKER, 1989, p. 295.
[209] DUSSAUD, 1936, I, pp. 13-14.
[210] DHORME, 1928, p. 71.
[211] DUSSAUD, 1936, I, pp. 362-363.

Arabic was interesting, but the weakness of this explanation was that the author does not give the original language of Haddad for a full understanding of the idea.

Mythological texts from Ras Shamra,[212] describe Baal as a storm-god who rides clouds and controls the seasons by providing rain, which enables the fertility of both land and animal. In the Asssyrian inscription dedicated to Adad, the Storm-god is known as ᵈIŠKUR, KÙ.GAL⁶ =Adad *gugallu* means "canal inspector," (CAD/g-*gugallu*, 1a: 121; Lipinski, 1994:35). ᵈIŠKUR is the Sumerian logogram which designates the God Adad, the Storm-god.[213] Another logogram is ᵈIM, (see Codex of Hammurabi IIIa: 55-59; XXVIIb: 64, cf. no.18).

The same epithet for Adad has been found in the Codex of Hammurabi XXVIIb § 64-71 (see also Finet).[214] He is the deity (Lipinski, 1994:38) "responsible for rainwater," and according to Finet,[215] *gugallum*, he is 'the water distributor.' The benefits of abundant water are the fertilization of the earth and the plants' sustenance:[216] "prosperity' ḪÉ.NUN=*nuḫšu* and 'as a source of wealth" for human beings.

In the fable of Nisaba, the Sumerian goddess of grain and wheat, BWL: 169, L. 17-18[217], is mentioned the same function attributed before to Adad:

L. 17*na-al-ba-áš šamê lib-ba-[tiq a-n]a ši-si-te* ᵈ*ad-di*

=Let the garb of heaven be rent at the cry of Addu

L. 18 *imbarum (im.dugud) liq-i-ma ur-qit* [*erṣetim* ᵗⁱᵐ] *lip-pát-qu*

---

[212] DUSSAUD, 1931, I, pp. 362-363.
[213] HUEHNERGARD, 2005, p. 534.
[214] FINET, 2004, 150 §: 69-80.
[215] FINET, 2004, 150 §: 80, note 1.
[216] LIPINSKI, 1994, p. 38.
[217] The translated by W. Gilfred Lambert, (1996).

= Let the rainstorm pour forth that the vegetation of [the earth] may be brought into being.

In order to discuss further the notion of Adad as god of rain and prosperity, we can read again the fable of Nisaba in BWL: 170-171, L.21: ^{d}Addu li-iḫ-mu-ma [li-ša-az-n] in nuḫša (ḪÉ.NUN): 'May Adad rumble and [rain down] prosperity' and CAD/Z: 43, zanānu b.1'). The words: nuḫša, nuḫšum, or nuḫuš (ḪÉ.NUN) mean, abundance, plenty, prosperity.[218] All these titles and epithets describing Adad as Storm-god prove that he is the deity that brings abundant rain, and breeds luxurious vegetation for all beings (animals and human beings) living on the earth.

In the Phoenician poem[219], especially in the tablet II AB, IV-V:L. 68; 70-71 of Ras Shamra, the identity and functions of Baal Hadad are discussed according to Dussaud[220] with the benefit of his rain: "he (Baal) gives voice in the clouds, he launched the lightning on the earth." We can declare that the tablets of Ras Shamra show that Baal Haddad is the god of storm, of lightning, and rain, being, therefore, indispensable for vegetation.[221]

4.1. The gods of storm: Haddad and Zeus on Mount Carmel

This three-line Greek inscription found on Mount Carmel is dedicated to Zeus by Gaius Julius, of the second and third centur AD (Avi-Yonah 1952:118).

---

[218] HUEHNERGARD, 2005, p. 511 ; CAD/N II: 319 nuḫšu)
[219] The translation and the commentary of this poetry was made by VIROLLEAUD, 1931 :193 "Un poème phénicien de Ras Shamra, La lutte de Mot, fils des dieux et d'Aleïn, fils de Baal.
[220] DUSSAUD, 1932, I, p. 256; 1935, p. 19; 1931, I, p. 362, L. 68 and L. 70-71.
[221] DUSSAUD, 1936, I, p. 249.

L-1 ΔΠ ΗΛΙΟΠΟΛΕΙΤΗΙ ΚΑΡΜΗΛΩ
L-2 Γ·ΙΥΛ·ΕΥΤΥΧΑΣ
L-3 ΚΟΛ>ΚΑΙΣΑΡΕΥΣ

Translation
L-1 -"A Heliopolitan Zeus (god) of Carmel
L-2 -by Gaius Julius Eutyches
L-3 -'Colonist of Caesarea"

It is interesting to see that during the Hellenistic period, the cult of Zeus was associated with Mount Carmel:[222] "Zeus is the only major god of the Greek pantheon. He is the father of humans and gods. "*Heliopolitan Zeus* is the same as Heliopolitan Jupiter. If Avi-Yonah,[223] concludes that the Baal dwelling on Mount Carmel before Zeus was Adad, the Storm-god; it is due to their identical function. As a matter of fact, Zeus is worshipped by the Greeks as an atmospheric god, the god of sky, storm, lightning and fertility. Similar to Baal Haddad, it is considered a mountain god.[224] We can conclude that it is not accidental that during the Hellenistic period, Mount Carmel was associated with Zeus, the Greek god of storm. The Baal of Mount Carmel could not in any way be Zeus. He came only after the Hellenistic period.

4.2. A seasonal god

The Semites made accurate observations about the rhythms of the seasons: summer would come to devastate the work of spring that made everything grow. Baal was nothing more than an auxiliary to the principles of fertilization. We must not forget the beneficial effects of the sun or the god Šamaš, which

---

[222] MCCARTER, 1999, pp. 1759-1761.
[223] AVI-YONAH, 1952, pp. 118-124.
[224] HERODOTUS, I, 131 :1.

they worshipped.[225] The gods have always had people around to serve them in perfect adoration. Baal, the Storm-god is a seasonal god. He dies during the summer heat, only to come back to life in spring. The cult of the continuous reincarnation of Baal had as a main goal obtaining rain, so necessary for keeping and perpetuating life on earth. Moreover, the analogous god named Baal Adonis, dies during the summer heat followed by a funeral liturgy.[226]

The cyclical character of the seasons aligned with the repetitive cycle of Baal who dies and is resurrected afterwards. This process manifests as an anniversary ceremony. The liturgy of Baal's death was marked by funeral ceremonies and wailers crying in lamentation over the effigy of the divinity.[227] The power of Baal is inseparable from the rain that brings fertility on the earth, and that allows people and animals to live.[228] The translation of the descent Baal in the inferno of CTA 5: II L.3-4 shows that the earth, the withered fruits of the trees, feared the almighty Baal, the rider of the clouds.[229] This fear is due to the usefulness of Baal as master of the rain indispensable to their life. We feel the anxiety expressed by god El in the expression of the following lamentation: [230] "What would become of all the people of Dagan's Sons? What would become the multitude (people)?" The phrase "people of Dagan's sons" is very significant. It refers to everything that grows or germinates in the soil due to the fertility given by the rain controlled by Baal. Dagan means wheat or grain. In the context of the myth and the lamentation of god

---

[225] LIPINSKI, 1995, p. 65.
[226] BARROIS, 1953, p. 338.
[227] BARROIS, 1953, p. 338.
[228] LIPINSKI, 1995a, p. 80.
[229] MATTER, 1980, p. 107.
[230] CAQUOT, et al., 1974, pp. 250-251.

El, it encompasses everything that grows. Baal is called in the mythology of Ugarit:[231] "the almighty, the sovereign master of the earth and king, rider of the clouds." He is a god that reigns over the clouds, the thunders, the lightning, the snow, and the rain. For Wyatt,[232] and many other scholars[233] the deity Baal is the "Charioteer of the clouds."

4.3. Baal a bellicose god

The iconographs of the Storm-god (Baal Adad) and his weapons like the sword, the mace or clubs and the thunderbolt used in different contexts proves the bellicose character of this deity.

4.4. Baal and his weapons

The weapons are surely the most characteristic of divine attributes. Moreover, in the Ugaritic myth of Baal and Yam (Sea) we can see how the divine artisan Kutaru made special weapons to help the God Baal Adad to defeat his enemy.[234] Baal is seen as a warrior god, due to his weapons. According to Vanel:[235] "He appeared as lightly dressed and brandishing a weapon sometimes a dagger, other times a mace or axe against his shoulder or at the level of his belt." Bunnens[236] affirms that the sword worn by Adad is, "the standard weapon of warrior of high rank." These weapons usually worn by the

---

[231] CAQUOT, et al., 1974, pp. 139; 152; 262.
[232] WYATT, 1998, p. 850.
[233] CAQUOT et al., 1974, pp. 136; 139; 152; 262; SMITH, 1994, p. 97; KTU 1.3 IV: 6-11.
[234] BUNNENS, 2006, p. 65; KTU 1. 2 IV, 11-27; BORDREUIL and PARDEE, 1993, pp. 63-70.
[235] VANEL, 1965, p. 55.
[236] BUNNENS, 2006, p. 66.

storm-god establish that he is a bellicose god. The simple fact that god Adad is seen brandishing a weapon, considered a symbol of attack, shows him as in the position of waging a war against an enemy. He performs the function of a warrior. De Vaux[237] confirms him to be a warrior god, a powerful hero. The features of his function as a bellicose deity are also related to climate changes. He is depicted as walking on mountains and seas, brandishing a mace pointing to the ground, and a spear whose shaft ends in the light. That suggests that the brandished lightning of Baal does not evoke a terrifying power but, on the contrary, it reminds us of the fertilizing rain accompanying the storms.

At Aleppo, the Storm-god affirms himself as a warrior god, even though there are a number of texts confirming the bellicose nature of the god, we choose to quote only two of them. The tablet 38 A. 1968 L. 5-7, presents the words of Adad that make reference to having given the country to Yadhun-Lim and because of his weapons none of his enemies dared to confront him in battle :[238] *um-ma-a-mi ^{d}IM-ma ma-a-tum ka la-ša a-na ia-ah-du-li-im ad-di-in ù i-na giš-tukul-meš-ia ma -hi-ra-am ứ-ul ir-ši*: "Thus spoke Adad: I gave all the country to Yadhun-Lim, and thanks to my weapons, he had no rival in battle." In the same text, the L. 2'-4': the Storm-god said that the weapons he had given to the king were identical to those he had used in the battle against the Sea Yam: *ú-te-er-ka giš-tukul-mešša it-ti te-em-tim am-ta-ah-sú ad-di-na-ak-kum-ì ša nam ri-ru-ti-ia* : "and the weapons I had used in battle against the Sea, I gave them to you."

In the Ebla texts, the god's weapons are mentioned. We notice the expression used by the

---

[237] De VAUX, 1971, p. 143.
[238] DURANT, 2002:134-135; 1993:44-45

Storm-god when he speaks about arming his allies in the war.The tablet 5 (A 1858) mentions the arrival of the god's weapons in Terqa:[239] "probably to participate in Zimri-Lim investure." In the Near Eastern tradition, the worship of the divine weapons was known, and this practice, "was meant to transfer divine power to the king and so legitimize his rule."[240] The weapons of the Storm-god are also worshipped among the the Hittites.[241] In another case, "at Emar, the weapon of Storm-god is mentioned in several rituals especially for the installation of the *entu*-priestess."[242] *The term Entu* is the high priestess.[243] According to the texts of Mari, (A.1968) L. 5:[244] *giš-tukul-há ša* ᵈIM, "the weapons of Adad". These weapons had to be stored in a safe place, in Terqa, in the temple of Dagan, considered as the ideal place as they could be easily accessed in time of need. The texts talk about the weapons of the Storm-god without naming actually them.

Therefore, the fact of having *giš-tukul ou giš-tukul-meš* in the tablets helps us understand the nature of Baal's weapons. In Akkadian, the word *giš* means "wood" and *tukul* "weapon."[245] Usually the word should be written in upper case: TUKUL, as it is the Sumerian ideogram borrowed from the Akkadian scribes; if not, the ideal name in Akkadian that refers to "weapon" is, *kakku* (CAD/K: 50, *kakku*). This means that the weapons that Adad talks about are weapons made out of

---

[239] DURAND, 2002, p. 15 ; BUNNENS, 2006, p. 65, note 45.
[240] WYATT, 1998, pp. 833-888 ; BUNNENS, 2006, p. 65.
[241] BUNNENS, 2006, p. 65.
[242] BUNNENS, 2006, p. 66; FLEMING, 1992, p. 50, note 7.
[243] LABAT and MALBRAN-LABAT, 1994, n° 556.
[244] DURAND, 2002, 15, L. 5; see also, L. 7, 2'.
[245] LABAT and MALBRAN-LABAT, 1994, p. 221; CAD/K: 57, *kakku*, 5b 2'.

wood. The word *giš* is linked to *tukul* or defines *tukul*. In Akkadian *giš* in relation to a word which helps to produce the name of the object suggests that in this case the object is made out of wood.

Concerning Akkadian grammar, Bodi[246] says, it is "determinative in front of names of trees and objects made out of wood," for example: *gišdaltum* or *gišIG* means "the door."[247] We can assume that the weapons were clubs. The armour of Baal could have evolved in time, and may have been made out of metal. Often, the club in the Ancient Near East was made with a wooden handle, and attached to it was a mace of a hard substance (stone, metal, ivory) according to the age and usage.[248] Therefore, the Ugaritic text of the battle between Baal and the Sea, explicitly names the weapons. Other authors, underlining the same sense in their research on the Ugaritic texts of the battle between Baal and *Yammu,* the Sea, note clearly that the text speaks about two types of clubs as weapons, where the first type is used to hit the shoulders and the chest, and was not very efficient, but the second type of weapon aimed at the head of the adversary, which could strike the adversary down.[249] The authors suggest the inefficiency of the first type of club, but the texts do not refer to that. On the contrary, they note their efficiency. The two weapons are mentioned (KTU 1.2 IV.4-30), were invented by the artisan god *Kutaru*: Thus *Kutaru* makes two "clubs" or "maces": *ṣmdm.*

---

[246] BODI, 2001, p. 63.
[247] BODI, 2001, p. 30.
[248] BRODREUIL and PARDEE, 1993, p. 68.
[249] CAQUOT et al., 1974, p. 112.

The Ugaritic word *ṣmd* is translated by "mace."[250] For Bunnens[251] the term *ṣmd* is translated as *"mace"* or (double) *"axe"* and Kutaru (the divine artisan) gives them their names.[252] "Your name is Yagrušu, Ô *Yagrušu* Expel *Yammu*. Expel *Yammu* from his throne …" "Your name is Ayyamurru, Ô *Ayyamurru,* throw out Yammu of his throne". Therefore, in the Phoenician inscription from Zincirli, we have divine names; one is BʻL ṢMD.[253] According to the research of scholars[254] this name Baal *ṣmd* means the: *"Lord of the Mace."* In the text A and B of Ras Shamra (Baal epic), *aymr* and *ygrš* are mentioned and employed by Baal to fight Yam (the Prince Sea). In the text A. L. 3 we have *ygrš* and in the text B. L.21 is *aymr.*[255]

The scholar Obermann[256] says: "The verb *grš* in the text A, is an optative perfect (*garraša*), "let him expel", while in B the verb is *mr*, another optative perfect (*marrā*), "let him force out", the agent in both verbs being Baal". For more explanation about the two verbs: *grš* and *ygrš*.[257] The two clubs or arms of Baal have symbolic names, and are possibly charged with magical efficiency.[258] We found the same idea about the signicance of the name of the clubs given by Obermann[259]: "Because the staff is to serve the same function in either incantation…" The only verbs

---

[250] VANEL, 1965, p. 108; BRODREUIL and PARDEE, 1993, p. 67; KTU 1.2 IV 11-12; OBERMANN, 1947, p. 202; BUNNENS, 2006, p. 65.
[251] BUNNENS, 2006, p. 65.
[252] BORDREUIL and PARDEE, 1993, pp. 63-64; WYATT, 1998, pp. 850-851.
[253] KAI, 24; ANET, 1969, p. 655; BUNNENS, 2006, p. 79.
[254] XELLA, 1995, p. 62; BUNNENS, 2006, p. 79.
[255] OBERMANN, 1947, pp. 200-203.
[256] OBERMANN, 1947, p. 202.
[257] OBERMANN, 1947, p. 202, note 22.
[258] CAQUOT, et al., 1974, p. 112.
[259] OBERMANN, 1974, p. 202.

"chase/expel" and "throw" used to expressed by the action of these weapons and the accomplishment of the withdrawal of Baal shows that the weapons were well feared and very efficient. According to Obermann's analysis, the two clubs of Baal have two verbs to show their different actions in the fight between Baal and Yam, the Prince Sea.

For more explanation Obermann[260] confirms that the aim is: "to expel" and "force out" his enemy, the Prince Sea "from his own top of Mount Ṣaphon", "his reign' and 'his throne". After this victory, Baal could take over his kingdom.

The text KTU 1.6 V 1-6 mentions *ktp* a third weapon, in parallel with *ṣmd* the "harpè."[261] This weapon *ktp* is translated by "the scimitar."[262] It was associated with "the club". Among all these weapons, "the club" remains the most powerful weapon of the god. It is with this that Baal wins his victory over Yam. All the weapons of the deity evoke his power over lightning with the exception of the scimitar. The mace suggests better the irresistible and decisive effect of the lightning. Vanel[263] explains that in the iconography the Storm-god raises the weapon with a threatening gesture instead of holding it to the front, explaining this idea of lightning power. The weapons of Baal are mythical representations of the lightning; Baal is the only master over it.[264] Being the master of his weapons, he holds the secret of their handling. This explains, therefore, that he would arm certain sovereigns in the wars against their enemies. He also praises his armour that makes the one who wears it

---

[260] OBERMANN, 1947, pp. 203 ; 206.
[261] BORDREUIL, and PARDEE, 1993, p. 65.
[262] VANEL, 1965, p. 108 ; BUNNENS, 2006, p. 66.
[263] VANEL, 1965, pp. 108-109.
[264] CAQUOT et al., 1974, p. 75.

invincible. The <u>axe</u>, the <u>sword</u> and the <u>thunderbolt</u> are also the weapons of the Storm-god. On many pictures of the Storm-god, he holds the <u>mace</u> in his right hand. The sword was the standard weapon of a warrior. The kings are portrayed with one.[265]

4.4.1. The Bellicose character of Baal of storm: its origin in mythology

The main symbols that we have looked at seem to attribute to the storm god "a terrible character, even devastating as he appears violently in storms". The god has a special relationship with the mountains, and on their peaks he prepares the rain. It is indispensable, because the abundance of the crops depends primarily on the rain. On the peaks of the mountains when "he is about to send lightning on earth, another spirit stores himself as well flashes of lightning."[266] This atmospheric god is viewed as being among the most important gods of the Babylonian pantheon together with Šamaš, Ištar and the god Šin. For Vanel,[267] the god Baal holds the title of: *bêl šamê ù irṣeti,* "lord of the sky and the earth." The same title of Adad appears in the Codex of Hammurabi (col, XXVIIb: 64-67).[268]

The bellicose character of the Storm-god has its origin in Ugaritic mythologies. It is due to his impetuous character that he rises up against the supreme god El who wants to build a palace to god Yam, the master of the seas covering the universe. Obviously, this project caused a stir among other divinities of the same status as Yam. Their worries were understandable due to the fact that the palace goes with the crowning of royalty. The

---

[265] BUNNENS, 2006, pp. 66-67.
[266] VANEL, 1965, p. 67.
[267] VANEL, 1965, p. 53.
[268] FINET, 2002, p. 150.

palace in fact is nothing less than the crowning of royalty. Building a palace to Yam means implicitly that he is chosen as the favourite of the great god El, making Yam the master over the other divinities. Despite their discontent and protest, the palace was finally built and Yam was crowned. But Baal showed his very strong discontent, making threats and going as far as predicting the sudden defeat of Yam. In order to do so, Baal made two clubs and began a war against Yam. He managed to defeat the monster of the sea and win his victory against Yam.[269] By resorting to a trick and taking advantage of the imprudence of his enemies, who with other divinities accepted an invitation to an inaugural banquet of the palace. In this way, he provoked and defeated them and in doing so he clearly stated "who is the lord of the earth."[270] Baal kept his bellicose nature through the passage of time. If Baal had lost this characteristic, than we could understand that he had become a penitent god.

4.4.2. The Storm-God: god with political outlook

The Storm-god takes a particular form. He conducts himself as the lord of Aleppo, in contradiction to the place he occupied in the Babylonian pantheon, where he was seen, without having the title of a dominant divinity, as an important god. Therefore, the god "Adad of Aleppo himself proclaims his absolute power."[271] He got involved in selecting political leaders, favouring and empowering them (giving them absolute power). Some cases followed: Yahdum-Lîm, the king of Mari who was favoured by Adad of Aleppo and received his absolute power. He was victorious in battles with enemies.[272] The nature and the functions of the Storm-god change in this

---

[269] CAQUOT et al., 1974, pp. 107-113.
[270] CAQUOT et al., 1974, p. 184.
[271] DURAND, 2002, p. 3.
[272] DURAND, 2002, p. 3.

particular area. Even so, he remains the Storm-god. He firmly proclaimed that the god of Aleppo was not interested in worldly goods but very much in justice. This is explained by the fact that the Storm-god of Aleppo was impartial and offered refuge to anyone seeking a refuge. He goes as far as giving his absolute power "independently of nationalist visions."[273]

The king of Mari, Zimri-Lim asked his counterpart of Aleppo for the extradition of one of his vassals who had had the nerve to address a written message to him in which he identified himself as his equal. The king of Aleppo refused, but after deciding on the guilt of the vassal, he made him swear under oath in the temple of Adad the Storm-god.[274] We conclude with the quotation from Mettinger where Baal is regarded as "*a weather god, warrior, and major figure of pantheon.*"[275] The Storm-god of Aleppo figures among the deities 'that are witnesses to the treaty concluded between Assur-nirari V and Mati-ilu of Arpad'.[276]

4.5. Death and resurrection of the Storm-god

The Storm-god Baal is also dying and rising deity. The resurrection of this god follows the seasons' cycle. The god dies during the summer and is reborn in spring. As a result of this cycle of the god who disappears and reappears following the seasons, there is a need to talk about the resurrection of the deity (Baal Hadad).

---

[273] DURAND, 2002, p. 3.
[274] DURAND, 2002, p. 4.
[275] METTINGER, 2001, p. 38.
[276] BUNNENS, 2006, p. 78; SAA II, n°2, L. 18.

4.5.1. Death and Resurrection: Myth worship or seasonality god?

Baal, the Storm-god, was one of the many divinities who would die and resurrect periodically. He was a seasonal god. The death and resurrection of the gods are generic titles attributed to all agrarian divinities in the Mediterranean societies. They are found among other myths and rituals attributed to them each year in order to celebrate their death and resurrection.[277] It is important to note that some elements are characteristic for such divinities; that is, the myths concerning their death and rebirth, the thematic correspondence of the cycle of seasonal changes and ritual series that serve as a context to the cult.[278] According to the Baal cycle, there are five interpretations of the Baal cycle, but no consensus over the interpretation. [279] Each interpretation has its characteristics and evidence:[280]

> "Five views of the Baal cycle which continue to influence strongly research on the Baal cycle. The first view (1) is the seasonal interpretation; (2) ritual interpretation; (3) the cosmogony theory; (4) the view of the Baal cycle as the struggle between the forces of life versus the power of death and chaos and (5) the view of the cycle as the exaltation of Baal as king".

In order to understand the nature or the character of Baal, we have to try to understand this myth better in order to understand the whole function of the divinity.

---

[277] METTINGER, 2001, p. 15.
[278] METTINGER, 2001, p. 37.
[279] SMITH, 1986, p. 313.
[280] SIMTH, 1986, p. 313; 1994, p. 59; 60.

4.5.1.a. The first hypothesis focuses on the seasonality of the myth.

It corresponds to the seasons, and the rites take place to express the religious aspect of the myth.[281] Therefore, the battle between Baal and Mot was inspired by the contrast between the mild autumn and the humid winds of September. The cycle of Baal explains the meteorological manifestations.[282] Virolleaud,[283] said that: Baal does not represent perpetual life but intermittent life, the life that is born and reborn every spring, that blooms during the summer only to wilt and disappear during autumn; Baal, therefore, is after all, the life of plants. The myth of Baal is a combination of nature and the places of cult, which tends to explain the alternation of seasons. Moreover, the origin of the Ugaritic cult was largely founded on the rites determined by the same seasons.[284] Such divinities are the personification of the seasonal cycle of the vegetation.[285] The cycle of Baal in the Ugaritic myth presents the alternation of seasons. Therefore, the teaching of Baal cycle according to Smith[286] is to tell "a vivid story of divine struggle and divine wisdom, divine power and divine death."

---

[281] SMITH, 1994, p. 64.
[282] GRAY, and CASSUTO, 1971, pp. 21-24.
[283] VIROLLEAUD, 1934, p. 317. „De toute façon, ce passage… établit nettement que Baal est, avant tout, un dieu de la végétation, et qu'il disparaît quand la végétation est fleutrie, à la fin de l'été", cf. (Virolleaud, 1934 :317). „Baal quant à lui, représente, non pas la vie perpétuelle, mais la vie intermittente, la vie qui naît ou renaît chaque printemps, qui s'épanouit durant l'été pour s'étioler et disparaître enfin à l'automne, Baal, en effet, c'est la vie des plantes", voir aussi Virolleaud, 1937, I :9 ;15.
[284] De MOORE, 1971, p. 68; SMITH, 1994, p. 65.
[285] METTINGER, 2001, p. 18.
[286] SMITH, 1986, p. 313.

4.5.1.b. Second hypothesis: the ritual interpretation

About the ritual interpretation, the scholar Smith[287] says: "The seasonal interpretation presupposes a correlation between the Baal cycle and the annual cycle of weather on the Syrian coast." Smith,[288] shows that there's a relationship between "rites or cultic acts which celebrated the divine deeds reflecting the vicissitudes of seasons." And according to Smith[289] and Gordon:[290] "the myth of the Baal cycle is a combination of nature-myth and a cultic myth to explain the origin of the alternating of the seasons as well as the origin of the Ugaritic cultic which was largely based on the rites determined by the same seasons." The only weakness of this interpretation lies in the fact that the god Yammu demands royalty and non-rain or flooding (CTA 2.1 and 2.4). Therefore, this weakness should not exclude the seasonal idea, because the conflict between Baal and Mot,:[291] can "lead up to the time of the autumn rains," or we can add that this Baal cycle purportedly reflects the autumnal New Year festival, and yet none of extant ritual...[292]

4.5.1.c. The third view is a cosmogony

This idea asks us to consider the cycle of Baal as illustrating the life in cosmos, and at the same time to regard the fight against Yam ('the Sea') and Mot as evoking the presence of death in the universe.[293] The death and resurrection motifs are very important to the cosmogony of the A.B. Cycle which describes the

---

[287] SMITH, 1986, p. 316; 1994, p. 63.
[288] SMITH, 1986, p. 316; 1994, p. 63.
[289] SMITH, 1986, p. 316; 1994, p. 60.
[290] C.H. GORDON, JNES, vol. 7, 1948, pp. 185-186.
[291] SMITH, 1986, p. 317.
[292] SMITH, 1994, p. 60; De TARRAGON, 1980, p. 184.
[293] SMITH, 1994, p. 75.

establishment of the cosmic order over the microcosm.²⁹⁴ The legitimation of both chaos ('Yam') and cosmos ('Ba'al') rule of the microcosm in turn by the creator god indicated that both forces are subordinate to El.²⁹⁵

4.5.1.d. The fourth view - life versus Death

The fourth interpretation found support in the effects which the death of Baal brings to the earth (in CTA 6.1=KTU 1.6 I 6-7 and CTA6.4.25-26=KTU1.6IV1-2. Mot ('Death') incarnates the power over life, and the conflict between Baal and his opponent. Baal represents the conflict between life and death.²⁹⁶ But Baal's battles with Yam ('Sea') and Mot are cast in terms of kingship in (KTU 1.1IV 24-25, 1.2IV10, 32, 1.6V5-6, and 1.6 VI 28-29, 33-35).²⁹⁷ This life is expressed by the human actions of the gods, and it is in this context that Baal emerges as the hero of the divine kingdom.

4.5.1.e. The fifth view - interpretation of Baal's kingship

Divine titles also show the dimension of the Baal cycle. Baal is called *zbl'arṣ* "lord of the earth". His title *'al'iyn* "mighty" and *'al'iyn qrdm,* "mightiest of warriors" "reinforce the picture of Baal as the great warrior battling against rival claimants for the divine throne."²⁹⁸ Mot through his own words proclaims in CTA 6.6 or KTU 1.6VI, 33-35. For Smith:²⁹⁹ "Let them

---

[294] WATERSTON, 1989, p. 425.
[295] WATERSTON, 1989, p. 425.
[296] SMITH, 1994, p. 59.
[297] SMITH, 1994, p. 59.
[298] SMITH, 1986, p. 323.
[299] SMITH, 1986, p. 339.

set Baal on the throne of his kingship, on the resting place, the seat of his domination." We can mention that the Yamm's epithet *'adn*, "lord" indicates the royal character, but his title *ṯpṭ* "judge" proves a function of kingship of *Yamm*.[300] The acquisition of his own palace by his battles against Mot and Yamm is another element that reflects the kingship of Baal.[301] In the same text, the author affirmed:[302]

> "Baal uses monarchy precisely because he is the deity who can mediate the blessings of the natural cosmos both to human society and to the company of the pantheon. The means of providing blessings are his rains, which the seasonal interpretation has emphasized. These rains revivify the world, duly noted by proponents of the cosmogony approach. Indeed, without the rains, there is no life. Baal's kingship brings life to the world, prevailing over the forces of the death and destruction, as stressed by those who view the Baal Cycle as a struggle between the forces of life and death."

This last view of Virolleaud[303] and Obermann[304] puts the interpretation of the Baal cycle in a historical and political context. They suggest "that Baal's defeat of Yamm ('Prince Sea') represents the historical victory over sea people which deserves notice". This interpretation can be made as well. The supporters of this interpretation argue that the conflict with Yam in KTU 1.2 IV was in reality a challenge between the people of the sea and those of the Syrian littoral late in the Bronze Age. The people of Ugarit managed to confuse and ruin their invaders from the oriental side of the Mediterranean Sea. This political and historical

---

[300] SMITH, 1986, p. 325; 1994, p. 59.
[301] SMITH, 1994, p. 60.
[302] SMITH, 1994, p. 96.
[303] VIROLLEAUD, 1946, pp. 498-509.
[304] OBERMANN, 1947, pp. 205-206.

factor has contributed to the birth of the Baal cycle in order to illustrate the reality of this rivalry.[305] This view has been pointed out by the scholar Virolleaud:[306]

> "In other words, in the light of the fragment which we have analysed, the narrator of 3 AB would appear to have incorporated in his version of building saga a myth designed to explain, etiologically, how the people of Ugarit succeeded in expelling a hostile invasion effected by the inhabitants of the sea region, say, on the eastern shore of the Mediterranean, how they routed and deranged the invader's forces, how they destroyed his ranks into ruin. That, by the medium of folklore, the struggle between two peoples may easily come to be remembered as the struggle between their respective gods and, in the present instance, between Baal, the most active and popular god of Ugarit, and Prince Sea, the real or popular name of the god worshipped by the invaders from the sea region."

The power of Baal had been showing in his lightning and rains manifestation (CTA 4.7 =KTU 1.4VII.25-31). According to all these interpretations, the seasonal interpretation struggles with influence researches and works. The Ugaritic mythology of Baal contains a number of references to the seasonal events that follow the course of the Ugaritic cultic year, which coincided with the Syrian agro-climatic year.[307] The texts KTU 1.4 V 6-9 and CTA 4.5 (KTU 1.4 VII) 26-31 refer to the rain of Baal, which gives life to the world. We can cite KTU 1.4V 6-9: [308]

> "L.6 And Baal now will fertilize with the luxuriance of his rain,
> L.7 The luxury of watering in turbulence (flow?)

---

[305] SMITH, 1994, pp. 87-91.
[306] VIROLLEAUD, 1947, pp. 405-509; OBERMANN, 1947, pp. 205-206.
[307] De MOOR, 1971, p. 67.
[308] SMITH, 1994, pp. 295-298; GRABBE, 1976, pp. 57-63.

L.8 And gives his thunder in the clouds,
L.9 Flashing lightning to earth'
Another reference is CTA 4.7=KTU 1.4 VII: 25-31:[309]
'L. 25 He (Baal) opened a window in the house,
L. 27 A window in the midst of pala[ce].
L. 28 Baal opened a break in the [clou]ds,
L. 29 Baal gave his holy voice
L. 30 Baal repeated the is[sue of] his lips,
L. 31 His holy voice, the earth [sho]ok"

This last passage in particular the L.28: "Baal opened a break in the clouds" refers to the manifestation of Baal's thunder and rain or the fall of rains:[310] "Each deity was sovereign over his domain. The divine conflicts symbolizes more than the alternation of seasons in the Syrian year".[311] For this alternation of seasons, in the summer period which Mot reigns over the nature, Baal is relegated to the underworld.[312] Baal descended into the underworld with his meteorological phenomena (KTU^2.1.5V.6b-11)[313]:

w'at. qh 'rptk. rhk. mdlkmtrk. 'mk. Sb't glmk. MTn. hnzrk 'mk.pdry. bt. 'ar 'mk. {t}tly. bt.rb.

"And you take your clouds, your wind, your chariot team, your rain; take with you your seven servitors and your eight boars, take Pidriya daughter of dew with you, and Taliya daughter of showers with you." Baal in the underworld is the time that Mot becomes king of the summer and exercises his omnipotence on nature during this period.

In this way we can read the tablet IAB, II, L. 24-25 [314] thus:

---

[309] SMITH, 1986, p. 315.
[310] DUSSAUD, 1932, I, pp. 298-300.
[311] SMITH, 1986, p. 317.
[312] DUSSAUD, 1937, II, p. 121.
[313] See also. DAY, 2002, p. 95.
[314] DUSSAUD, 1935, I, p. 55.

"L. 24 les plaines sans (l'eau) des cieux
L.25 (sont) dans la main de Mot, le fils divin."

It is supposed that the reign of Mot retains water from heaven to fall over the earth; it also occurs at the time of the death of Baal. According to Eusebius of Caesarea, (*P. Ev.*, III: 12-17),[315] Adonis (Mot) is the god, the spirit of harvest. He is the deity who lets it be known when the cereals, ears of corn and grains achieve ripeness. So, Mot becomes king over nature during the summer, when Baal dies at the time of harvest.

4.5.2. Baal and Mot

The conflict between Baal and Mot takes place at the inaugural banquet of the palace (1.4 V-VII). Among all the gods, only Mot refuses to bow before the power of Baal. Instead, he claims to be entitled to reign. Baal does not hesitate to summon his rival to renounce his claim. He even sends him Gapan and Ougar as ambassador messengers with cautious and precise instructions to go to the underground dwelling of Mot: "But be careful divine servants, when you approach divine Mot, so that he does not turn you into a lamb in his mouth,"[316] The reason why the ambassadors are sent to Mot is not clear. He had to bring homage to the greatness of Mot and admit that he is the king of gods, protector of life on earth I.4.VII: 49-52.[317] We believe that the messengers were sent to force his rival to give up on his claim to reign, since at the banquet Mot himself refused to bow before Baal. However, the instructions given to the messengers warning them not to approach the house

---

[315] DUSSAUD, 1932, I, p. 249.
[316] CAQUOT, et al., 1974, p. 220.
[317] METTINGER, 2001, p. 57.

of Mot, puzzle us. Could they have sent their message from a distance? Nothing is less certain. They came back to Baal with a message, this time from Mot, the personified death, the sovereign of the infernal world, inviting the king of gods, Baal, to his table.[318] Baal responds positively. Baal himself, who warned his ambassadors not to get too close to Mot, ignores his own advice by accepting this invitation. The evidence has been pointed out by Smith:[319] "the Baal and Mot conflict speaks about the symbol of dying and reviving god. The end of the cycle describes ritual wailing for Baal as projection of the seasonal ululation."

4.5.3. The death of Baal: A limit of its glory

Baal has just signed his death warrant. Accepting an invitation from Mot and descending into the afterlife means metaphorically the death of Baal.[320] It seems that the invitation was not a metaphor, but a reality, and would speak to twisting the minds of instructional or educational myth. To be a metaphor, there must be a transposition of a direction A to B or the expression of the abstract by a concrete word. Accepting the invitation of his fierce rival, Mot requires the submission of Baal. Baal, once in the home of Mot, adopts an unusual posture, humble in contrast to his fiery temper, and bragged of being the lord of gods. The scholar Waterson[321] said: "Hail Divine Mot, I am your slave, I am forever", (KTU1.5 II:4-12). Once at the table with Baal, Mot gives notice that he will put his host Baal in the graveyard of the divine land. The will of the lord of the kingdom of hell has been accomplished, Baal is dead.

---

[318] CAQUOT, 1974, p. 243-245.
[319] SMITH, 1986, p. 317; 1994, p. 61.
[320] METINGER, 2001, p. 61.
[321] WATERSON, 1989, p. 431.

The death of Baal is not seen everywhere in the same way. The idea of an alternative is mentioned. Baal's daughters would be killed by Mot.[322] Waterston[323] disagrees with the argument that rejects the death of Baal. According to him, if the death of Baal were real, there would be no sense in subsequent events. Besides, the narrative KTU 1.5 V implies that one of Baal's daughters was given to Mot not as part of a substitution, but rather as a gift or as a sacrifice. It is true that Mot requested Baal to come with his entourage including his two daughters who are *Pidray* "the bright." *Pdry*, one of daughters of *Ba'lu* (Baal), is probably the eldest, because she was always mentioned first and was revered as an independent goddess in Ugarit. Her name $^{d}pi\text{-}id\text{-}ra\text{-}i'$, in *AOAT 16*, 1971:82; (see also II AB, I, L. 18) *Pdr (y)*, "fille de la lumière" means the "daughter of the light,".[324] The daughter *Taday* means "the rainy".[325] According to Dussaud[326] the word *pdr(y)* could have a connection with the "the mace" and *Pdr* symbolizes the "lightning" especially since *Pdr(y)* has been connected with a light. He clarifies that *Pdr* could have two meanings: 'the mace' and 'the lightning'. Virolleaud,[327] concurred, and says that *Pdr* is the synonym of *brq* (*barāqum*): "a flash of lightning." The rest of the story does not provide more details. Baal would go to his rival Mot's city with his two daughters. What has become of them? The myth tells about the death of Baal, burial and mourning. We believe the idea is president of a substitute or the death one of the Baal's daughters instead of him. One of Baal's

---

[322] METTINGER, 2001, p. 39.
[323] WATERSON, 1989, p. 431.
[324] DUSSAUD, 1937, II, pp. 127; 129.
[325] CAQUOT, et al., 1974, p. 248.
[326] DUSSAUD, 1937, II, pp. 127; 129.
[327] VIROLLEAUD, 1936, p. 44, notes 3.

daughters is given to Mot for sacrifice. Nevertheless, if Baal did not die, why was the supreme god El informed? Why did Anat, Baal's sister mourn her brother? Why look for his body? All that proves the preparation of Baal's funeral rites (1.5. 1.6:I-VI) and certifies the death of Baal.[328] Baal's death restores an understanding of the attitude of Supreme god El and goddess Anat in mourning and the funeral of Baal. For Waterson[329] who argue that a daughter of Baal was given to Mot, the following question appears: which one? The choice of one daughter of Baal at the expense of another requires a preference or a choice that was necessary for the sacrifice they suggest. In addition, what sacrifice? All these unanswered questions leave a confusion in the mind.

4.5.4. The mourning of Baal

The supreme god El will be informed about the death of Baal, and it does not help to lament it. Caquot said:[330]

> "El ... descends from his throne. He sits on the step and sits down. He spreads on his head filth of mourning, the dust on his head where he rolls. He covers his loins with sackcloth; he slashes the skin with a stone ... What will happen to the people of the Son of Dagan? What will become of the multitude?"

Following the death of Baal, El and Anat expressed similar words. They had identical reactions, only they were different in their objections: falling from the throne, El (KTU 1.5 vi 12-14) for using ash and dust (KTU 1.5 vi 14 -16).[331] Baal died, Anat, looked for his body and with the deity Šapaš assistance of the deity

---

[328] CAQUOT, et al., 1974, pp. 250-253.
[329] WATERSON, 1989, pp. 425-434.
[330] CAQUOT, et al., 1974, pp. 250-251.
[331] WYATT, 1998, p. 129.

Šapaš. They finally found his body. He was buried on Shaphon Mountain.[332] Parallels can be drawn between the mourning of Baal by Anat and El, and mourning through the Old Testament, the appeals to sit down and spread dust on the dead body's head (Josh 7:6; 1 Sam 4 12; Job 2:12; Ezek 27:30; Amos 2:7).

4.6. Ritual and worship

4.6.1. Burial and funeral rites of Baal

With the help of Šapaš, Anat traces the body of his brother on the mountain Shaphon where Baal was buried. According to the text, it was in the divine cemetery of earth where Anat buried his brother Baal. The role of Šapaš by the side of Anat in finding the body of Baal is not unimportant, because he is the conductor of souls in the after life (KTU1.161).[333] This mountain was very important in the worship of Baal. The sacrifices for the funeral were held there (KTU 1.6.i:15-31).[334] The animals which were sacrificed were oxen, wild cattle, sheep, deer, goats, donkeys, and animals of each species in a number equivalent to seventy (KTU 1.6i.15-20).[335] It is difficult to know the liturgy ritual, and how it was done. The corpus of Ugaritic ritual texts contains no reference to the death and resurrection of Baal. [336] Looking at the texts of the mythology on the Baal cycle, we find that there was no resurrection of Baal. Some authors said that the Ugaritic royal ritual concerning funerals shaped

---

[332] METTINGER, 2001, p. 58.
[333] See also METTINGER, 2001, p. 58.
[334] METTINGER, 2001, p. 62.
[335] CAQUOT, et al., 1974, pp. 254-255.
[336] SMITH, 1994, p. 290.

the Baal worship.[337] If the ritual of Baal is modelled on the Ugaritic kings' ritual, then we must recognize that Baal is portrayed as the king of the gods and the greatest of all.[338] On the other hand, it should be noted that in this mythology, Baal comes back to life, but the human king who dies never comes back to life.

4.6.2. Royal Funeral Ceremony KTU 1.161 or RS. 34.126[339]

1-*spr. dbḥẓlm*	The document of the feast for *I-almu:*
2-*qritm. rpi. a[rṣ]*	You are invoked, O rpu arṣ
3-*qbitm. qbṣd[dn]*	You are summoned, 0 assembly of Didanu!
4-*qra. ulkn. rp[u]*	Ulkn, the *rpu* is invoked,
5-*qra. trmn. rp[u]*	Trmn, the *rpu* is invoked,
6-*qra. sdn. w. rd[n]*	Sdn-w-Rdn is invoked,
7-*qra. ṭr. 'llmn[ ]*	Tr-'llmn is invoked,
8-*qru. rpim. qdmym[ ]*	The ancient *rpum* are invoked.
9- *qritm. rpi. a[rṣ]*	You are invoked, O rpu arṣ
10-*qbitm.qbṣ ddn*	You are summoned, 0 assembly of Didanu!
11-*qra. 'm1tmr. m[l]k*	Ammi! tamru the king is invoked,
12-*qra. u nqmd [.] mlk*	Niqmaddu the king is also invoked.
13-*ksi. nqmd f.] ibky*	O throne of Niqmaddu, be wept for,
14-*w. ydm'. hdm. p'nh*	May his footstool be shed tears for;
15-*l pnh. ybky. ṯlḥn. mlk*	May the king's table be wept for before it,

16-*'dmt. w. 'dmt. 'dmt*	Misery! Misery of miseries!
17-*iḫšn špš.*	Burn, 0 šapšu!
18-*w. iḫšn.(19) nyr. rbt.*	Burn, 0 Great Light!
19-*'ln.Špš tṣḥ*	May Sapsu cry from above:
20- *aṯr. [b]'lk. l. ksh*	'To the place of your lord,

---

[337] METTINGER, 2001, pp. 38-39.
[338] CAQUOT, et al., 1974, p. 183.
[339] BORDREUIL and PARDEE; 1982:121-128; TSUMURA, 1993:42-43, translated by Tsumura.

	before his throne,
21- a*t*r (21) b'lk. arṣ rd.	To the place of your lord, descend to the underworld,
22- arṣ rd. (22) w. špl. 'pr.	Descend to the underworld, and be low in the dust!
23- t/ht (23) sdn. W. rdn.	Go down, O Sdn-w-Rdn,
24- t/ht *t*r. (24) 'limn.	Go down, O *T*r-'llmn,
25- t/ht. 'm*t*tmr. Mlk	Go down, O Ammi!tamru, the king,
26- t*h*m. u. nq[md]. Mlk	Go down too, O Niqmaddu, the king!
27-'šty. W. *t*'y.	One and make an offering,
*t*n.] W. *t*'y.]	two and make an offering,
28-tlt W. *t*'y[.]	Three and make an offering,
a[rb]'. w. *t*'[y]	four and make an offering,
29-*h*mš w. *t*'y.	Five and make an offering,
tt[w.] *t*'y.	six and make an offering,
30-- šb' w. *t*'y.	Seven and make an offering.
tqdm 'ṣr (31) šlm	Offer a bird as a slm-offering.
31- šlm 'mr [pi]	Peace to Ammurapi,
32-w. šlm. bnh.	and peace to his sons!
Šlm. [*t*ryl	Peace to Tariyelli;
33- šlm. bth.	Peace to his house!
šlm. u[g]rt	Peace to Ugarit;
34- šlm *t*g̊rh	Peace to its gates!

Mettinger[340] said that god Baal is modelled on the perception of the fate of Ugaritic kings who descended into hell as their destiny. His main thesis is based on the liturgy in royal funerals KTU 1.161 and literary elements in KTU1.5-6. Baal's death reflects the death of the Ugaritic kings, but his return to life can be excluded from the living king's role, to ensure peace in the world to the living people. In Mesopotamia, there was a ritual of substitution when the king died whereby a substitute took his place to avoid bad omens for the king. This substitute received royal funeral ceremonies and was buried. The royal palace was purified by the substitute's death to exclude potential danger against the king. After that ceremony, the king could return to his palace to play his usual or an official role and resume his public

---

[340] METTINGER, 2001, p. 82.

life.³⁴¹ If the funeral ceremonies of Baal were modelled on the usual king on KTU1.161, we can identify the royal funerary ritual. The KTU 1.161 text dimensions are: (11 cm x 13.5 cm). The scholars Caquot and De Tarragon³⁴² call this document: "a liturgical book" of the ceremony of "funeral of a king who dies". Bordreuil and Pardee³⁴³ speak about a deceased king's sacrificial booklet Niqmadu III.

The study of this text (KTU. 1.161) leads us to subdivide the liturgy into five parts (5): L. 2-12, appeal to the Rephaim or spirits of the ancestors. "The ancestors (the *rapa'a ù 'arsi*) were invited to the banquet offered to them at the king's death,"³⁴⁴ There existed some material proving the relationship between the Storm-god and dead kings. On the statue from Gerçin (northeast of Zincirli in Turkey), was found an inscription, from which we read the following first line:³⁴⁵

"I am Panamuwa, son of QRL, king of Y'DY, who erected this statue for Hadad in my eternal above".

In the work and translation of Niher,³⁴⁶ Y'DY is read Yādiya and QRL is to read Qarli. This means that the statue of the Storm-god Hadad was present in all dead kings' tombs. In the same inscription on the lines L. 17-18, we found the legitimate successor making offerings and praying to the dead spirit of the king *Panamuwa* who may eat and drink with the god Hadad' confirms:³⁴⁷ "May the spirit of *Panamuwa* [eat] with thee, and may the spirit of *Panamuwa* drink with

---

[341] BOTTERO, 1987, pp. 281-282.
[342] CAQUOT, and De TARRAGON, 1989, p. 103.
[343] BRODREUIL and PARDEE, 1982, p. 126.
[344] HUSSER, 1995, p. 115.
[345] BUNNENS, 2006, p. 57, fig. 82.
[346] NIHER, 2014, p. 185.
[347] NIHER, 2014, p. 184.

thee". The same idea has been repeated in the inscription on the statue of Gerçin in the lines L. 21-22. In this text, the king *Panamuwa* partakes in the meal with the Storm-god Hadad.

In the text KTU1.161, (L. 13-17), there is prescription of the ritual lamentation, and in lines L.18-26 there is a prayer to the god Šapaš, the solar deity, to lead the deceased to the realm of death.[348] The dead king Niqmadu III has been invited by god Šapaš after this funeral meal to follow the Rephaim and their ancestors when they descended in שְׁאוֹל "the underworld". See in the L. 18-22; the role played by the deity Šapaš is commanded by the dead Niqmadu to descend in the underworld.[349] Some similar ideas about the journey of gods in the underworld were added:[350]

> "In ancient Mesopotamia, the sun was thought to travel from west to east through a subterranean tunnel during the night. On that journey the solar deity took with him the spirits of the deceased as well as the offerings for those already dwelling in the nether world".

For Spronk:[351]

> "The conception of the sun-goddess ruling the dead...The sun was believed to travel through the netherworld during the night. So it is not difficult to understand why the sun-deity was associated with the spirits of dead staying there."

The question is, why is the night travel time chosen by the goddess to meet the dead spirit? Spronk proposes the answer, and says it was: "the usual time for the spirits of the dead to appear (1 Sam 28:8)."

---

[348] HUSSER, 1995, pp. 115; 120; TSUMURA, 1993, p. 45.
[349] TSUMURA, 1993, p. 52.
[350] De MOOR, 1976, p. 330 see notes 52; TSUMURA, 1993, p. 54.
[351] SPRONK, 1986, p. 163.

In L.27-30, we found offerings, and finally in the L.31-34 is the whole blessing. This ceremony takes place over a period of seven days.[352] The king celebrated in this ritual was Niqmadu III, since he was the predecessor of king Ammurapi, his successor.[353] About this tablet[354] Bordreuil and Pardee said: it "was referring to the ritual performed for the funeral of Niqmadu III. The end of the text alludes to a salutary sacrifice... for the successor, the new king Ammurapi to be alive." The dead man was on the verge of descending into hell; even a king did not yet have the status of ancestor. At this stage, it cannot grant safety, strength, and prosperity to the living. To become a *rapa'a u arsi,* it is necessary for the entire process of death to take place, including the rites of burial. Without this process, the wandering soul of the deceased represents a danger for the living ones.[355]

Here is what the worship of Baal might look like, as shown in the Ugaritic royal liturgy booklet about funerals. Nevertheless, without physical evidence of the worship of Baal, it is difficult to prove the reality of it. There is no certain proof of animal sacrifices offered during the ceremony, even if this ritual is implicitly expressed during this period of seven days of funeral ceremonies. If we agree with this point of view, we cannot accurately name the animals sacrificed for the worship of Baal, or the place where the ceremony was celebrated. That leaves us perplexed once again, and makes us wonder what usually happened during the seven days' ceremony. There is a great lack of information regarding this process, even if we look closely at the liturgical

---

[352] CAQUOT and De TARRAGON, 1989, p. 103.
[353] HUSSER, 1995, p. 115 ; TSUMURA, 1993, p. 47.
[354] BORDREUIL and PARDEE, 1982, p. 128.
[355] HUSSER, 1995, p.115.

interpretation of the facts. This difficulty does not stop us from making progress in our research, and undertaking the comparative study between the funeral rites of Baal as described in the myth and the Ugaritic royal ritual about funerals.

4.6.3. Worship Staff of Baal and prophecy

We must admit that it is difficult, in our quest to find materials concerning worship of the deity Baal in the kingdom of Ugarit, like our predecessors who have studied the ritual corpus. However, De Tarragon said: "the corpus of ritual tablets delivers only a small number of references on the worship ritual, aside from being the person of the king". Not only, the class of priest does not deliver any secret or information on the worship of Baal's death or resurrection, but we also have few items of the personal side of this cult. He continues his argumentation on the next page, saying that: "The king acts as chief of worship in a number of rituals." He proclaims himself as "king-priest."

Apart from the king, other people were known to be priests of the cult. Among them, we can mention *inš ilm* qualified as an agent of worship more often called, "besides the king", whose function remains unclear, but who was often appointed in various rituals.[356] The term '*khnm*' which means "priest", is less often mentioned than its predecessor and it is never attested to in the ritual texts. In his own words, he (De Tarragon)[357] concludes: "this is a surprise". He explains that this was a junior staff member, not part of the temples of the priests, who were not named in worship services, but they were employed in

---

[356] De TARRAGON, 1989, p. 133.
[357] De TARRAGON, 1989, p. 134.

administrative lists, among other professional groups which were far from being religious.[358] Given this lack of written word informing us about the rituals of Baal, we decided to proceed by making an analogy between the mythological ritual of god Baal and the Ugaritic royal rite on funerals. Therefore, this comparison is based on the thesis that the cult of Baal was designed after the cult of royal ritual. By this comparison, we can deduce the worship elements in the Baal booklet. We are hoping that a debate will be opened from this thesis. However, we recognize and speak about both cases, the funeral liturgy celebrated for a human king who dies, followed by mourning the death of the king of the gods. However, said:[359] "in the mythology of Ugarit, being essentially religious, as always in the ancient Near East, the main actors are gods."

On the prophecy of Baal, the stele of the Ahmar/Qubbah made of stone black basalt erected by Hamiyata king of Masuwari (Til-Barsib), the Storm-god named Tarhunza had the prophet whose role is to deliver a message.[360] This stele was discovered according to Bunnens:[361] "in the Euphrates River at some distance downstream from Tell Ahmar, near the village of Qubbah." For the period and the date we have the proposal of Hawkins:[362] "in the later tenth or early ninth century BC," or according to Bunnens[363] the date was Neo-Hittite, or Late Hittite or Syro-Anatolian. This deity was the "Storm-god", (see the commentary of L.7),[364] and he (Storm-god) was also known as the "god of the

---

[358] De TARRAGON, 1989, p. 134.
[359] De TARRAGON, 1980, p. 11.
[360] BUNNENS, 2006, p. 2.
[361] BUNNENS, 2006, p. 1.
[362] HAWKINS, 2006, p. 11.
[363] BUNNENS, 2006, p. 58.
[364] HAWKINS, 2006, p. 21.

Vineyards."[365] This Storm-god (Tarhunza) was a prophet messenger according to L. 22 of the stele inscription:[366] "the god-inspired (one) said to me". We found another interesting comparison in the text of Mari published by J.-M Durand.[367] In this text, someone named Abya was known as the *āpilum*, the priest/prophet of the Storm-god, lord of Halab (Aleppo). He delivers the prophetic message to Zimri-Lim king of Mari: *¹a-bi-ia* **a-pí-lum** *ᵈIM be-el ha-la-a[bᵏⁱ]* 'Abya, "the answerer of Adad lord of Aleppo." The word *āpilum*, came from the verb **apālu** which means "answer", see CAD/AII: 162, *apālu*, 2a.- *āpilum* (male) and *āpiltum* (female).

Robinson[368] (1950:104, L. 26) in his works about the prophecy of Adad, lord of Kallassu, we found this: *LÚ a-pí-lum ša* ⁱˡAdad *be-el Ka-al-la-súᵏⁱ* the "answerer/Prophet of Adad, lord of Kallassu". CAD/AII: 170, *āpilu* A.1b; (RA, 78, L. 29; 31).[369] About "the prophet of the God Adad", see the tablet A1121+A 2731.:[370]

In the same oracle, they mention a male and a female who played the role of prophets. The author of the tablet said that when he resided in Mari, he sent to his master (Zimri-Lim) all oracles from the male and female prophets: ᵃʷⁱˡ*a-pí-lumù* ˢⁱⁿⁿⁱˢᵃᵗ *a-pí-il-tummi-im-ma a-wa-tam ša i-qa-[ab-bu] nim a-na be-li-ia ú-ta-ar:* "I used to report to my lord whatever the male and female were saying." Both male and female can be prophets of God Adad.

---

[365] BUNNENS, 2006, p. 58.
[366] HAWKINS, 2006, pp. 15 ; 27.
[367] DURAND, 1993, p. 45; 1988, pp. 377-452.
[368] ROBINSON, 1950, p. 104.
[369] LAFONT, 1984.
[370] LAFONT, 1984, *RA*, 78, p. 9, L. 29, 31 and 35.

4.6.4. Comparative table of mythic ritual and royal burial ritual[371]

This table is a comparison between the funeral ritual of mourning Baal in mythology and the royal Ugaritic ritual on burial. Since most authors argue that the worship of Baal would be physical evidence, modelled on the Ugaritic royal funeral rituals, this table aims to find common elements, as well as the differences between the two views. The following text (KTU.1. 5-6) is the Ugaritic fragments of the Baal Cycle of Myth.[372] It concerns the reactions and the mourning of the God El and the goddess Anat after the death of Baal, the Lord of earth, the winner against Yam, (the Sea deity).

The mourning of the God El.

KTU.1.5 vi. 1:	[They rolled back the tent of **El**]
	And came to the pavilion of the King,
	The Father of the Bright One.
	[They lifted up their voices and cri]ed:
	We travelled to [the ends of earth],
1.5 vi. 5	To the edge of the abyss;
	We came to 'Paradise' the land of pasture,
	To 'Delight', the steppe by the shore of death.
	We came upon Baal fallen to the earth:
	Dead was Valiant Baal,
1.5 vi. 10	Perished was the Prince, Lord of the earth:
	Then the Wise One, the perceptive god,
	Went down from his throne:
	He sat on his footstool.
	And from his footstool
	He sat on the ground.
KTU.1.5 vi. 15	He poured the ashes of affliction on his head,
	the dust of grovelling on his skull
	For clothing he put on a loin-cloth
	His skin with a stone he scored,
	his side-locks with a razor;
	he gashed cheeks and chin

---

[371] CAQUOT et al., 1974, pp. 250-254.
[372] CAQUOT, et al., 1974, pp. 250-254.

1.5 vi. 20	He ploughed his collar-bones, he turned over like a garden his chest, like a valley he ploughed his breast He lifted up his voice and cried: Baal is dead! What has become of the Powerful One? The Son of Dagan!
1.5 vi. 25 Mourning of Anat 1.5 vi. 30 Anat	What has become of Tempest? After Baal I shall go down into the underworld. **Anat** also went out, and searched every mountain in the midst of the earth, Every hill in the midst of the steppe. She came to 'Para[dise', the land of] pasture, 'Delight', the steppe by the [shore of] death. She f[ound] Baal, fall[en to the ea]rth. [For clothing] she put on a loin[-cloth].
KTU.1.6 i. 1 Anat 1.6 i. 5 Anat Help of Šapaš to find the corpse of Baal 1.6 i. 10 1.6 i. 15 Burial of Baal in a graveyard of gods Animal sacrifice	Her skin with a stone she scored, her side-locks [with a razor], She gashed cheeks and chin. She [ploughed] her collar-bones, she turned over like a garden her chest, like a valley she ploughed her breast. 'Baal is dead! What has become of the Powerful One? The Son of Dagan! What has become of Tempest? After Baal we shall go down into the underworld. With her went down the Luminary of the gods, **Shapsh.** Until she was sated she wept, Like wine she drank (her) tears. Aloud she cried to the Luminary of the gods, **Shapsh:** 'Pray, load on to me Valiant Baal!' The Luminary of the gods, **Shapsh,** obeyed: she lifted up Valiant Baal; On to the shoulders of **Anat** did she set him. She took him up into the uttermost parts of Saphon, she wept for him and buried him. She placed him in a _grave of the gods_ of the underworld She slaughtered seventy wild bulls

KTU.1.6.i. 20	[as a fun]eral offering for Valiant Baal.
	She slaughtered seventy oxen
Animal sacrifice	as a funeral offering for Valiant Baal.
	[she slaugh]tered seventy sheep
----||----||----	[as a fu]neral offering for Valiant Baal.
	[She slau]ghtered seventy stags
1.6 i. 25	[as a funeral offering for] Valiant Baal.
	[She slaughtered se]venty mountain-goats
	[as a funeral offering for Valliant Baal.
----||----||----	[She slaughtered seventy an]telopes
	[as a funeral offer]ing for Valiant Baal.
KTU. 1.6 i. 30	Her [sacrifi]ce she placed in the fu[rrows],
	her [off]ering $^{(?)}$ as a gift for the god(s).
	[The]n indeed she set her face
	towards El at the source of the rivers,
	at the midst of the springs of the two deeps.

COMPARATIVE TABLE

Mourning of Baal in mythology	Royal funeral ritual
KTU.1.5vi-1.6 i. 1-30	KTU 1.161 :1-34
	The invocation of Rephraim or of
X	ancestors- L2-12:
	2-*You are invoked, O rpu arṣ*
X	3-*You are summoned, 0 assembly of Didanu!*
X	4- Ulkn, the *rpu* is invoked,
	5- Trmn, the *rpu* is invoked,
	6- Sdn-w-Rdn is invoked,
	7- Tr-'llmn is invoked,
	8- The ancient *rpum* are invoked.
	9- *You are invoked, O rpu arṣ*
	10- *You are summoned, 0 assembly of Didanu!*
	11- *Ammi! tamru the king is invoked,*
	12- *Niqmaddu the king is also invoked.*
Ritual lamentation of El and Anat	**L13-16:Lamentation**
KTU. 1. 5 vi. 20- 25 (Lametation of El)	
…He lifted up his voice and cried:	13- *o throne of Niqmaddu, be wept for,*
Baal is dead!	14- *May his footstool be shed tears for;*
What has become of the Powerful One?	15-May the king's table be wept for before it,
The Son of Dagan!	16-Misery! Misery of miseries!
What has become of Tempest?	
KTU. 1.6 i. 5: (Lamentation Anat)	
…Baal is dead!	

What has become of the Powerful One?
The Son of Dagan!
What has become of Tempest?

Praying to god Šapaš -KTU. 1.6 i. 5-10 With her went down the Luminary of the gods, **Shapsh.** Until she was sated she wept, Like wine she drank (her) tears. Aloud she cried to the Luminary of the gods, **Shapsh:** 'Pray, load on to me Valiant Baal!' The Luminary of the gods, **Shapsh,** obeyed:	**L17-24** 17- *Burn, O šapšu!* 18- *Burn, O Great Light!* 19- *May Sapsu cry from above:* 20-' *To the place of your lord,* - *before the/his throne,* 21- *To the place of your lord,* *descend to the underworld,* 22- *Descend to the underworld,* *and be low in the dust!* 23- *Go down, O Sdn-w-Rdn,* 24- *Go down, O Ṯr-'llmn,*
Burial- KTU. 1.6 i. 15 On to the shoulders of **Anat** did she set him. She took him up into the uttermost parts of Saphon, she wept for him and buried him. She placed him in a *grave of the gods* of the underworld	**L22-26 is this an interpretation of burial?** *Descend to the underworld,* *and be low in the dust!* *Go down, O Sdn-w-Rdn,* *Go down, O Ṯr-'llmn,* *Go down, O Ammi! tamru, the king,* *Go down too, O Niqmaddu, the king!*
Funeral and animal sacrifice-KTU.1.6 i.20ff [as a fun]eral offering for Valiant Baal. She slaughtered seventy oxen as a funeral offering for Valiant Baal. [she slaugh]tered seventy sheep [as a fu]neral offering for Valiant Baal. [She slau]ghtered seventy stags [as a funeral offering for] Valiant Baal. [She slaughtered se]venty mountain-goats...	**L 27-30 offerings** *Go down too, O Niqmaddu, the king!* *One and make an offering,* *two and make an offering,* *Three and make an offering,* *four and make an offering,* *Five and make an offering,* *six and make an offering,* *Seven and make an offering.* *Offer a bird as a slm-offering.*
X X	**L 31-34: Final blessing** *Peace to Ammurapi,* *and peace to his sons!* *Peace to Tariyelli;* *Peace to his house!* *Peace to Ugarit;* *Peace to its gates!*

Acts of mourning of El	
-1.5 vi. 10: Then the wise one… Went down from his throne…	
KTU.1. 5vi. 15 He poured the ashes of affliction on his head,	X
the dust of grovelling on his skull…	X
his side-locks with a razor; he gashed cheeks and chin	X
Acts of mourning of goddess Anat	X
KTU. 1. 5 vi. 30: …[For clothing] she put on a loin[-cloth].	
KTU. 1. 6 i. 1 Her skin with a stone she scored, she gashed cheeks and chin. She [ploughed] her collar-bones,	
KTU. 1. 6. i. 5 she turned over like a garden her chest, like a valley she ploughed her breast.	

In this comparative table, we can see some common elements like the lamentation, prayer to the god Šapaš, the offerings, and burial. However, there is an invocation of Rephraim or ancestors and the blessings are not present in the myth. In the royal funeral ritual, there are no mourning acts. It is important to show the role of the sun-goddess Šapaš in the myth of the Baal Cycle. She is named the "Luminary of the gods", (KTU.161:18; KTU. 1. 6 i. 5-10).[373] She helps Anat to recover the corpse of Baal in the netherworld and bury him in a cemetery of the gods. The netherworld is "the land without return" (*erṣet lā tāri*). In Akkadian. *erṣtum*, means "the Land", or "the earth" and the word *tārum* means "to return."[374] About "the netherworld."[375]

---

[373] WYATT, 2002, p. 129, note 65.
[374] HUEHNEGARD, 2005, pp. 494; 526.
[375] CAD/E, p. 310-2a.

4.6.5. Resurrection of Baal

After a few days, Anat had trouble accepting the death of her brother Baal. She went to Mot to demand that he give her her brother. Given Mot's boasting and the fate he imposed on Baal, his sister Anat could not stand the words of the king of hell (Mot). She took the body of the god and cut him into pieces. The myth continues with the vision of the great god El who predicted the imminent return of Baal to life.[376] We note that curiously Baal has received a funeral rite, in which various animals were sacrificed for his grief. The next myth does not refer to a ritual of resurrection of Baal. The corpus of the Ugaritic ritual texts contains no reference to the death and resurrection of Baal.[377] We should also add that the myth tells us about a dream in which the great god El was warned about Baal's revival.[378] So, if no text of the corpus mentions a ritual of death and resurrection of Baal, and if the mythology adds nothing more, we simply conclude that the divine resurrected without any particular rite. It can only be said that Baal's death reflects the death of an Ugaritic king, and his return to life, makes him a peace-keeping king in the world.[379] Smith[380] talks about the relationship between the cosmic aspect of the cycle of Baal, the royal human dimension and the realities of seasonal Ugaritic society. We can conclude that the conflict between Baal and Mot seems to be natural phenomena related to the change of seasons.

---

[376] CAQUOT et al., 1974, pp. 258-262.
[377] METTINGER, 2001, p. 55.
[378] CAQUOT, 1974, p. 261-262.
[379] METTINGER, 2001, pp. 38-39.
[380] SMITH, 1994, p. 61.

4.6.6. Iconographical representations of the Storm-god

In the Ancient Near East, all deities have different representations, in the glyptic or iconographies. Thus, the Storm-god is no exception. The goal of our research does not focus on inventories of God Adad representations. But this thesis will show a few different aspects of all representations of the Storm-god Adad.

Around 2000 BC, the bull and the dragon were two of the most recognized symbols, but we also have to mention the dragon called *ušumgallu*, which appeared long before the bull symbol for the Storm-god:

> "L'ušumgallu, ce dragon spécifique du dieu de l'orage dans la glyptique agadéenne et héritier de l'aigle léontocéphale et du lion ailé de la période dynastique archaïque mésopotamiennes. A partir de l'époque néo-sumérienne et peut être sous influence amorite, l'ušumgallu semble avoir été supplanté par le taureau aussi bien comme monture habituelle du dieu de l'orage que comme symbole de fertilité."[381]

It has been observed that the bull symbol progressively replaced the lion-dragon in the seal iconography carved on different supports in the second half of the Ur III dynasty, and became the main animal attributed to the god in the Old Babylonian period.[382] The Storm-god of the Akkad powers is linked to the rain. He is the master of all elements on which the fertility of the earth depends:

> "Dans la région chaude et sèche du Sumer et d'Akkad, le dragon symbolise les averses de pluie bienveillante qui gonflent les ruisseaux et les rivières et produisent une luxuriante verdure et abondante récolte, son image

---

[381] VANEL, 1965, p. 160.
[382] BUNNENS, 2006, p. 69; VANEL, 1965, pp. 30; 32; 47; DUSSAUD, 1931, II, p. 363, 1935, I, p. 11.

est regardée comme un talisman qui évite la sécheresse, un heureux présage d'abondance et de bénédiction.[383]

On a cylinder Seal of Ur dating from the Isin-Larsa period fig. 9, (Vanel, 1965) we can see the symbol of fertility represented by the lightning held by the God as a fire falling on the earth.[384]

Illus. 17. The cylinder Seal from Ur. The god holds the lightning, Vanel, 1965:173, fig. 9. See Legrain, 1951, Pl.31, 473 (U 3080).

In the iconography, the Storm-god Baal is depicted as a bull, in an anthropomorphic appearance, with a horned headdress holding a flash of lightning.[385] The Storm-god with the appearance of a man stands on the back of the bull.[386] This iconography was "found towards the end of the Bronze Age in the Carchemish region, especially in

---

[383] VANEL, 1965, p. 28 note 3.
[384] VANEL, 1965, pp. 22; 23.
[385] LIPINKI, 1995a, p. 80.
[386] BUNNENS, 2006, p. 35.

Carchemish town and in Emar."[387] The author of this stele added a winged disc and crescent and guilloche to the motif of the Storm-god standing on a bull (see figs. 18 and 19). The winged disk is an ancient symbol in the Near East. It's possible that this symbol derived from Egypt.[388] Primarily it was a solar symbol, and secondly it became a symbol of power both on the earth and in heaven. The third symbol was the symbol of kingship as the military power and victory.[389] The disc represented by the sun and the wings can be understood to be the celestial vault.[390]

---

[387] BUNNENS, 2006, p. 36.
[388] FRANKFORT, 1939, 208.
[389] BUNNENS, 2006, p. 71.
[390] FRANKFORT, 1939, pp. 209-210; BUNNENS, 2006, pp. 71; 75; 82.

Illus. 18. Storm-god standing on the back of the bull. Front (side A) of the Ahmar/Qubbah stele, (Bunnens, 2006, figs. 7 and 8).

The guilloche "refers to the cosmic ocean representation on which the earth was floating."[391] The winged disc shows the celestial power of Storm-god and the guilloche proves the domination of the deity over the cosmos, symbolized by the cosmic ocean.[392]

---

[391] BUNNENS, 2006, p. 74.
[392] BUNNENS, 2006, pp. 75; 82.

The bull ridden by Adad cannot be considered as a simple setting or frame for the God. The bull is an animal symbolizing fertility,[393] and "is generally associated with the fecundity and often presents itself in a verdant setting."[394] The bull is known for "his role as provider of fertility [395] but in other cases the animal emphasizes the god's strength. We concluded that the bull is not simply related to fertility or fecundity, but it indicates, as well, the impetuous and terrifying character of the divine "It is the animal which he rides and which leads the god through the clouds and his bellowing can produce thunder".[396] On the following Seal, we have the thunder of the Back of the Bull.

Illus. 19. The Seal, the thunder on the back of the bull, Vanel, 1965:40, fig. 19. See De Clercq, I, Pl. XVIII, 169.

There is also the question of the "lightning of Baal in the skies" in the Ugaritic texts.[397] The lightning is, as a consequence, the symbol of ^{d}IM *par excellence*. Nevertheless, initially, the most used form associated with the manifestation of the Storm-god

---

[393] VANEL, 1965, p. 55.
[394] VANEL, 1965, p. 13; AMIET, 1961, fig. 1269.
[395] BUNNENS, 2006, p. 83.
[396] VANEL, 1965, p. 65.
[397] CAQUOT, et al., 1974, p. 170.

was the flash of lightning that tore apart the clouds.[398] According to Frankfort[399] the roar of the whip of the Storm-god evokes the crack of thunder. The Storm-god cracks his whip as the lightning tears the sky.

The whip of ^{d}Iškur (Storm-god) is then a symbol of the roar of the lightning.[400] The two or three zigzag lines can be lightning, which is the lightning in the skies of Adad.[401] The Hititte stele of Malatya (Arslan Tepe), is 1m 30 long, and 0 m 90 high. On this stele the Storm-god was presented in an anthropomorphic form. He marches with his left leg foward. He holds in his left hand lightning with three branches.[402]

In some representations of the Storm-god, cf. fig. 56, stele B and fig.58 stele A[403] from Tell Amar, we have on these steles the motif of the Storm-god standing on a bull holding in his right hand an "axe" ḫaṣṣinnu[404] and in his left hand the trident-thunderbolt. Baal wears a belted kilt and a sword. It should be noted that the thunderbolt held by the Storm-god is the materialization of the lightning that tears the skies.

---

[398] VANEL, 1965, p. 54.
[399] FRANKFORT, 1939, p. 125.
[400] VANEL, 1965, p. 21; 23, FRANKFORT, 1935, p. 1939, 127 note 3.
[401] VANEL, 1965, pp. 31-32.
[402] VIEYRA, 1946:131-132.
[403] BUNNENS, 2006, p. 111.
[404] BUNNENS, 2006, FLEMING, 1992, p. 50 see note 7.

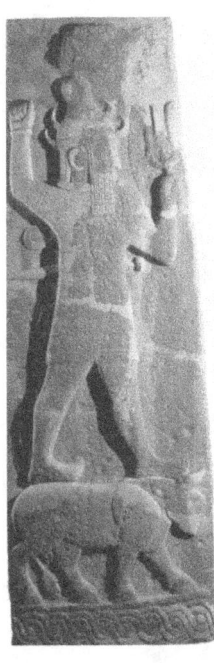 

Illus. 20. Storm-god stele B from Tell Ahmar, (Bunnens, 2006:111; 156, fig. 56). 3.03 m x 0.98 m.

Illus. 21. Storm-god stele A from Tell Ahmar, (Bunnens, 2006:111; 157, fig. 58). 2.06 m x 0.83 m.

In the iconographic representation of the Storm-god, instead of the mace or the lightning present in the region of Mari in Syria, XVIIIth century, the God holds sometimes in his hand the vegetal symbol, a stylized branch, certainly a palm.[405] According to Vanel,[406] Adad is striking the ground with his lance in order to ensure the birth of vegetation.

In the eighth century, a relief of Ivriz in the Neo-hititte region called Tyana, a stele was found. It was erected by order of Tyana's king, Warpalawas (730-710 BC?). Tyana or Tabal was the Neo-Hititte state in South-central Anatolia (modern Turkey). On this stele,

---

[405] VANEL, 1965, pp. 78-79, figs. 34; 36.
[406] VANEL, 1965, p. 84.

the king faces the Storm-god, Hadad, fig. 69.[407] The cap of that deity is on two pairs of horns. His beard is curly, his hair is bouclé, and he has bulging muscles. He holds in his left hand an ear of wheat and in his right hand, he holds grapes.

Illus. 22. The Storm-god Hadad on the stele from Tyana, (Vanel, 1965:183, fig. 69).

On another stele from Niğde, fig. 87,[408] appear a bunch of grapes and ears of wheat associated with the Storm-god. He stands on his two feet in the greenery in the attack position, and holds in his right hand the axe and in his left hand the trident-thunderbolt. In this verdant [picture] of the Ears of Weat and bunches of Grapes there is an indication of the symbol of Storm-god as god of the rain and the

---

[407] VANEL, 1965, fig. 69.
[408] BUNNENS, 2006, p. 112.

fertility of the earth. In the Ancient Tabal, the Storm-god with bunches of Grapes and Ears of Wheat was associated him with fields and vineyards,

Illus. 23. The Storm-god. Stele from Niğde, (Bunnens,2006:163, fig. 87).
0.62 m x 0.30 m

The God Adad was correlated with the mountain, fig. 16.[409] In this picture we can see the Storm-god, Adad, standing on the hills and it seems he is preparing to strike the earth while a small genie holds in his hands other barrels in reserve. The fig. 15 by the same author shows the God placing one foot on a mountain.

---

[409] VANEL, 1965; DUSSAUD, 1936, I, p. 7.

Illus. 24. Storm-god and the small genie, (Vanel, 1965, fig.16).

Illus.25. The Baal stele from Ugarit, (Bunnens, 2006:67, fig. 31). The lightning held by the Storm-god "terminates as spear with which the god is hitting the earth."

This illus. 25, the Baal stele from Ugarit, is dating from the Middle or from the Late Bronze Age.[410] According to De Vaux,[411] Adad "is depicted as walking on mountains and seas." The mountains are the most favourite places of Adad. "The mountains are the privileged places where the storm reveals better than anywhere else the power of Baal".[412] On the Ras Shamra tablet IIAB, IV-V, L. 85, we have this inscription: *'m B'l m r y m Ṣ p n* "to the heights of Saphon" (*Saphon Mountain*),[413] where was erected the palace of Baal. "Quickly shall you buil[d] the house, quickly shall you erect the pal[ace], Amid the summit of Sapan", (KTU. 1.4V:53-55).[414] The "Mount Ṣapon, is the domain of Baal."[415] On the mountains, the Storm-god Adad can flash or strike with lightning. "The mountains evoked the highest parts of the world."[416] In Akkadian the verb *barāqum* "to flash, to strike with lightning" has been used in correlation with the Storm-god, Adad, (See *barāqum*.[417] And another text said: *ṣābit kippat šārē mukīl mê nuḫši mušaznin zunni mu-šab-ríq NIM.GÍR mušabšû urqēti* which means: "(Adad), who controls all the winds, who keeps the waters in abundance, who causes rain and lightning, who breeds the vegetation.[418]

---

[410] SCHAEFFER, 1949, p. 46-49.
[411] De VAUX, 1971, p. 143.
[412] LPINSKI, 1995, p. 80.
[413] DUSSAUD, 1935, I, p. 21.
[414] SMITH and PITARD, 2009, p. 82.
[415] OBERMANN, 1947, p. 196.
[416] BUNNENS, 2006, p. 62.
[417] CAD/B, p. 103, 1.
[418] IRAQ, 24 93, p. 5; CAD/B, p. 104, b2.

Illus. 26. The Storm-god, Stele from Babylon. Date: late 10th – early 9th century. Bunnens, 2006:113; 159, fig. 64. 1.28 m x 0. 53 m. Only one pair of horns is attached to the god's helmet. The god holds the spikes of the trident-thunderbolt.

Illus. 27. The Storm-god. Orthostat from Zincirli. Date: 10th century. 1.35 m x 0.83 m. Bunnens, 2006:115; 160, fig. 68. The god's helmet has no horns. The sword is pointing forward and attached to the left side of the deity.

Illus. 28. Stele from Arslan Tash. Bunnens, 2006:116-117; 161, fig. 73. 1.36 m x 0.54 m. Date: 8th century. The Storm-god portrayed in the Assyrian style, with his tiara and standing on the back of the bull. The God brandishing the double lightning as the Asssyrian Storm-god usually does.

Illus. 29. Relief K from the Lion Gate at Arslantepe/Malatya, (Southeastern Turkey). Bunnens, 2006:128; 166, fig. 102. Dating perhaps from the 11th or early 10th century, (cf. Bunnens, 2006:123, fig.89). 0.87 m x 1.95 m. The Storm-god is shown twice. Once is jumping in a chariot and once standing and in front of him stands the king PUGNUS-Mili making the libation. Behind the king comes an attendant with bull.

A

B

Illus. 30.A. Stone block from Tell Ashara. Storm-god figure. H.: 0.90 m. Bunnens, 2006:129; 167, fig. 104. The Storm-god fighting a serpent (monster). The god holds an axe in his right hand. With his left hand he is grasping the serpent by its throat.

Illus. 30.B. Drawing of the entire relief. A human figure in fish garb and on the third side of the block stands another human holding three ears of wheat.

Illus. 31. Orthostat from the Aleppo Citadel. Height 2 m. Storm-god facing a king. The Storm-god wears a conical helmet with two pairs of horns and a kind of disc at the top, (Bunnens, 2006:130; 168, fig. 106).

All these iconographic representations of Adad mentioned above, are not unique. There is another symbol of the Storm-god like: ᵈIM-DUGUD^{mushen} (the eagle-headed-lion).[419] The eagle-headed-lion is a hybrid animal and has two wings with the lion head.

---

[419] LABAT and MALBRAN-LABAT, 1994, p. 185, N°207.

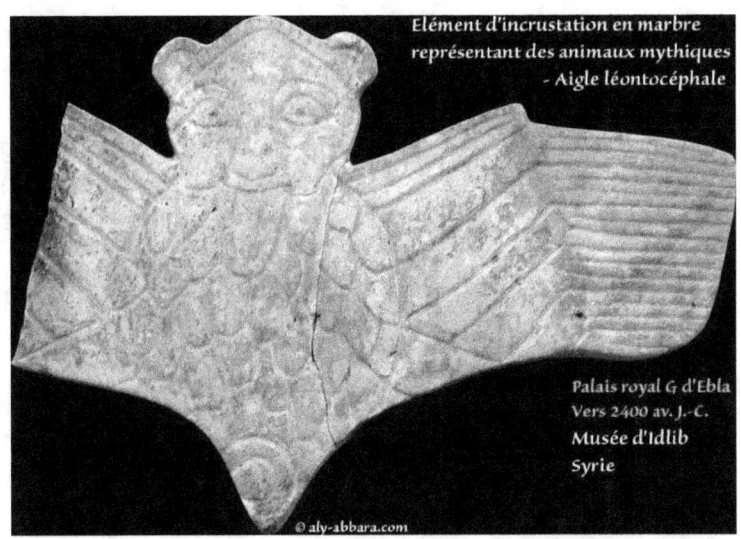

Illus. 32. The eagle-headed-lion. King's palace G of Ebla around 2400 BC. From Idlib Museum, Syria. © Dr Aly ABBARA.[420]

According to Dhorme,[421] DUGUD means: heavy, thick or powerful. IM-DUGUD= (in akk. *imbaru*) can be translated by: "wind, fog, powerful". It's possible to see here the force of storm compared to the quick flight and the power of the eagle.[422] For Jacobsen, the word *imbaru* means: "thunder-shower" and says ^dIM-DUGUD ^{mushen} corresponds to the personification of the storm cloud.[423] This hybrid animal (the eagle-headed-lion) was conceived as a big raptor soaring with his wings in the sky. The thunder was another symbol of the Storm-god and was compared to the lion roaring. That is why this monster has a lion head.

---

[420] http://www.alyabbara.com/voyages_personnels/syrie/Ebla/images/museum/element_incrustation/e_incrustation_aigle_leontocephale (Visited: 09/09/2014).
[421] DHORME, 1949, p. 103.
[422] VANEL, 1965, p. 12.
[423] JACOBSEN, 1953, pp. 167-168 see also note 27.

It was the symbol of the Storm-god. It also plays the role of the guardian and the protector of the animals.[424] How do we justify the relationship between the eagle-headed-lion and the Storm-god? During the period of king Akkad around 2300 BC, was a time of change for the civilization and the glyptics. At that time, the eagle-headed-lion disappeared and gave place to the Storm-god accompanied by his consort (Astarte), the rain goddess.[425]

We have chosen to show these few representations of Baal the Storm-god, but not all. We will come to this consort of Baal, Astarte, in our synthesis and conclusion. The goddess Astarte was present in 1 Kings 18:19, and has four hundred (400) prophets.

4.6.7. Preliminary conclusion

We set out here a partial conclusion of this part of our research. We note that Melqart Baal, the patron of Tyre and Adad Baal, the Storm-god had all the titles of a king. The worship of the two deities on their death and resurrection was well modelled on the alternation of seasons. They are both worshipped as atmospheric deities. However, the Ugaritic mythological texts mention only the death of Baal, in mourning for the supreme god El and Anat Baal's sister and the funerals. We do not have details of his worship and especially his death and resurrection. The study of both gods, and analysis with the internal evidence of the discursive elements of the prophet Elijah (1 Kgs 18: 1-46) suggest that the master of Mount Carmel could be the Baal Melqart. However, there are some shortcomings in this interpretation.

---

[424] VANEL, 1965, p. 14, note 2.
[425] WARD, 1912, p. 50, N°150; VANEL, 1965, p. 19, note 1.

The biblical text does not provide us with any information about the specific months during which the scene at Mount Carmel occurred, and the sacrifice of the bull does not indicate whether it was really a sacrifice for the epiphany that was supposed waking Melqart from sleep during the time that the searing heat of summer lasted. However, if in the Carmel event there is no distinction between the ritual fires, we can nevertheless say that this scene of confrontation between Elijah and prophets of Baal on Mount Carmel was an ordeal. And for this reason, some elements of the ceremony Melqart could not be highlighted in the text. All this does not mean that the Melqart god was not the god of Carmel. The elements of Baal Adad related to the biblical text are not confirmed.

CHAPTER 5

BAAL MELQART: GOD OF MOUNT CARMEL?

Melqart is a name that originates from the title *milk qrt,* meaning "the king of Tyre" or "king of the city."[426] An Aramaic inscription on a stele dating from the ninth century AD, makes reference to Melqart as being the king of Tyre, (KAI, 201). The majority of scholars present Melqart as the product of the first millennium, and hence his evolution is due to the marine power of Tyre. He was venerated like Hercules of Tyre.[427]
We come across his name in the Akkadian inscriptions, *ᵈMi-il-qar-tu and Mil-qar-te* meaning "king of the city."[428] Melqart was venerated, as his name suggests, as "king of Tyre". This title makes reference to a legendary past,[429] where Melqart appeared as the founder of the city of Tyre.[430] Information from Dionys confirmed that Heracles/Melqart was the founder of Tyre city, (Nonnos Dionys, XL: 429-573) and especially in 439 Heracles said: "son of the earth" φιλόπτολιν οἰστρονάέξων "Me, (Heracles), I

---

[426] BONNET, 1999, p. 19.
[427] BONNET, 1999, p. 226.
[428] BONNET, 1999, p. 227.
[429] GRAS, et al., 1989, p. 49.
[430] EUSEBIUS of CAESARAE P.E.I, 10, pp. 10-11.

145

harboured the desire to found a city". Is the patron of Tyre really the god of Mount Carmel? Some authors[431] said that Baal Melqart has been cited as the true god of Mount Carmel. Their first argument rests primarily on the dynastic-diplomatic marriage between Jezebel and Ahab. We detect, obviously, a political reason in this union. It is basically related to the desire to maintain a good neighbouring relationship between the two kingdoms. These authors support their affirmation by means of the text of 1 Kings 18, the episode of Carmel and the conflict between the prophets of Baal and Elijah, the Yahvist. The text of 1 Kings 18 affirms that these Baal prophets shared the table with Jezebel of Tyre (1 Kgs 18:19). Melqart had been enthroned in Samaria during the reign of King Ahab, (Ant. J. VIII, 13: 1; IX, 6:5; 1 Kgs 18:31-32). The biblical text of 1 Kings 18 presents certain elements of irony on the part of the prophet Elijah: "Baal has fallen asleep", "he is travelling", "he is busy" (1 Kgs 18:27). As we will develop in the following chapters, these hints make allusion to certain attributes of Baal Melqart and his wakefulness.

The intervention of fire cannot be considered as a trivial matter. It could allude to the fire of a pyre as part of the resurrection ritual of Baal Melqart. The fire could also suggest the capacity of Baal Melqart as an atmospheric god, a god of lightning and storm.[432] If the introduction of Baal in Samaria was a consequence of new alliance with Tyre by the Ahab-Jezebel marriage, as we have just suggested, then

---

[431] BONNET, 1988:19 explains that everyone identifies this divinity with the god regent in Tyre (Baal Melqart); see also pp. (136-140); DUSSAUD, 1948, pp. 205-230; De VAUX, 1941, pp. 7-20; RIBICHINI, 1999, pp. 563-565.
[432] DUSSAUD, 1946-1948, p. 209.

Baal Melqart, in his dominant position in the pantheon of Tyre as the great god and king of Tyre, could represent the city officially and internationally. We should add that Baal Melqart played an important role in the economy and navigation.

The ordeal of Mount Carmel, opposing the prophets of Baal and Elijah (1Kgs 18:26-27), took place in accordance with the discursive elements of Elijah, the prophet of YHWH. The elements make reference to certain realities of the god Melqart, the patron of Tyre. The dance of the Baal prophets, the sleep, the travel, and the concerns of Baal are hints that lead us to believe that the god in question is Melqart, patron of Tyre.

Before examining the verses regarding the competition between YHWH and Baal on Mount Carmel (vv. 21-40), we should mention some elements of the scenery and other foundational elements of the chapter 1 Kings 18. Basically, we will disgress slightly. No polemical discussion will be made on the origins, composition, or author of the story told as such. Thus, we will examine it in light of its theological function, to see how these elements might be articulated in our study.[433] It is important to keep in mind the considerable difficulties we have encountered while dealing with this particular biblical text.

5.1. Brief study on the context of the pericope

Our aim here, it is to show the context of the story of Mount Carmel, (religious, social and political context) of 1Kings 18.

---

[433] ASURMENDI, 1989, p. 8.

5.2. The structure of the text 1 Kings 18:1-46

Chapter 18 tells the story of the confrontation on the grounds of a religious and political crisis between the prophet Elijah, King Ahab, and the prophets of Baal. This confrontation sets up two groups, each representing their god (Elijah for YHWH and the prophets of Baal for god Baal). We can distinguish three main parts.

First scene: Elijah is on the road, in the middle of a drought (v. 1-20). In this episode, YHWH sends Elijah with precise instructions: look for King Ahab and deliver to him a promise of life: the gift of rain, preceded by a confrontation on Mount Carmel. Hugo affirms that "the instruction given to Elijah by God to present himself before Ahab matches a different fulfilment of a promise by the end of the chapter (v. 45). A reminder of the famine replaces the fulfilment of the promise by contrast (v. 2b)"[434] Instead of announcing the coming of rain, Elijah will convoke a sacrifice contest on Mount Carmel. Did the prophet exceed his mission? Or is it that YHWH got tricked by his own prophet?

At the instruction of YHWH, Elijah made a detour and presented himself before Obadiah. Then he saw Ahab, who was out searching for livestock forage in this period of severe drought. The actors that take part in this first scene are: the prophet, the king and his servant. The fourth character in the shadows, who plays an appreciable part in the events, is the first lady of the kingdom, Queen Jezebel (vv.4:13 and 19). The king was deeply concerned with the problem of the drought as mentioned in 1 Kings 18:5. The drought had caused so much damage that the king himself had to get out of his palace. In this sense, he

---

[434] HUGO, 2006, p. 306.

was more preoccupied with maintaining his military power than caring for horses and mules. The animals represented important military equipment, as revealed by the inscription of king Salmanazar III (858-824 BC).[435] The king was only looking to preserve his cavalry and his military camp. Thus, preserving his military power and consolidating the state were the only reasons that guided the priorities of King Ahab in this period of drought and famine, (Hugo, 2006:279). The misery of his people was concealed or masked by the king, as well as by the narrator of the story, in the silence surrounding the living conditions of the people at that time.

In a subsequent scene, the pericope describes in detail "the sacrificial competition of the Baal prophets and of Elijah and also the ordeal of Carmel that witnessed the manifestation of YHWH's power together with the massacre of the Baal prophets (vv.21-40)". The problem of the famine announced in the beginning of the biblical text introduced by the famine then fell upon Samaria (v. 2b) is not resolved in the text. However, the promise of YHWH indicated the end of the drought by the return of rain, and that represented the mission that Elijah was given.[436] The mission of the prophet Elijah was to announce the return of rain, but we are forced to observe that during the ceremonial sacrifice on Mount Carmel the problem of the drought and rain is not mentioned. "The drought seems far from Mount Carmel; the true god, after all, was to make himself known by producing fire, not rain."[437] The king Ahab disappears in this part of the story of Mount Carmel (1 Kgs 18:21-40) and then appears again (1 Kgs 18:41-46). The same is true for the theme of rain

---

[435] NOCQUET, 2004, p. 115 ; ANET, 1969, pp. 276ff.
[436] JYRKI, 2001, p. 58.
[437] COGAN, 2008, p. 445.

and drought that was supposed to govern all the text; it is quite clear that this theme disappears after the verses 1 Kings 18:1-2a and comes back at the end of the text (1 Kgs 18:41-46).

In a third scene, the biblical text tells us about the falling of rain (vv.41-46). The text of 1 Kings 18 is marked by the presence of the drought (1 Kings 17:1) and the promise made by YHWH on the recurrence of rain (1 Kgs 18:1).

The homogeneity and the literary unity are marked by the theme of drought, (chapters 17 and 18, starting from 1 Kings 17:1 and ending in 1 Kings 18:41-46). The LXX (v. 45) mentions the fact that King Ahab "cried", ἔκλαιεν (√κλαίω) and went to Israel, whereas MT talks about his departure for Yizre'el.[438]

5.3. Questions and difficulties of the text

Many questions may arise on reading this thesis. Who provided the two bulls for the sacrifice (v. 23)? In verse 18, the prophet used the name בְּעָלִים "Baalim"; is it the plural form of Baal? Did he want to evoke the plurality of Baal's personality worshipped in Israel? The prophet uses בְּעָלִים by contrast to YHWH who is an unique God. It may refer as well to different local appellations of Baal worshipped in Canaan.[439] According to Gray, it refers to the same god, but at the same time he clarifies the concept of plurality in the god's divinity. He says that בְּעָלִים "The plural of Baal" indicates the various local manifestations of the "paramount" the Canaanite fertility-deity Adad, Baal (lit. "Lord"). The vv. 22 and 40 mention only four hundred and fifty prophets of Baal. The narrator said nothing about

---

[438] HUGO, 2006, p. 285.
[439] GRAY, 1970, p. 393

four hundred prophets of Asherah. Only prophets of Baal were killed (v. 40)? If we admit that the drought lasted three years, where did the assembly find excess water to pour over the holocaust of Prophet Elijah (vv. 34-35)? The simple answer is that even in a drought, there is water, and in this case, the happening is right next to the sea. Therefore, the narrator, did not need to tell us precisely where people drew water for this ordeal on Mount Carmel. How long did the drought last, three years or three and a half years (v. 1)? A number of authors of the New Testament say that the drought lasted three and a half years (Luke 4:25; Jas 5:17). Was the prophet Elijah himself able to kill the two bulls and prepare the sacrifice without the help of the people (v. 33)? For our view, it is impossible. However, after Baal failed the ordeal, the people help the prophet Elijah to kill the bull and prepare the sacrifice.

Only the LXX attributes the title of prophet to Elijah Ηλιου ὁ προφήτης 'Elijah the prophet' whereas the MT simply refers to him as the Tishbite, אֵלִיָּהוּ הַתִּשְׁבִּי (1 Kings 17:1). In both cases, we see that the man of YHWH comes onto the scene without genealogical references. We recognize that the introductory phrase of the prophet is אֲשֶׁר עָמַדְתִּי אֱלֹהֵי יִשְׂרָאֵל Josephus called Elijah a prophet. He started the story of 1 Kings 17:1 calling Elijah a prophet but does not mention the name of Elijah. Προφήτης δέτις τοῦ μεγάλου θεοῦ ἐκπόλεως Θεσσεβώνης τῆς Γαλααδίτιδος ... "There was now a prophet of God Almighty, from Thisbi, a country in Gilead, that came to Ahab, and said to him, that God foretold he would not send rain nor dew in those years upon the country but when he should appear", (Ant. VIII: 319). Another source, namely the Samaritan chronicles, said that Elijah presented himself as prophet, (Macdonald, 1969:163): "Now Elijah the Tishibite, of Tishbe of Gilead in those days called himself a prophet, claiming that the Lord spoke with him". In this verse the LXX (17:1) mentions two important theological terms Ηλιου ὁ προφήτης ανδ ὁ θεὸς τῶν δυνάμεων But these theological terms are not mentioned in the MT. In verse 36 of the MT we only find אֵלִיָּהוּ הַנָּבִיא "the prophet Elijah". Despite the theological importance of these terms and their impact in the opening narrative of the story, they do not change the portrait of Elijah and God.[440]

The time indicator "from morning to noon" is missing from the LXX, and we are not able to understand its absence. "The variant of LXX should not be considered because of the narrative importance of the story's time references."[441] Why does verse 32a use the term וַיִּבְנֶה "and he built" or verse 30 וַיְרַפֵּא אֶת־מִזְבַּח יְהוָה הֶהָרוּס 'and he restored the altar of *YHWH* which was in ruins'? Does it refer to the destroyed altar of YHWH that was being restored or are we witnessing a new altar built for YHWH? It refers to the altar of the Lord which was destroyed; its time reference and religious background will have to be researched.

5.3.1. The beginning of Elijah's mission

1 Kings 17:1 אִם־יִהְיֶה הַשָּׁנִים הָאֵלֶּה טַל וּמָטָר כִּי אִם־לְפִי דְבָרִי
"There will not be dew or rain these years except by my word".

"Just as in 1 Kings 17:1, the sinfulness of Ahab and Israel in worshipping Baal is not specified as the reason for the coming of the

---

[440] HUGO, 2006, p. 211.
[441] NOCQUET, 2004, p. 92.

drought, so here the reader is not told that the victory of Yahweh over Baal, which is soon to be achieved, is the reason for the return of the rains. There is only a hint of things to come", (Allan and Russell, 1990:23). חַי־יְהֹוָה אֱלֹהֵי יִשְׂרָאֵל "YHWH lives, God of Israel" (1 Kgs 17:1). Elijah claims here that the status of YHWH is "the God who lives" and that He is God of Israel; חַי־יְהֹוָה אֱלֹהֵי 'the God YHWH lives...' "The invocation of the deity sanctions the oath, asserting the truth of the words spoken, lest there be punishment for falsehood."[442]

אֱלֹהֵי יִשְׂרָאֵל אֲשֶׁר עָמַדְתִּי לְפָנָיו "The God of Israel before whom I stand" is the proof that Elijah is not a magician but someone who has a close relationship with his God, and the consequences of his acts depend on the latter and not on him.[443] About the prophet Elijah, "His authority for doing this is that he stands in YHWH's presence."[444] "There will be no dew or rain these years, except by my word" (1 Kgs 17:1). "Elijah standing with YHWH is depicted as being of sufficient merit and maturity that by his word alone the drought will be determined."[445] The expression אֲשֶׁר עָמַדְתִּי לְפָנָיו makes reference to the prophetic vocation of Elijah and shows that he has received the authorization from YHWH. Elijah was the mediator in the mission ordered by YHWH. The power to stop rain belongs to YHWH who lives.[446] The words spoken by Elijah to Ahab came from YHWH. If they were not true, why would the Lord take precautions to safeguard his prophet? YHWH sends Elijah in a place where he promises to take care of him and save him

---

[442] COGAN, 2001, p. 245.
[443] JYRKI, 2001, p. 15.
[444] DUNN and ROGERSON, 2003, p. 261.
[445] COGAN, 2001, p. 425.
[446] ALLAN and RUSSELL, 1990, p. 13.

from the consequences of drought. YHWH said to Elijah: וְאֶת־הָעֹרְבִים צִוִּיתִי לְכַלְכֶּלְךָ שָׁם "I have ordered the ravens to feed you there" (1 Kings 17:4). According to verse 6, הָעֹרְבִים "the ravens" brought to Elijah bread and meat in the morning and bread in the evening. The prophet will have to face the possibility of his death due to the drought he has called upon the land, but to save him YHWH commands him to leave and go to Cherit (1 Kgs 17:3).

Kings 18:1 וְאֶתְּנָה מָטָר עַל־פְּנֵי הָאֲדָמָה

"and I (YHWH) will send rain on the land"

This sentence is the proof that Elijah himself is not responsible for the drought but YHWH, because He will stop the drought and send the rain again upon the face of the land. "These words again affirm YHWH's power as the God of life and death, the God who can send rains when he wills."[447] He "will be able to send rains and overcome the famine."[448]

5.3.2. Dialogue between Elijah and Obadiah

When Obadiah was trying to find some grass and water for the horses and mules of his master King Ahab, he met Elijah. He bowed down and said: אֵלִיָּהוּ הַאַתָּה זֶה אֲדֹנִי "Is it really you, my lord Elijah?" (1 Kings 18:7). This attitude and reaction of Obadiah is rather respectful. [449]

הַאַתָּה זֶה אֲדֹנִי אֵלִיָּהוּ "Is it you my lord Elijah?" (1 Kgs 18:7) הַאַתָּה זֶה "Is it you" is rhetorical, for Obadiah had recognized Elijah. The demonstrative זֶה adds

---

[447] ALLAN and RUSSELL, 1990, p. 23.
[448] ALLAN and RUSSELL, 1990, p. 24.
[449] JYRKI, 2001, p. 57.

emphasis, almost "Is it really you"? (cf. v.17). We have in the Hebrew Bible the same style of question with זֶה הָאַתָּה (cf. Gen 27:17). Isaac asked Jacob בְּנִי עֵשָׂו אִם־לֹא הָאַתָּה זֶה "It is you really my son Esau or not?" In the fratricidal war in Israel, when Avner, the commander of Saul's army was pursued by Asahel, in his flight he asked: הַאַתָּה זֶה עֲשָׂהאֵל "It is really you Asahel?" (2 Sam 2:20).[450] By this rhetorical question הַאַתָּה זֶה אֲדֹנִי אֵלִיָּהוּ "Is it you my lord Elijah?" Elijah responds הִנֵּה אֵלִיָּהוּ 'Elijah is here' or 'yes I am Elijah'. (1 Kgs 18:8).

After this, Elijah ordered the servant of King Ahab to inform his master about the prophet's presence, לֵךְ אֱמֹר לַאדֹנֶיךָ הִנֵּה אֵלִיָּהוּ (v. 8). He brought fear into the heart of Obadiah (v. 12). The prophet Elijah had commanded Obadiah to say to his master Ahab הִנֵּה אֵלִיָּהוּ "Behold, Elijah", and Obadiah twice repeated these two words (vv.11, 14) in order to understand what Elijah had commanded him to say. While these two words may initially seem innocuous, they carry a double meaning, since הִנֵּה אֵלִיָּהוּ can also mean, "Behold, my God is Yahweh". Understood in this way, the words which Elijah asks Obadiah to speak to Ahab would be a direct confession of Obadiah's allegiance to Yahweh'.[451] It is possible that these words could be a direct confession of Avadayahou, but given that Ahab considered Elijah to be the troublemaker of Israel, Elijah's name pronounced by Obadiah could not be the cause of confusion. He was afraid for his own life because he would put himself in a dangerous situation. The contrasting dialogue between the man of YHWH Elijah and the manager of the royal palace presents Obadiah as a righteous or pious man. "He is a man who has acted on

---

[450] COGAN, 2001, p. 437.
[451] ALAN and RUSSELL, 1990, p. 26.

conscience but who is also an ordinary man with understandable fears and hesitations."[452] The character of Obadiah in this dialogue corresponds to a man who is "dichotomic and inconsistent... the first time he is a brave man jeopardizing his life and career in order to save Yahweh's prophets and the second time he is described as a creeping coward before Elijah, begging for mercy and making excuses."[453] This hesitation was the tension between Obadiah's desire to serve YHWH and his desire to be loyal to Ahab. Obadiah's name means "servant of YHWH". He had a desire to remain in the king's favour and save his life, and also to remain faithful to YHWH. This presentation of Obadiah is an image of the individual persons in Israel who desired to remain faithful servants of YHWH but who did not have Elijah's courage.[454] Like Obadiah, "who had difficulty deciding whether to follow Elijah's command and be openly faithful to Yahweh or to follow the voice of his own fear and avoid placing himself in a dangerous position, the people of Israel did not know what to do." We can see this in Elijah's words in verse 21: עַד־מָתַי אַתֶּם פֹּסְחִים עַל־שְׁתֵּי הַסְּעִפִּים "How long will you limp upon two crutches?"

5.3.3. The fear of Obadiah

Obadiah is justified in his fear of obeying Elijah's command . This fear of Obadiah is that the "Spirit of the Lord" may carry Elijah away when he informs Ahab הִנֵּה אֵלִיָּהוּ "Elijah is here"; then the prophet may not be found anywhere, (1Kgs 18:4, 13).[455]

---

[452] ALTER, 1981, p. 73.
[453] JONES, 1984, p. 313.
[454] ALAN and RUSSELL, 1990, p. 37; ALTER, 1981, p. 73.
[455] ATTRIDE, 1996, p. 364.

וַיֹּאמֶר מֶה חָטָאתִי כִּי־אַתָּה נֹתֵן אֶת־עַבְדְּךָ בְּיַד־אַחְאָב לַהֲמִיתֵנִי

'What is my sin that you would give your servant into the hand of Ahab, to cause my death'? Verse 9) "What is my sin?" explains clearly Obadiah's fear. From Qumran cave 4, a piece of the biblical text (4Q382 frg.1) has been found with this text. It is probably a biblical paraphrase based on 1 Kings 18-19 with a quotation from 1 Kings.

4Q282
Frg. 1.] ∘∘∘ ∘∘∘ ∘ [

חמשים חמשים ויחביאים

[∘∘ ומאחאב איזבל מ ירא]∘

ל ישראל בארץ בדיה/עו]

Translation
L. 1] - - - - - - - - - - - - - - -[
L. 2] and he hid them by fifties
L. 3] he feared Jezebel and Ahab [
L. 4 O]badiah in the l[an]d of Israel [

In this fragment of the biblical text of 1 Kings 18 from Qumran, we can see that Obadiah feared his master Ahab and his wife Jezebel. This fear of Obadiah did not depend on the king's character, but on a possible disappearance of the prophet Elijah: "so when I go and tell Ahab, and he cannot find you, he will kill me" (v.12). He attributed this disappearance of Elijah to an action of the Spirit: יְהוָה יִשָּׂאֲךָ עַל אֲשֶׁר לֹא־אֵדָע וְרוּחַ "the spirit of YHWH will carry you to somewhere I don't know" (v. 12, cf. also 2 Kgs 2:16). He is afraid to obey Elijah's command, but his problem is that Elijah will not be found:

וְלֹא יִמְצָאֶךָ "you will not be found" (v. 12). He will be taken for a liar. The consequence of this will cause "my death" וַהֲרָגְנִי, "he will slay me" or "he will kill me": וַהֲרָגְנִי (Qal pret. 3rd person masc. sing. + suffix 1st cs) "to be killed" הָרַג = 'to kill'. The Qal expressed a type of active action.

So Obadiah, when he said וַהֲרָגְנִי, implies a violent death. By contrast, in verse 9, Obadiah, when speaking to Elijah used the word לַהֲמִיתֵנִי (hiphil) מוּת, 'die, kill, have one executed'. The hiphil is used to express a causative type of action. It means that Obadiah's death would be caused by Ahab. Therefore הָרַג "swear to be sure that they do not lie to him by hiding Elijah in their territories (1 Kings 18:10) to kill" appears twice, in (vv. 12, 14). Obadiah remembers how King Ahab treated kingdoms and nations; he made them swear. If Ahab would do such a thing for kingdoms and nations, imagine what could be the punishment that he would inflict on one man? The reaction of Obadiah is not only to express his fear, but also to describe the character of his master Ahab. He described his master, Ahab as violent and a shedder of blood, a monarch capable of condemning to death arbitrarily (v. 9).

In this dialogue between Elijah and Obadiah, the protests of Ahab's manager make it clear that he wants to be sure that when he tells his master הִנֵּה אֵלִיָּהוּ 'Elijah is here' Elijah will, in fact be found. When Elijah said in verse. 15 יְהוָה צְבָאוֹת אֲשֶׁר עָמַדְתִּי לְפָנָיו כִּי הַיּוֹם אֵרָאֶה אֵלָיו חַי "As the Lord Almighty lives, whom I serve, I will surely present myself to Ahab today." We have חַי יְהוָה only in 1 Kings 17:2 and 1 Kings 18:10 and 15, used by Elijah and Obadiah. Both times the use of this expression חַי יְהוָה means that Elijah and Obadiah swear by the living God YHWH. They take Him as their witness. In 1 Kings 18:15 he added צְבָאוֹת to יְהוָה חַי. And why this addition of צְבָאוֹת which means "armies?" It may "allude to the armies of Israel or to the heavenly hosts over whom YHWH presides", (Cogan, 2001:438).The LXX translated חַי־יְהוָה צְבָאוֹת by ζῇ κύριος τῶν δυνάμεων "the Lord of power lives".

In the LXX σαβαωθ is the transcription of צְבָאוֹת, pl. of צָבָא (army) in a name applied to God. κύριος in the LXX = יהוה צְבָאוֹת Yahweh Lord of the armies, Lord of hosts, almighty, all-powerful, one who is powerful over all (Isa 1:9; 25:6; Zech 13:2; 1 Sam 1:3; 11:20; 15:2; Josh 5:4; Rom 9:29). The word σαβαωθ was not used by the LXX. It decided to translate צְבָאוֹת by δυνάμεων. צְבָאוֹת /σαβαωθ is the divine epithet of YHWH. In this case, Elijah used חַי־יְהוָה צְבָאוֹת to reassure Obadiah or to convince him that he stood before the Lord of armies. He could not disappear and would not be afraid to present himself to Ahab. Obadiah obtained the guarantee that Elijah would be found when he announced to his master:

הִנֵּה אֵלִיָּהוּ

"Elijah is here"

The attitude of King Ahab before facing Elijah is totally paradoxical. He had sufficient authority to impose a decree in order to extradite Elijah from the territory if he wished to do so. The extradition of fugitives was often practised in Ancient Near Eastern texts and treaties. The persons wanted were those who had made mistakes or incited revolt or rebellion against the king.[456] When we compare the MT and LXX particular: "He swore on the kingdom and nation" (v.10), the end of this (v.10) shows a difference between LXX and MT. At the end of the LXX (1 Kings 18:10) we have" καὶ ἐνέπρησεν τὴν βασιλείαν καὶ τὰς χώρας αὐτῆς ὅτι οὐχ εὕρηκέν σε "then has he set fire to the kingdom and its territories, because he has not found thee". But the MT said,

---

[456] ANET, 1969, p. 660b.

וְה שְׁבִּיעַ אֶת־הַמַּמְלָכָה וְאֶת־הַגּוֹי כִּי לֹא יִמְצָאֶכָּה "he made them swear they could not find you." We cannot say what the reason is for this difference. It is possible that this part of verse10 in the LXX is due to another manuscript used by the LXX other than the MT. These two actions (to swear or to set fire) both prove the power of Ahab. It's also possible that the difference came from the corruption of LXX.[457] The king, described as passionate by his servant, was a monarch who used the diplomatic pressures of his time to ensure that the countries interrogated about the presence of the prophet would not lie to him (v.10),[458] LXX הִנֵּה אֵלִיָּהוּ was omitted). Informed about the presence of Elijah, King Ahab rushed out to welcome him (v.16). Such an attitude does not correspond to royal dignity, but rather to a position of submission.[459]

5.3.4. Observations and critical analysis

The observation, and the critical analysis of the pericope of 1Kings 18 :1-46 help us to understand certain discursive expressions and the different role and functions of different personages mentioned in this text.

5.3.5. Elijah the order giver

When reading the text, several questions are worth exploring. There are certain discursive expressions indicating that it is Elijah who does the commanding in the story. He organises the course of events. Elijah is given an order by YHWH to go and present himself before King Ahab and to give him the

---

[457] HUGO, 2006, p. 263.
[458] HUGO, 2006, p. 279.
[459] HUGO, 2006, p. 276.

good news of the returning of the rain (v. 1), אֶל־אַחְאָב לֵךְ הֵרָאֵה. That is the imperative of YHWH, but we become aware that Elijah is making a detour and goes to see עֹבַדְיָהוּ the famine was severe, Ahab had been intently seeking for him. According to 1 Kings 18:13a Obadiah's name means "servant of YHWH." His name seems to be paradoxical as he is the administrator of Ahab's royal lands, a king described as impious and idolatrous. Yet all his actions are very much conducted as shown in the nature of his name, because he protects a number of YHWH's prophets against the persecution of Jezebel. He had hidden prophets of YHWH as YHWH hid Elijah.

In this sense, Obadiah confirms the etymology of his name. That Elijah announced the coming drought is directly responsible for the persecution of his colleague's prophets by Jezebel. And because, "Obadiah is astonished that Elijah has not been informed of his heroic deed."[460] He is the person held responsible for the famine in Israel.[461] Elijah gave his first order when facing Obadiah: לֵךְ אֱמֹר לַאדֹנֶיךָ הִנֵּה אֵלִיָּהוּ "Go tell your master, Elijah is here" (v. 8). In verses 17-18, we witness an argument between Ahab and Elijah as they mutually accuse each other of having brought the misfortune upon Israel. It is then (v.19) that Elijah gives a new order, this time to King Ahab: וְעַתָּה שְׁלַח קְבֹץ אֵלַי אֶת־כָּל־יִשְׂרָאֵל "Now summon the people from all over Israel." שְׁלַח: this word means simply to "send". But in this context it has a more precise meaning: "send in mission or assign an order." Ahab was assigned by Elijah to gather all Israel. The verb is in the imperative form. קְבֹץ means "summon, gather" but there is another word, אָסַף, that has the same meaning. Not only does Elijah give the order to Ahab

---
[460] JYRKI, 2001, p. 46.
[461] DUNN and ROGERSON, 2003, p. 262.

to assemble all the people of Israel, but he names the place of gathering as well, that is, on Mount Carmel.

In verse 20 we see that Ahab follows the order like a simple subject: וַיִּשְׁלַח אַחְאָב בְּכָל־בְּנֵי יִשְׂרָאֵל וַיִּקְבֹּץ. As if to insist on the obedience of King Ahab, verse 20 voluntarily uses verbs such as "send" and "summon", verbs of order used by Elijah in verse19. In front of all the people assembled (vv.21-25), Elijah decided upon the occurrence of the sacrificial act. It is remarkable that during this period he had the function of a leader. Verse 26 shows that the prophets of Baal followed the instructions fixed by Elijah. In verse 30, the prophet intervened in order to end the final test of his adversaries' sacrificial act.

"Then וַיֹּאמֶר אֵלִיָּהוּ לְכָל־הָעָם גְּשׁוּ אֵלַי וַיִּגְּשׁוּ כָל־הָעָם אֵלָיו Elijah said to all the people, come here to me and they came to him." This is another order by Elijah obeyed by all gathered people. With the phrase "The hour that was given to you to prove the might of your god has come to an end" all the people would fix their eyes upon Elijah, who would praise the glory of YHWH.

In verse 40 the order is given by Elijah to seize the prophets of Baal: אֶת־נְבִיאֵי הַבַּעַל אִישׁ אַל־יִמָּלֵט מֵהֶם וַיִּתְפְּשׂוּם וַיֹּאמֶר אֵלִיָּהוּ לָהֶם תִּפְשׂוּ "Seize the prophets of Baal! Do not let one of them escape. So they seized them". תִּפְשׂוּ: the imperative plural masculine form of תָּפַשׂ means "seize" or "hold by force". Elijah demands that all the prophets of Baal be held by force by all the people. It is what the conjugation Qal (suffix masculine plural) of the verb וַיִּתְפְּשׂוּם indicates. Literally: "And they seized them", that is, "And the people seized them". Once more the entire mob obeyed without reservation the orders of YHWH's man. Verse 41 attests to the presence of Ahab on Mount Carmel, but he seems to be reduced to silence. He received the last orders of

Elijah: וַיֹּאמֶר אֵלִיָּהוּ לְאַחְאָב עֲלֵה אֱכֹל וּשְׁתֵה "Then Elijah said to Ahab, Go up, eat and drink" and the king obeyed וַיַּעֲלֶה אַחְאָב לֶאֱכֹל וְלִשְׁתּוֹת (v. 42) "So Ahab went up the mountain to eat and drink."

5.4. The courage of Elijah in front of Ahab, 1 Kings 18:17-20

Verses 17-18 present to us the hero, Elijah, or the protected by the Lord, in front of his adversary, Ahab.[462] This episode tells how King Ahab and the prophet Elijah accuse one another of the misfortune of Israel. The prophet and the king are seen as two irreconcilable adversaries.[463] The king refers to Elijah as a troublemaker who disrupts the order imposed by the religious rule of Ahab. The interference by Elijah proves to be justified if we take into consideration the essence of Israel as a nation that worshipped the God YHWH. Elijah disturbed the relationship between Baal and his followers, and deprived the people of the blessings expected from this god.[464] The prophet Elijah is to be the only one to oppose the religious rule of the king (1 Kgs 18:18). Due to this opposition, he remains in the eyes of the king a disrupter of the relationship between god Baal and his followers, depriving the latter of the divine benedictions.[465] Elijah is seen as having provoked the scourge of Israel.

הַאַתָּה זֶה עֹכֵר יִשְׂרָאֵל "It is you who troubles Israel" (v.17) or "it is you who brings unhappiness to Israel". This reaction of Ahab is reproachful, contrary to the reaction of Obadiah before Elijah, הַאַתָּה זֶה אֲדֹנִי אֵלִיָּהוּ Is "it really you, my lord Elijah"? (v.7), which is

---

[462] ASURMENDI, 1989, p. 6.
[463] ASURMENDI, 1989, p. 6.
[464] BUIS, 1997, p. 142.
[465] BUIS, 1997, p.143-145.

respectful.[466] Ahab addresses Elijah as if he were a magician, a disrupter, and not a prophet of YHWH.[467] The term עֹכֵר Qal, singular, active participle of the verb עָכַר means disturb, cause unhappiness' (1 Sam 14:29; Judg 11:35; Gen 34: 30). The verb עָכַר is used in (Josh 6:18) referring to the misfortune of Israel. The king points the finger at Elijah as the one who carries misfortune or the one responsible for the unhappiness of the people caused by the drought in Israel.

On this word עֹכֵר as it is used by Ahab to describe Elijah as "the troublemaker of Israel",[468] comments: "The troublemaker of Israel denotes one who, like Achan in Joshua's invasion (Josh 6.18; 7.25), is an infectious influence". The verb is found in Arabic denoting the pollution of water by mud. It is used to denote ritual disability which excludes a man from society, as Jacob was excluded from fellowship with the people of Shechem through the violence of Simeon and Levi (Gen 34.30), and Israel's harmonious and successful co-operation with Yahweh was disrupted through Achan's breach of taboo at the fall of Jericho… It is also used of the disability brought on Israel by Jonathan's breach of the taboo imposed by Saul, for which the latter is held responsible (I Sam 14:29).

וַיֹּאמֶר לֹא עָכַרְתִּי אֶת־יִשְׂרָאֵל כִּי אִם־אַתָּה וּבֵית אָבִיךָ בַּעֲזָבְכֶם אֶת־מִצְוֹת יְהוָה וַתֵּלֶךְ אַחֲרֵי הַבְּעָלִים

"And he said: I do not trouble Israel, on the contrary, it is you and your father's house who trouble Israel, in that you have forsaken the commandments of the Lord and you have followed the Baals.

Elijah responds (v. 18).

---

[466] JYRKI, 2001, p. 57.
[467] JYRKI, 2001, p. 64.
[468] GRAY, 1970, p. 392.

The prophet, in turn, accuses the monarch Ahab of interfering with the relationship between YHWH and his people, attracting the malediction of the alliance.[469] There are two personal pronouns used in the verse: one is second person plural and the other is second person singular. The second person plural pronoun is used to refer to the king and the house of his father considered responsible for the apostasy of the people in rejecting YHWH as God of Israel. The second person singular points out to the responsibility of the king regarding the religious situation of Israel. The texts of 1 Kings 16:23-24; 22:39-40 describe the king's family in negative terms. The calamity of the drought and the severe famine was attributed directly to King Ahab and his family, who promulgated practices of idolatry. Omri and Ahab followed the sin of Jeroboam. The prophet proved his heroism in front of King Ahab.

The narrator shows that Elijah does not try to excuse himself in front of the king or flatter him in any respect, but simply avoids his anger (Ant. J.VIII: 335). He does not have to defend himself against anything; he rejects the accusations of Ahab and courageously states that it is Ahab's sins that have brought upon Israel the terrible disaster: "I do not bring trouble to Israel", he says, "on the contrary it is you who abandon the Lord in order to rally with Baal", see (1Kings 18:18).

Elijah does not announce the good news that the drought is to end. Instead, he asks the king to summon all the people on Mount Carmel, together with all the prophets of Baal and of Asherah. Verse 19 starts with: וְעַתָּה "And now". This temporal gap used by Elijah is followed by the orders given to King Ahab שְׁלַח קְבֹץ "send, summon". The prophet intended to say

---

[469] BUIS, 1997, pp. 143-144.

that "now" would suffice in terms of words used. The argument between the two ends. They have to react to the urgency of the situation. The king accepts the order since the distress was great and he needed the drought to end no matter the price.

The tension between Elijah and Ahab turns into a collaboration in order to assemble the people on Mount Carmel (vv.19-20), as the use of these two verbs shows וַיִּשְׁלַח וַיִּקְבֹּץ "He sent" "and gathered". The king obeyed straightaway. Ahab submitted to the orders of Elijah without any question.[470] The intervention of the prophet was indispensable for the attaining of two objectives: 1. To show the ending of the curse originated from YHWH. 2. To act for the purification of the people. The king had only the role of accessory when the actors were all gathered; he and the rest of the people were just spectators and had to draw the conclusions of the duel.[471] However, the religious affiliation of the people will be known through the presentation of v. 21:[472] "if the Lord is God follow him; but if Baal is God, follow him. The people gathered at Mount Carmel for this ordeal are at the centre of the competition between the gods (YHWH and Baal)".

Therefore, when Elijah said in v. 24 בָּאֵשׁ הוּא הָאֱלֹהִים הָאֱלֹהִים אֲשֶׁר־יַעֲנֶה "The god who answers by fire, he is God", all the people gathered on Mount Carmel responded quickly: וַיַּעַן כָּל־הָעָם וַיֹּאמְרוּ טוֹב הַדָּבָר "Then all the people said": "What you say is good" or "the matter is good". The same sense was used by Shimei in 2 Kings 2:38, 42. Were the Baal prophets tricked by the answer of the people "your words were good" (1Kings 18:24) and (therefore) unable to backtrack?

---

[470] JIRKY, 2001, p. 74.
[471] BUIS, 1997, p. 145.
[472] NOCQUET, 2004, p. 103.

Were the prophets of Baal forced to save the honour of their god because of the action of the people? If not, we can say that they joined their voices to the voice of the people and said: "the matter is good". For Alan and Russell, (1990:40): "the people's quick response" "what you say is good" reveals their fear and "ambivalence". This ambivalence was earlier presented (v. 21) as a means of showing the threat that 'both death and Ba'al pose to Yahweh". It is not only the problem of ambivalence, but also the radical choice of faith to follow God YHWH or Baal.

The "religious limping" of the people constituted a handicap to their responding. If they said YHWH was the true God, why did they follow Baal? If they said Baal, why was he not able to send rain as the god of thunder and rain should? Why had he not stopped the drought during these three years? They had a passive attitude, waiting silently for the outcome of the challenge. Once YHWH answered by "fire" (v. 38) the people took an aggressive attitude and became the advocate of YHWH (v. 39):

יְהוָֹה הוּא הָאֱלֹהִים יְהוָה הוּא הָאֱלֹהִים "The Lord he is God! The Lord he is God," (Alan and Russell, 1990:40). The name of Elijah which means "YHWH is my Lord" is expressed paradoxically in Israel during Ahab's reign because YHWH was not in fact recognized as Lord. Thus, Elijah's role was to put an end to the religious paradox in Israel. The people of Israel were cured of their religious limping.

Therefore, the assumption that YHWH and Baal could refer to the same divinity (Buis, 1997:147) is not convincing. We can see the same point with Hosea (Hos 2:18). If the prophet Hosea uses the name of Baal in this verse, he does so in the context of Hebrew and other Semitic languages, as Baal can refer to both proper and common nouns such as:

master, owner, possessor of a person or object, examples: owner of a house (Exod 22:7), of a bull (Exod 21:28; Isa 1:3), of wealth (Eccl 5:13), citizen of a city (Josh 24:11) and also a woman's husband (Exod 21:3). It is by virtue of the last meaning that the prophet Hosea uses the term, in saying that the Lord is the Husband of Israel, who is his wife.

5.4.1. Table of comparison between MT and LXX

We are not comparing all the verses here, just some of them. Our intention is to highlight some differences between these two sources of our research.

MT Translation		LXX Translation
1 Kings 18:21 וַיִּגַּשׁ אֵלִיָּהוּ אֶל־כָּל־הָעָם וַיֹּאמֶר עַד־מָתַי אַתֶּם פֹּסְחִים עַל־שְׁתֵּי הַסְּעִפִּים אִם־יְהוָה הָאֱלֹהִים לְכוּ אַחֲרָיו וְאִם־הַבַּעַל לְכוּ אַחֲרָיו וְלֹא־עָנוּ הָעָם אֹתוֹ דָּבָר	Elijah went before all the people and said, 'How long will you limp with these two crutches? If the Lord is God, follow him; but if Baal is God, follow him.' But the people said nothing.	21 καὶ προσήγαγεν Ηλιου πρὸς πάντας καὶ εἶπεν αὐτοῖς Ηλιου ἕως πότε ὑμεῖς χωλανεῖτε ἐπ' ἀμφοτέραις ταῖς ἰγνύαις εἰ ἔστιν κύριος ὁ θεός πορεύεσθε ὀπίσω αὐτοῦ εἰ δὲ ὁ Βααλ αὐτός πορεύεσθε ὀπίσω αὐτοῦ καὶ οὐκ ἀπεκρίθη ὁ λαὸς λόγον
וּק רֹאתֶם בְּשֵׁם אֱלֹהֵיכֶם וַאֲנִי אֶקְרָא בְשֵׁם־יְהוָה וְהָיָה הָאֱלֹהִים אֲשֶׁר־יַעֲנֶה בָאֵשׁ הוּא הָאֱלֹהִים וַיַּעַן כָּל־הָעָם וַיֹּאמְרוּ טוֹב הַדָּבָר	Then you will call on the name of your god, and I will call on the name of the Lord. The god who answers by fire he is God.' Then all the people said, 'What you say is good'.	24 καὶ βοᾶτε ἐν ὀνόματι θεῶν ὑμῶν καὶ ἐγὼ ἐπικαλέσομαι ἐν ὀνόματι κυρίου τοῦ θεοῦ μου καὶ ἔσται ὁ θεός ὃς ἐὰν ἐπακούσῃ ἐν πυρί οὗτος θεός καὶ ἀπεκρίθησαν πᾶς ὁ λαὸς καὶ εἶπον καλὸν τὸ ῥῆμα ὃ ἐλάλησας
וַיִּקְחוּ אֶת־הַפָּר אֲשֶׁר־נָתַן לָהֶם וַיַּעֲשׂוּ וַיִּקְרְאוּ בְשֵׁם־הַבַּעַל מֵהַבֹּקֶר לֵאמֹר	v. 26 So they took the bull given them and prepared it. Then they called on the name of	26 καὶ ἔλαβον τὸν μόσχον καὶ ἐποίησαν καὶ ἐπεκαλοῦντο ἐν ὀνόματι τοῦ Βααλ ἐκ πρωίθεν ἕως

וְעַד־הַצָּהֳרַיִם	Baal from morning till noon. 'O Baal, answer us!' they shouted. But there was no response; no one answered. And they danced around the altar they had made.	μεσημβρίας καὶ εἶπον ἐπάκουσον ἡμῶν ὁ Βααλ ἐπάκουσον ἡμῶν καὶ οὐκ ἦν φωνὴ καὶ οὐκ ἦν ἀκρόασις καὶ διέτρεχον ἐπὶ τοῦ θυσιαστηρίου οὗ ἐποίησαν
עֲנֵנוּ וְאֵין קוֹל וְאֵין		
עֹנֶה וַיְפַסְּחוּ עַל־הַמִּזְבֵּחַ		
אֲשֶׁר עָשָׂה		
וַיֹּאמֶר אֵלִיָּהוּ לְכָל־הָעָם	v. 30 And Elijah said to all the people, 'Come here to me'. They came to him, and he repaired the altar of the Lord, which was in ruins.	30 καὶ εἶπεν Ηλιου πρὸς τὸν λαόν προσαγάγετε πρός με καὶ προσήγαγεν πᾶς ὁ λαὸς πρὸς αὐτόν
גְּשׁוּ אֵלַי וַיִּגְּשׁוּ כָל־הָעָם		
אֵלָיו וַיְרַפֵּא אֶת־מִזְבַּח		
יְהוָה הֶהָרוּס		

Now, it is important to take note of some of the differences between MT and the LXX. In verse 21, we find this expression in MT 'Elijah went before *all the people*' כָּל־הָעָם but the LXX has πρὸς πάντας before all. In verse 30 we find in the MT, לְכָל־הָעָם *to all the people*, the LXX for the same verse says πρὸς τὸν λαόν *to the people*.

It is not impossible to think that MT wants to emphasize the extensive presence of people on Mount Carmel as in verse 39 (MT. = LXX).[473] If we accept this assumption, then why did the MT not have the word "people" in verse 40, whereas in the LXX it is present? Many times verbs in MT do not correspond to verbs in the LXX, for example: verses. 21, 24, 37, and 39. But the phenomenon is not identical to what is found in verse 26. In fact, in those cases the subject is a collective and Hebrew is not consistent with itself regarding related verbs. For example in verse 24 the verbs correspond to the subject in singular: *people,* עָם. One verb is in singular

---

[473] HUGO, 2006, p. 219.

and another verb is in plural: וַיַּעַן כָּל־הָעָם וַיֹּאמְרוּ[474][475] "*and all the people answered and said*". In French, we can see the difference between the singular and the plural of the verbs of our translation: *"et tout le peuple répondit et ils dirent"*. In the LXX we have the harmonization of this (v. 24): *kai. ἀπεκρίθησαν πᾶς ὁ λαὸς καὶ εἶπον καλόν* "And all the people answered and said"; *ἀποκρίνομαι*= "to answer". *ἀπεκρίθησαν*: verb, indicative, aorist, passive, 3rd person plural. The Greek word *εἶπον* "said" is the indicative, aorist, active, 3rd person plural of the verb *λέγω* "to say".[476]

According to the LXX, Baal's prophets are the subject, and they are plural, as are the verbs. It is they who built the altar. But is there a problem with using the singular in verse 26? Is Elijah the subject of the verb עָשָׂה "to make"? Why does the MT have the subject and verb in singular? Maybe it is possible that in this verse we have the impersonal form: "altar that had been done."[477] The MT used עָשָׂה the 3rd person singular, which had been translated in the LXX by *ἐποίησαν* the 3rd person plural. We can conclude that the LXX explains the Hebrew verb עָשָׂה with the Greek *ἐποίησαν* to refer to the context or to the sentence in which the subject is the prophets of Baal. Between these two texts, the likely original and preferable choice is the LXX.[478]

---

[474] יֹּאמְרוּ Qal imperfect, the 3rd person masculine plural of the verb אָמַר to say.
[475] יַּעַן Qal imperfect, the 3rd person singular masculine of the verb עָנָה to answer, to respond; Targum עֲנָא.
[476] HUGO, 2006, p. 224.
[477] BARTHELEMY, 1982, p. 371.
[478] COGAN, 2001, p. 435.

5.4.2. The ordeal on Mount Carmel

In verse 23 the schedule of the competition is presented, each prepares their holocaust and waits for the fire to come down from the sky and consume the holocaust. Through this test, the winner would be named as the servant of the real God, and his adversary, an impostor. It is an ordeal, a judgment made by the gods. The two gods, YHWH and Baal, were obliged to respond to the challenge and prove their power to the people. Barrois[479] explains that the ordeal practices were used in antiquity in order to decide the innocence or the guilt of contestants or protagonists. People would resort to the judgment of the river, also called the ordeal of the river. The name of the river was preceded by a divine name. In Akkadian (*nārum*=river/ canal or in Sumerian= ÍD, I_7); ÍD.DA.ḪI.A (the Euphrates). The river is a river-god/river-deity or deified river [^{d}ÍD].[480] Before an ordeal, watchmen must guard those who had been suspected or accused. *ERÍN.MEŠ maṣṣartu ša ina iddi ^{d}ÍD ultu šimētān adi namāri elišunu izzizū.* "the watchmen stood guard over the persons undergoing the ordeal on the bank of the river from evening to morning", (Wilfred, 1965: 6 iv 8). Wolfram[481] said:

> "The ordeal was employed as a further means of proof when someone was accused of murder or adultery without adequate substantiating evidence. It was occasionally used also in cases of suspected theft; in Babylonia, Assyria, and Nuzi, this was always a river ordeal. Apparently, at that time no one considered the possibility that someone could actually swim in the river. Therefore, people could be persuaded that the river god always threw the innocent up on land yet he would at the same time let drown either the one who committed the crime or a person who brought a false charge."

---

[479] BARROIS, 1953, p. 339.
[480] Black et al., 2000, p. 242.
[481] WOLFRAM, 1994, p. 143.

If the person thrown in the river was guilty, the river would engulf him. Moreover, if the person was innocent, the river god would spare his life. The Mosaic Law prescribes an ordeal ceremony when a woman is suspected of adultery. The priest would prepare a beverage in which he would put tabernacle dust, which he would then dissolve with a papyrus while chanting imprecations. Afterwards, he would administer it to the woman. Judging by the effects produced, she would be declared innocent or guilty (Num 5:11-31). But here, there is a judiciary duel taking place between Baal and YHWH, who are invited to prove their right to be worshipped as a God and master of Israel.

In this Carmel episode, the central point of the ordeal is this phrase:

הָאֱלֹהִים אֲשֶׁר־יַעֲנֶה בָאֵשׁ הוּא הָאֱלֹהִים "The god who answers by fire, he is God" (1Kings 18:24). Between YHWH and Baal, who is able to send fire to burn up the sacrifice? The two deities will be in competition. "The gods themselves will solve the dilemma."[482] The winner will be known as God, and will be followed without hesitation or suspicion by all the people gathered on Mount Carmel.

5.4.3. The healing of the altar (v. 30bMT) = (v. 32bLXX)

In this ordeal on Mount Carmel, the altar plays an important role in the competition. "The story underlines the reconquest of a Yahvist sanctuary which had been thrown down somewhere on Mount Carmel, and which had become a place of Baal worship."[483] This reconquest took place through the

---

[482] TROMP, 1975, p. 497.
[483] NOCQUET, 2004, p. 117.

restoration of the ruins of the altar of YHWH (v. 30b MT), and also by the construction of an altar by the prophets of Baal (v. 26 MT) about which they danced. The reconquest of Mount Carmel is not simply that YHWH is jealous of Baal, who had previously deposed Him in the demolition of His altar and the occupying of Mount Carmel; it is also the religious conquest of all the people of Israel. The reconquest of the people, who had abandoned the Lord and His commands, to follow Baal, was accomplished by the restoration of YHWH's altar upon Mount Carmel. The altar is a cultual element of worship for both gods (Baal and YHWH). On that, account there is some confusion in the order of elements in the episode.

The verse 30b MT uses the verbs רָפָא and בָּמָה, and in verse 32b of the LXX οἰκοδομέω 'to build' and ἰάομαι 'to heal' are employed. וַיְרַפֵּא אֶת־מִזְבַּח יְהוָה הֶהָרוּס 'And he repaired the altar of the Lord that had been torn down'. The different literary character appears more clearly between the MT and the LXX, (Hugo, 2006: 228).This part of the verse in MT appears when Elijah calls all the people to come near to him:

וַיֹּאמֶר אֵלִיָּהוּ לְכָל־הָעָם גְּשׁוּ אֵלַי "And Elijah said to all the people come here to me "(v. 30a). He repaired an altar that had broken down. But in the LXX, this statement is in verse 32b; after Elijah had built up the stones in "the name of the Lord", he repaired the altar of the Lord which had been broken down. By reading this section (vv. 30-32) in both the MT and the LXX we find that there is greater harmony and consistency of the narrator or the author of the MT. Most Bible translations[484] followed the MT. Two verbs רָפָא and

---

[484] NIV=New International Version, NJB=The New Jerusalem Bible, NKJ=New King James, ESV=English Standard Version, VUL=Latin Vulgate, OABA=Oxford Annotated Bible with Apocrypha...

בָּמָה, in this section (vv.30-32) 'repair' and 'build' the altar of YHWH lead us to ask some questions. How we should understand, the existence of a ruined altar of YHWH on Mount Carmel in a period that there was not one of "high places", since there had already been a centralization of the cult of YHWH? Verbs referring to "to repair" and "to build" the altar of YHWH suggest an abandonment of the altar due probably to Israel's infidelity. We find an explanation in a "destroyed altar of YHWH" mentioned by Elijah in 1 Kings 19:10-14. In this passage, the same words are used about the demolition of YHWH's altar as in 18:30.[485] The same הָרַס "demolish"or "destroy" is employed in (18:30; 19:10-14).

10 וַיֹּאמֶר קַנֹּא קִנֵּאתִי לַיהוָה׀ אֱלֹהֵי צְבָאוֹת כִּי־עָזְבוּ בְרִיתְךָ בְּנֵי יִשְׂרָאֵל אֶת־מִזְבְּחֹתֶיךָ הָרָסוּ וְאֶת־נְבִיאֶיךָ הָרְגוּ בֶחָרֶב וָאִוָּתֵר אֲנִי לְבַדִּי וַיְבַקְשׁוּ אֶת־נַפְשִׁי לְקַחְתָּהּ

"I have been very zealous for the Lord God Almighty. The Israelites have rejected your covenant, **broken down** your altars, and put your prophets to death with the sword. I am the only one left, and now they are trying to kill me too'. (1 Kings 19:10-14, NIV).

The existence of an altar on Mount Carmel as a high place introduces the problematic question of the centralization of the cult of YHWH according to the Deuteronomistic concept (Deut 12:4-7).[486] However, the fact that Elijah restored the altar in *the name of YHWH* (v. 32) means that he must have received the authorization or permission from YHWH.[487] For Hugo,[488] "to construct" בָּמָה, (v.31-32) an altar with

---

[485] JYRKI, 2001, pp. 106-107.
[486] HUGO, 2006, p. 231.
[487] HOGO, 2006, p. 237.
[488] HOGU, 2006, p. 231.

twelve stones creates a tension with the healing of the altar (v. 30b). If we refer to the MT and these two verbs רָפָא and בָּמָה, we find that the sections are complementary, both referring to Elijah's action. He "repaired" what was to be repaired there on the ruins of the altar of YHWH and 'built' or 'rebuilt' it with the twelve stones according to the twelve tribes of Israel. This was to indicate the particular role of this altar, in memory of the twelve sons of the patriarch Jacob, whose name had been changed to Israel.[489] It is not that Elijah built two altars, as posited by Nocquet.[490] For us, the LXX in its narrative construction seems to indicate otherwise. It shows two different actions on the altar of YHWH in ruins at Mount Carmel. First of all there is the verb οἰκοδομέω "to build" the altar with twelve stones, and a second action ἰάομαι "to heal" or "to repair" the altar of YHWH.

The narrative construction of the text of the LXX can distinguish two different actions in connection with the altar. Hugo,[491] argues that there was a single altar which served the prophets of Baal, the very same one that "they made" (v.26). It had been defiled by the pagan Baal sacrifices offered by his prophets. So to reclaim it for the sacrifice to YHWH, Elijah had to 'heal' it. In conclusion, Hugo, [492] said that:

---

[489] NOCQUET, 2004, p. 106.
[490] NOCQUET, 2004, pp. 106; 108.
[491] HOGO, 2006, p. 235.
[492] HUGO, 2006:236 „En conclusion, la différence majeure des deux mises en récit réside dans le fait qu'en LXX il n'est question que d'un seul autel servant à la fois aux prophètes de Baal et à Elie, alors que TM parle de deux autels distincts et préexistants. La guérison de l'autel n'a pas la même fonction narrative. En LXX, elle apparaît comme la ré-consécration d'un autel païen. En TM, au contraire, il s'agit de la restauration d'un autel Yaviste déjà édifié sur le Mont Carmel, détruit soit en raison de la centralisation du culte comme l'avait été celui de Béthel (1 R 13, 1-5 ; cf. Dt 12, 4-7)-, soit à cause de l'apostasie du peuple (cf. 1

"The major difference in the two stories is the fact that there is, for the LXX, one altar serving both the prophets of Baal and Elijah, whereas MT speaks about two separate altars. The healing of the altar hasn't the same narrative function. Contrary in the MT, it is the restoration of a yahvist altar already built on Mount Carmel, destroyed because of the centralization of worship that was in Bethel (1 Kgs 13:1-5; Deut 12:4-7) or because of the apostasy of the people (1 Kgs 19:10 and 14)".

Therefore, for Elijah to rebuild the altar of YHWH is to signify that YHWH is back again upon this mountain, symbolizing his dominion over Carmel.[493] But the sequence of actions in verse 32, first "he built", ᾠκοδόμησεν then "healed", ἰάσατο sows confusion over the event concerning the existence of one or two altars on Mount Carmel. However, if the LXX suggests the existence of an altar used by the prophets of Baal and Elijah, then the question is why the Greek text (LXX) employs again ᾠκοδόμησεν "he built" (v. 26)? The Greek text should have simply said that Elijah 'healed' in the sense of purifying the altar before it was used for YHWH. This argument is unconvincing. If we compare τοῦ θυσιαστηρίου οὗ ἐποίησαν "the altar which they had made" (v.26) and καὶ ᾠκοδόμησεν "and he built" (v. 32a) we can add that: "the altar of the Lord, which was in ruins" (v. 30) is not touched by the prophets of Baal because at this time they had built their own altar (v. 26). Elijah alone was able to restore it and use it to avenge the honour of his God. It is hard for us to see how Elijah, the champion of YHWH, and the prophets of Baal, the champions of their god Baal, would accept competing on the same altar. We think, on the contrary, that according to the order of verbs in the LXX text where Elijah is the subject of

---

R 19. 10.14)."
[493] NOCQUET, 2004, p. 126.

ᾠκοδόμησεν "he built" and ἰάσατο "he healed" or "repaired", there are two independent actions. After Elijah had built the altar, he healed or repaired it.

In summary, we can say that when we compare the forms of each of our ancient sources, we find that narrative elements are substantially identical, although the sequence of events and organization of the story are different.[494]

5.4.4. Variants between the MT and the LXX of vv.31-39

This passage of the biblical text displays some variation between the MT and the LXX in the organization of the verses. We will make use of this table to compare the corresponding passages from the MT and the LXX.

MT	Translation	LXX	Translation
וַיֹּאמֶר אֵלִיָּהוּ לְכָל־הָעָם גְּשׁוּ אֵלַי וַיִּגְּשׁוּ כָל־הָעָם אֵלָיו	v. 30a The Elijah said to all the people: 'Come here to me' and they came to him'.	v. 30 καὶ εἶπεν Ηλιου πρὸς τὸν λαόν προσαγάγετε πρός με καὶ προσήγαγεν πᾶς ὁ λαὸς πρὸς αὐτόν	v. 30 And Elijah said to the people, Come near to me. And all the people came near to him.
אֶת־מִזְבַּח יְהוָה הֶהָרוּס וַיְרַפֵּא	v. 30b and he repaired the altar of the Lord, which was in ruins.	v. 32b καὶ ἰάσατο τὸ θυσιαστήριον τὸ κατεσκαμμένον	v. 32b and repaired the altar that had been broken down.
וַיִּקַּח אֵלִיָּהוּ שְׁתֵּים עֶשְׂרֵה אֲבָנִים כְּמִסְפַּר שִׁבְטֵי בְנֵי־יַעֲקֹב אֲשֶׁר הָיָה דְבַר־יְהוָה אֵלָיו לֵאמֹר יִשְׂרָאֵל יִהְיֶה שְׁמֶךָ	v. 31 Elijah took twelve stones, one for each of the tribes descended from Jacob, to whom	v. 31 καὶ ἔλαβεν Ηλιου δώδεκα λίθους κατ' ἀριθμὸν φυλῶν τοῦ Ισραηλ ὡς ἐλάλησεν	v. 31 And Elijah took twelve stones, according to the number of the tribes of Israel, as the Lord spoke to him,

---

[494] HUGO, 2006, p. 233.

	the word of the Lord had come, saying, 'Your name shall be Israel.'	κύριος πρὸς αὐτὸν λέγων Ισραηλ ἔσται τὸ ὄνομά σου	saying, Israel shall be thy name.
וַיִּבְנֶה אֶת־הָאֲבָנִים מִזְבֵּחַ בְּשֵׁם יְהוָה	**v. 32** With the stones he built an altar in the name of the Lord,	**v. 32a** καὶ ᾠκοδόμησεν τοὺς λίθους ἐν ὀνόματι κυρίου	And he built up the stones in the name of the Lord,
וַיַּעַשׂ תְּעָלָה זֶרַע סָבִיב לַמִּזְבֵּחַ כְּבֵית סָאתָיִם	and he dug a trench around it large enough to hold two seahs of seed.	**v. 32c** καὶ ἐποίησεν θααλα χωροῦσαν δύο μετρητὰς σπέρματος κυκλόθεν τοῦ θυσιαστηρίου	and he made a trench that would hold two measures of seed round about the altar.

Looking carefully at the manuscripts of the LXX we find several variants in verses 30-32 and in the prayer of Elijah (vv. 36-37). In verse 32a of the LXX[L] 'in the name of the Lord' is absent. We see that in verse 31 the MT mentions the name of the patriarch Jacob who is not in the LXX, and the prayer of Elijah (v. 36 LXX[A]) particularly mentions the name of the patriarch Jacob who is absent in other manuscripts. We can conclude that: LXX[A] has faithfully followed a manuscript compatible with MT.

It is not inconsequential to see that Elijah evokes in his prayer the Lord of the patriarchs Abraham, Isaac, and Jacob. It would thus depend on faith in YHWH, whom their ancestors had faithfully obeyed, and of whom all the people of Israel claimed to be the progeny. Only in verse 36 MT do we find Elijah with the title of prophet: אֵלִיָּהוּ הַנָּבִיא "Elijah the prophet". We do not understand what purpose the Hebrew editors would have had in deleting this title, which is very important from a theological and narrative point of view.⁴⁹⁵ In addition, this same verse 36 of the manuscript LXX^L shows some difference, especially towards the end:

καὶ ἀνεβόησεν Ηλιου εἰς τὸν οὐρανὸν καὶ εἶπεν κύριε ὁ θεὸς Αβρααμ καὶ Ισακ καὶ Ισραηλ ἐπάκουσόν μου κύριε ἐπάκουσόν μου σήμερον ἐν πυρί καὶ γνώτωσαν πᾶς ὁ λαὸς οὗτος ὅτι σὺ εἶ νόμος κύριος ὁ θεὸς Ισραηλ κἀγὼ δοῦλός σου καὶ διὰ σὲ πεποίηκα τὰ ἔργα ταῦτα καὶ σὺ ἐπέστρεψας τὴν καρδίαν τοῦ λαοῦ τούτου ὀπίσω σοῦ.

This part ["and turned the heart of the people back to you again"] is the end of verse 37. It could be an accident on the part of the editor of LXX^L but possibly it is deliberate.⁴⁹⁶ We find νόμος "only" in LXX^L preceded by "Lord the God of Israel". This word is absent in others manuscripts of the LXX, but this word νόμος "only" in the prayer of Elijah, for the editor of LXX^L, puts an accent on the fact that YHWH is the only God and Lord in Israel. Unfortunately, in this context, it is because Israel follows other deities, הַבְּעָלִים "the Baals". Elijah asked YHWH in his prayer (v. 37) to manifest himself as God in Israel, as the national God.⁴⁹⁷

Another difference comes from Elijah's prayer in the text of the Targum of 1 Kings 18:37 which mentions 'fire' but also adds "rain":

"קַבֵּיל צְלוֹתִי בְעוּתִי יוי בְאִישָׁתָא קַבֵּיל צְלוֹתִי בְעוּתִי יוי בְמִטַר *Receive my prayer, YHW with the fire; receive my prayer, YHW, with rain ...*" ⁴⁹⁸ In the Talmud of Jerusalem (1Kgs 18:36-37), we have this: "*exauce-moi d'abord en faisant descendre du feu du ciel, et exauce-moi encore en ce qu'on ne dise pas que j'ai fait de*

---

⁴⁹⁵ HUGO, 2006, p. 204.
⁴⁹⁶ HUGO, 2006, p. 239.
⁴⁹⁷ NOCQUET, 2004, p. 124.
⁴⁹⁸ SPERBER, 1959, p. 260 ; TARGUM of Jonathan of Former Prophet, vol. 10, 1987, p. 252.

sorcellerie.'⁴⁹⁹ It is understandable that the "fire" is the element of the challenge of Elijah (v. 24). We are not able to justify why the Targum adds "receive my prayer *YHWH* with rain". In verse 36 LXX we find in the prayer of Elijah only the mention: ἐπάκουσόν μου σήμερον ἐν πυρί "answer me this day by fire". It is possible that this mention of 'rain' is a progressive development of the text.⁵⁰⁰ It can be assumed that the editor of the Targum 1 Kings 18 reintroduced in verse 36 the problem of the lack of rain caused by drought, for the drought was, after all, a consequence of the apostasy of King Ahab and the people who are summoned to help solve that very problem on Mount Carmel.

5.4.5. Context and theological implications

The quarrel between Ahab and Elijah resulted in a sacrificial competition on Mount Carmel, commanded by Elijah and witnessed by all the people of Israel and the prophets of Baal. The aim, according to our pericope, is to reveal which god is the most powerful, and therefore, deserves to be worshipped in Israel. The status of "authentic god" would be recognized by the one who would manifest its power in descending the "fire of the sky" to devour the offering.⁵⁰¹ The fire, but also the lightning and the rain, represented a characteristic of a god. 'In a stele depicting the storm god Baal, the storm is symbolized by this stylized branch, evoking the storm, emblematic for Baal, the rider of the clouds'.

---

[499] Le TALMUD de Jérusalem, vol. 1, 1960:243; 257. Cet ajout du Talmud de Jérusalem à la fin du v.37 : „qu'on ne dise pas que j'ai fait de la sorcellerie", "est une précaution qui vise à écarter tout d'idée de qualifier le prophète Elie de magicien."
[500] HUGO, 2006, p. 240.
[501] ASURMENDI, 1989, pp. 10; 12-13.

In the epic Gilgamesh, IV/III: 17 or (L.97), we find the following: *[ib-r]iq birqu innapiḫ išātum* "The lightning flashed, the fire broke out". Here is another way that fire can be a divine intervention, (AAA20 88:150): *ᵈGiš.BAR (Girru) ultu šamê imqutma...uqalīšunūti* "upon the divine intervention, fire fell from the heavens and consumed them."

According to Black and Green,[502] the deity ᵈGiš.BAR (Girru) is the Babylonian god of fire. He is represented by fire in all its aspects: as destructive force and as the burning heat of the Mesopotamian summer, as well as a creative force. At Ešnunak, the fire burned the temple of Hurrian, the storm god, but we do not know the reason: *išātum ana bīt ᵢₗTišpak ina Ešnunna ᵏⁱ imqutma innaḫizma kali mūšim īkul* "The lightning struck the temple of the god *Tišpak* at *Ešnunak*, the fire spread and ravaged the building all the night.[503] This demonstrates the frequent occurrence of the storm in connection with fire. "It is especially noteworthy that fire is used as the means whereby Baal and YHWH are known to indicate their power as gods. In Canaanite mythology Baal, as part of his role as god of rain and fertility,... Baal failed to produce fire."[504] Storm-god Baal must have control over fire and lightning. The Baal also failed to let his believers understand his voice וְאֵין קוֹל "but no voice" of Baal (v.26). Jesse,[505] said: "There is no voice of thunder from the powerful god of storm... Baal, the god of thunder and lightning, fails his test. He is unable to put fire on the sacrifice. He is, in fact, no god at all."

---

[502] BLACK and GREEN, 2006, p. 88.
[503] DOSSIN, 1939, p. 121.
[504] HUSSER, 1990, p. 40; JYRKI, 2001, p. 97, note 8.
[505] JESSE, 2002, p. 216.

If Elijah asked Baal to send his fire and consume the holocaust it was because Elijah wanted to point out one of the characteristics of Baal. Baal could light the fire which was followed by rain, since Baal was considered to have control over the clouds, the thunder and the rain. The fire in 1 Kings 18:38 is presented as an instrument of divine judgment, an ordeal in the ritual competition that opposed Elijah to the prophets of Baal. The response of YHWH proves that he is "YHWH of fire."[506] In this ordeal Elijah said: יַעֲנֶה בָאֵשׁ הוּא הָאֱלֹהִים הָאֱלֹהִים אֲשֶׁר "The god who shall answer by fire, he is God" (1 Kgs 18:24). That means that according to Jyrki, [507]: "the real god is expected to be able to set the sacrifice on fire. This means, vice versa, that the God who does not answer by fire is not God."

In this particular religious context where YHWH is not recognized as a real god, the name of the prophet Elijah אֵלִיָּהוּ is significant as its translation renders the meaning "my God is YHWH." The name of Elijah contains the wholeness of his mission.[508] It is a confessional name and it means: "YHWH is my God." We can define this narrative as an ordeal: a divine intervention that decides which of the two parties in a litigation is right. These two parties are Elijah and the prophets of Baal, acting as constitutional bodies. YHWH was represented by Elijah and Baal represented by his prophets.[509] This competition ends with the declared victory of Elijah and God YHWH together with the confession of all the people who would cry out aloud יְהֹוָה הוּא הָאֱלֹהִים יְהֹוָה הוּא הָאֱלֹהִים "It is YHWH who is

---

[506] HEINTZ, 1973, p. 73.
[507] JYRKI, 2001, p. 97.
[508] VISCHER, 1951, p. 417.
[509] RUSAK, 2008, p. 29.

God, it is YHWH who is God"(1 Kgs 18:39b). It is as if the confession made by the people represented, on the one hand, the religious correction of Israel, and, on the other hand, the recognition of the prophet who carried the confessional name that would, from that moment forward, correspond to a religious paradox in Israel.

Before the prayer of Elijah, he asked the people to pour water on the offering and on the wood (v. 33). Ordering this action proves the faith of Elijah in his Lord YHWH and His power. We can say that to follow the Lord implies faith in Him; to believe YHWH implies belief in His power. The faith of the followers of any god and faith in the power of this god, is the crux of theological point of the relationship between believers and their god. Here Elijah wants to demonstrate his faith in the Lord as the almighty and true God. "Pouring water over the sacrifice is an extravagant demonstration of belief that nothing is too hard for Yahweh."[510] According to Tromp[511]: "The prophet's gesture intends to remove any suspicion that he will bring about a kind of spontaneous ignition by natural but secret means." It is also "an expression of confidence."[512] The text of 1 Kings 18:1-46 is marked by the motif of the drought in 1 Kings 17:1, and the return of rain in 1 Kings 18:1-2, 41-46. The return of the rain shows that Baal could not be the master of the rain. The one who had the power over the rain could invoke it anytime he decided.

---

[510] DUNN and ROGERSON, 2003, p. 262.
[511] TROMP, 1975, p. 486.
[512] GRAY, 1970, p. 400.

5.5. Irony of the Prophet Elijah or reality of the god?

Is the Baal of Mount Carmel, in the ordeal, is the chief god of Tyre, the Baal Melqart? Or does the irony of Elijah in 1Kings 18:27 describe the reality of Baal Melqart? What evidence is there to support this assumption or this view? This assumption is that the Baal of Mount Carmel is the Baal Melqart. Basically, three main points of comparison have been made. First, Elijah's allusion to the possibility that Baal is daydreaming and that Baal might be on a journey (1 Kgs 18:27) has been compared to the description of Herakles with whom Melqart was equated. Another bit of evidence is that Elijah said "Baal is sleeping and must be awakened", (1Kings 18:27). We will develop all the evidence for these ideas in the following paragraphs.

5.5.1. The sacred dance of the Baal prophets

וַיְפַסְּחוּ עַל־הַמִּזְבֵּחַ אֲשֶׁר עָשָׂה "and they danced on the altar that they had built" (v. 26). What could the choreography of this dance be? Laforgue,[513] says that the Phoenicians adored their divinities by kneeling before their statues and making signs of adoration with their hands. He adds that these were the religious rites of fertility. According to Heliodorus, (IV, 17:1) a hopping/jumping dance was a practice attested to in the cult of Hercules of Tyre, a god identified with Melqart, the patron of Tyre. The dance accompanied by music is described as a dance, accompanied by a fast, in which worshippers would jump lightly in the air, sometimes kneel close to the ground, and other times turn to each other as if they

---

[513] LAFORGUE, 1956, p. 27.

were possessed.[514] The verb פָּסַח meaning "limp or wobble", is also found in 1 Kings 19:18 where *YHWH* promises Elijah to spare "all whose knees have not bowed down to Baal." The similarity found in the two texts reaffirms the meaning of the dance.

The LXX translated this word as χωλαινειν which means "to crouch down" or "bend the knees". In the second century AD, there was still the limping dance performed in Israel to avert the drought. The scholar Caquot,[515] brings a testimony about this dance against drought and for the return of rain:

> "During a drought, Levi fasts, and the rain never came. Levi says: You are Master of the world and you're High in the upper seats, but the rain did not come, you do not have mercy on your children. The rain came (finally) but Levi was lame, [Talmud Babli, Ta'anit 25a]".

Does this mean that Levi had danced against the failure of his fasting for rain? If so, Levi used dance, and the passion in this dance made him a cripple. The context shows that the priests performed the ritual dance, or sacred dance, which was intended to wake the sleeping god, but without effect.[516] According to John Chrysostom, the fast and the dance have been attested to during the period of drought among the Jewish of Antioch.[517] If we go by this meaning, we can

---

[514] BRIQUEL-CHATONNET, 1992: 304 : „Je les laissai là à leurs airs de flûte et à leurs danses, qu'ils menaient d'une manière Syrienne, au son des cordes, sur un rythme rapide : tantôt ils s'élevaient en l'air avec des bonds légers, tantôt ils s'accroupissaient (*epoklazontes*) à ras de terre et tournoyaient de tout leur corps comme des possédés."

[515] CAQUOT, 1963, p. 130: „Lors d'une sécheresse, Lévi observa le jeûne, et la pluie ne vint pas. Lévi dit : Maître du monde, tu t'es élevé et tu sièges dans les hauteurs, mais la pluie n'est pas venue, tu n'as pas eu pitié de tes enfants. La pluie est venue (enfin), mais Lévi était boiteux."

[516] De VAUX, 1967, p. 487; FENSHAN, 1980, p. 232.

[517] CAQUOT, 1963, note 3; Migne *Patrologiae Gracae,* XLVIII,

assume that the prophets of Baal were performing an ecstatic dance in order to obtain the gratification of their god.

The verb פָּסַח "suggests a wavering movement and of rhythmic genuflections."[518] Another meaning that can be applied is 'float religiously", "be undecided."[519] From this perspective, Elijah, by using the verb "waver" refers to all those who want to serve both YHWH and Baal. This idea is more explicit in the discourse of the prophet if we look at verse 21:

וַיֹּאמֶר עַד־מָתַי אַתֶּם פֹּסְחִים עַל־שְׁתֵּי הַסְּעִפִּים "How long will you waver between two opinions?" Elijah uses סְעִפִּים meaning "branches", (Ezek 31:6), "opinions" or "opposite thoughts."[520] On the other hand, this phrase may mean "hobbling between two forks."[521] The noun הַסְּעִפִּים is difficult to interpret. Its root is סָעִף, meaning branch, Isa 10:33; 17:6). For Hugo,[522] in the context of our biblical text, סְעִפִּים probably means "branches, or crutches". Reymond,[523] translates it as "branches, hocks, *crutches*" but he mentions that the exact meaning remains unknown. Therefore, the LXX translates the word *ταῖς ἰγνύαις* which means "hocks". This word has the meaning of trotting by bending the knees alternately before the two divinities (*YHWH* and Baal).[524]

The scholar Burney,[525] says in reference to this verse that: "the attempt to combine two religions as incompatible as Yahweh-worship and Baal-worship is

---

Col. 846.
[518] BONNET, 1988, p. 141.
[519] SENDER and TRENEL, 1987, p. 585.
[520] BUIS, 1997, p. 147; HUGO, 2006, p. 220; gray, 1970, p. 396.
[521] GRAY, 1970, p. 396.
[522] HUGO, 2006, p. 220.
[523] REYMOND, 1991, p. 265.
[524] BUIS 1997, p. 147; BURNEY, 1903, p. 223.
[525] BURNEY, 1903, p. 223.

compared to the laboured gait of a man walking upon legs of different length". In conclusion, the prophet Elijah asks the people: "How long will you waver between two religious opinions, that is, between the cult of YHWH and of Baal?" By this expression, the prophet shows that the people were in religious hesitation or in religious limping.

Caquot,[526] talks about the dance and translates this phrase by: "How long will you totter with two legs?" meaning "Until when will you dance both for YHWH and for Baal?" He said that the movement suggested is that of a hopping from one foot to another or a swaying of the hips and a rebound movement developed in succession. He also says that in Deir-el-Qal'a near Beirut, there was a sanctuary dedicated to Baal Marqod, which is Baal of the dance.[527] Buis and Gray[528] also believe that verse 26 makes reference to a ritual dance. De Vaux,[529] says that Apuleius has described a procession of Syrian goddesses accompanied by dance, music to the sound of flutes and tambourines:

> "They started screeching, heads tilted, their necks twisting in movement, audacious, their hair loose, they turned round and sometimes attacked their own skin

---

[526] CAQUOT, 1963, p. 130.
[527] CAQUOT, 1963, p. 130; GRAY, 1970, p. 397.
[528] BUIS, 1997, p. 147; GRAY, 1970, p. 396.
[529] De VAUX, 1967 :489-490 : Apulée a décrit un cortège de la déesse Syrienne accompagnée de danse, de chants et aux sons des flutes et tambourins. „Ils éclatent en hululement, tête penchée, le cou tordu en mouvement, audacieux, les cheveux pendants, ils tournent en rond et parfois ils attaquent des dents de leur propre chair. Finalement avec le glaive à double tranchant, qu'ils portaient chacun se taille les bras. Cependant, l'un d'eux le plus exalté que les autres tirant du fond de sa poitrine de fréquentes soupirs, comme s'il était rempli d'un esprit divin, simulait une démence…dans un oracle bruyant il se met à se charger lui-même et fini par s'accuser de crimes imaginaires puis se flagelles."

with their teeth. Finally, with their two-edged sword that each one had they cut their arms. Meanwhile, one of them who was more exalted than the others sighing repeatedly from the bottom of his chest, as if being under the spell of a divine spirit, simulated an act of dementia...in a loud oracle he took upon himself the task and finished by accusing himself of imaginary crimes and then flagellating his own body".

The self-laceration was also known in Roman times. The Phrygian fertility god Attis, consort of Cybele, was celebrated in Rome. During the festival:[530]

"The third day, the twenty-fourth of March, was the Day of Blood: the Archigallus or highpriest drew blood from his arms and presented it as an offering. Nor was he alone in making this sacrifice. Stirred by the wild barbaric music of clashing cymbals, rumbling drums, droning horns, and screaming flutes, the inferor clergy whirled about in the dance with waggling heads and streaming hair, until, rapt into a frenzy of excitement and insensible to pain, they gashed their bodies with potsherds or slashed them with knives in order to bespatter the altar and the sacred tree with their blood. The gastly rite probably formed part of the mourning for Attis and may have been intended to strengthen him for the resurrection".

The self whipping and self laceration with knives, self biting, or "use the knives to cut their tongues", "lacerate themselves with knives," "tossing their long hair" and "frenzied dance" have been attested to for agrarian cults, the cult of the Syrian goddess and of Cybele.[531] For Lightfoot,[532] see the commentary of Lucian of Samosate, *The Syrian Goddess* section 50: "On set days the multitude gather the crowds in the temple of Galli and the sacred persons I mentioned before and they perform the rites, cutting their arms and beating one another on the back. Many stand

---

[530] FRAZER, 2009, p. 821.
[531] LIGHTFOOT, 2003, p. 277.
[532] LIGHTFOOT, 2003, p. 506.

beside and pipe an accompaniment, many clash the drums, and others sing inspired and sacred songs. This takes place outside the temple, nor do those who perform these rites enter the temple".

In section49 Lucian of Samosate, (The Syrian Goddess) talks about the 'Fire-Festival' celebrated at the beginning of spring, when people came from Syria and surrounding countries. According to Caquot:[533] the whips and lacerations are known in the various cults from agricultural origins, like that of Attis and the Syrian goddess. "So they shouted louder and slashed themselves with swords and spears, as was their custom, until their blood flowed" (1Kgs 18:28). For Alan and Russell,[534] (1990:45) the prophets of Baal cutting themselves with knives and swords or lances until their own blood gushed out is a prophecy or an image of their own death. "In verse 28 they ... and shedding their own blood the prophets of Baal present an image suggesting the death of the Baalistic movement and anticipating their own death at the hands of Elijah and the people of Israel (v. 40)." This argument is very interesting, but does not convince us. It is not a prophetic action of priest of Baal. Verse 28 presents this practice as a ritual of their customs (כְּמִשְׁפָּטָם.). We can conclude that self-laceration or multilation was known as ritual and religious practices in the Ancient Near East world. For example $a\underline{h}\underline{h}\grave{u}a$ kìma ma$\underline{h}$-$\underline{h}$e-e damì šunu ramku: "my brothers are drenched in their own blood like ecstatics" (CAD/M1:90b). Self-laceration was practised to arouse the god's pity and his response. However, mutilation or self-laceration was forbidden by YHWH (Lev 19:28 and Deut 14:1).

---

[533] CAQUOT, 1963, p. 130.
[534] ALAN and RUSSELL, 1990, p. 45.

5.5.2. Baal worries, he is travelling

Another bit of evidence is that Elijah said Baal is asleep and must be awakened (1 Kings 18:27b-c). This has been compared to the fact that there was a ceremony of awaking Melqart in the month of Peritius (February-March) from his winter sleep: καθελών τε τὰ ἀρχαῖα ἱερὰ καὶ ναὸν ᾠκοδόμησε τοῦ Ἡρακλέους καὶ τῆς Ἀστάρτης πρῶτός τε τοῦ Ἡρακλέουςἔγερσιν ἐποιήσατο ἐν τῷ Περιτίῳμηνὶ "he had pulled down the ancient temples, he built both the temple of Heracles and that of Astarte; and he was the first to celebrate the resurrection of Heracles in the month of Peritius" (Menander of Ephesus in Josephus).[535] Heracles is the name in Greek of Baal-Melqart.[536] The word שִׂיג means *"matter, pursuit, departure or absence"* and שִׂיחַ means *"meditation, thought or worry."*[537]

The scholar Hausmann,[538] explains that: "in connection with Elijah's mockery of Baal, שִׂיחַ in its traditional semantic context means someone being "in thought", meaning that Baal is in this sense not present or is en route". The majority of translations propose: "he is meditating, or he is busy, or he is on a journey" (KJV). "He is deep in thought, or busy, or travelling" (NIV).[539] The LXX translates this χρηματίζειν meaning "take care of business". Rendsburg,[540] has given another view in the

---

[535] Ant. J. VIII. 146; Apn. 1:119; De VAUX, 1941, pp. 7-20; RIBICHINI, 1999, p. 564; COGAN, 2000, p. 441; DUSSAUD, 1948, pp. 205-230; LIPINSKI, 1970a, p. 30; DAY, 2002, p. 74.
[536] LIPINSKI, 1970a, p. 31; EUSEBIUS OF CAESAREA, 1: 10. 27).
[537] REYMOND, 1991, p. 366; BURNEY, 1903, p. 224.
[538] HAUSMANN, 2004, p. 87.
[539] „Il a des préoccupations, il a dû s'absenter, il a du chemin à faire" (TOB). „Il a des soucis ou des affaires ou bien il est en voyage." (Bible de Jérusalem), *translator's note.*
[540] RENDSBURG, 1988, pp. 411-417.

translation of the words שִׂיחַ and שִׂיג. This new view gives another angle on the sense of irony of Elijah. The word שִׂיחַ means "conversation" or "meditation", based on the well-known Hebrew root שִׂיחַ. The LXX translates it as ἀδολεσχία ("meditation, talking"). The better translation is not from Driver,[541] who proposed the meaning of שִׂיחַ as "to dig a hole," an euphemism for "to defecate[542]"This means that Baal goes away to defecate or to excrete. therefore, an alternative and better translation is offered by Rendsburg. For Rendsburg,[543] the verb שִׂיג bears the meaning "go aside, move away". The sense again implies a euphemism to say that Baal has gone aside to "ease himself". We can say that this is a good interpretation, because it is hard to see Elijah speaking about the "defecation of Baal" in this context to all the people gathering upon Mount Carmel. We think that Elijah's mockery points to the intrinsic character of the Baal deity himself. But, surely to insult Baal is the whole point of the exercise.

The god Baal Melqart was a god who had to take care of business; he had an economic role in the life of his followers.[544] Elijah's irony makes us think of the role occupied by Baal Melqart in the Phoenician colonies as the protector of navigation.[545] He was the god who brought the best fortune to people. The navigators and ship owners counted on his blessings.[546]The Phoenicians had a thalassocracy, (domination over the seas).[547] Baal Melqart

---

[541] DRIVER, 1957, pp. 66-67.
[542] GRAY, 1970, p. 398.
[543] RENDSBURG, 1988, p. 415.
[544] RIBICHINI, 1999, pp. 564-565, GRAY, 1970, 397.
[545] BONNET, 1988, p. 141.
[546] BRIQUEL-CHATONNET, 1992, p. 306.
[547] GRAS, ROUILARD and TEIXIDOR, 1995, p. 24.

accompanied the merchants and the settlers of Tyre in their distant travel. This work of the deity in taking care of the business of his worshippers was indicated by the representation on the oldest Tyrian coins from the Persian period of the god Melqart on a seahorse.[548] According to the scholar Hayman,[549] Symmachus translates this part: "he is engaged in business". We can say that verse 27 describes the nature of the normal activities of Baal.[550] The words of Elijah suggest that Baal was kept from answering their cries, especially that of his prophets, because he was a god very much preoccupied by absorbing and exhausting activities.

5.5.3. Baal sleeps

אוּלַי יָשֵׁן הוּא וְיִקָץ "Maybe he is sleeping and must be awakened" (v. 27d). The derision of the god who sleeps refers, according to a number of authors, to the *egersis* of Melqart, the celebration of his death and his resurrection.[551] De Vaux,[552] says the Pharaohs of Egypt had gods in their temples; the priests came in each morning and greeted them by singing and invoking incessantly "wake up in peace." The sleeping of Baal, requiring him to be awakened, may also refer, according to some, to an annual ritual of Baal Melqart as a vegetation deity, who was awakened from his sleep of winter.[553] This Baal Melqart deity is known as the god of fertility and rain. The *egersis* of Melqart is the fertility-cult. In these ceremonies, worshippers celebrated the awakening of

---

[548] GRAY, 1970, p. 397
[549] HAYMAN, 1951, p. 57.
[550] TROMP, 1975, p. 481.
[551] BONNET, 1988, p. 141.
[552] De VAUX, 1941, p. 16.
[553] GRAY, 1970, p. 398.

Baal Melqart from his sleep of winter. יָשֵׁן means 'sleep' and may refer to the sleep or death phase of Melqart during the heat of the summer. The god Melqart is the dying and rising deity. There was a ritual in which Melqart was resurrected and celebrated.[554]

An inscription in Greek has been found in Amman in the temple of Hercules which is dedicated to the gymnasiarch, named Maphan, exerting the function of "the resuscitator of Hercules" ἐγεροέιτημν τοῦ Ἡρακλέους ,[555] About the sleeping of Melqart, Mettinger[556] says:

> "Since sleep may be a metaphor for death, it is natural that the term meaning 'awakening' could refer to the resurrection. The term, however, has also been understood in other ways. There are a number of references to a m(y) qm 'lm ('raiser of the deity'), which, in its turn, has been understood as referring to a cultic function: a participant who carried out a rite serving to resuscitate the god".

Mettinger,[557] continues that the ritual of the resurrection of Melqart involves an officiant as resuscitator. There was in the Phoenician mainland and in Palestine, in Hellenistic times, a cultic celebration referred to as the ἔγερσιν "resurrection" of god, a celebration in which some agent was referred to as ἐγεροέιτης "resuscitator" of Heracles.

The term יָקִץ can be translated as "wake." A number of translators[558] propose "awake"[559] which

---

[554] METTINGER, 2001, p. 83; LIPINSKI, 1970A; p. 31; MAY, 1931/2, p. 73.
[555] LIPINSKI, 1970a, p. 31; ABEL, 1908, p. 573.
[556] METTINGER, 2001, p. 88.
[557] METTINGER, 2001, p. 91.
[558] 'Réveiller' Bible du Semeur 2000, Bible de Jérusalem, et Louis GEGOND.
[559] 'Wake' translated from the French s'éveiller and 'awake' from the French réveiller. Translator's note.

goes well with the context. Verse 27 shows Melqart on the whole as inactive and powerless to answer his prophets in the conflict with YHWH.[560] The ἐγέρσιν is the ceremony at which followers of this deity celebrate to call him into activity, sending rain, and producing grasses and plants useful for animals and for human beings. If the god Baal could sleep, it is because he was regarded by his worshippers as someone who, after a period of great fatigue, should rest or sleep in order to build up new strength.

---

[560] NOCQUET, 2004, p. 123.

CHAPTER 6

THE NATURE AND FUNCTIONS OF BAAL MELQART

6.1. Melqart: Religious ideology and geostrategy

The god Heracles was very ingenious, and he advised the Tyrians to build their first ships and guided them into navigation. According to Nonnos Dionys the god Heracles says: τεύξατέ μοι ξένον ἅρμα βατῆς ἁλός "Build for me an unusual tank to walk on the sea", (XL: 444). Later on, the god Heracles adds: σχεδίην πρωτόπλοον ᾗ διὰ πόντου ὑμέας ὀχλίζειε The ships will be used for the first navigation: "it will carry you through the sea."[561]

De Vaux,[562] said that this Baal would accompany its people in all their work. Ribichini,[563] has made the same remark: "Melqart had a remarkable role in the religious ideology of commercial expansion of the people of Tyre towards the West and its cult was very popular in all the

---

[561] NONOS DIONYS, XL : 449.
[562] De VAUX, 1971, p. 492.
[563] RIBICHINI, 1999, p. 564.

Phoenician colonies." In addition, scholars like Aubet,[564] explain that Melqart was the god of the settlers and presided over all the colonial business done by Phoenicians. The religion was used for political ends, because the worship of Melqart in the Tyrian colonies played an important role through intermediary priests. According to Aubet:[565]

> "Tyrian custom demanded that a temple should be built in honour of Melqart. This created a religious bond between the colony and the metropolis, and the presence of the god in distant lands that ensured the tutelage of the temple of Tyre in the enterprise. In other words, the presence of Melqart guaranteed or drew attention to the intervention of the monarchy in every distant commercial activity".

The presence of their god in other regions of the earth allowed them to appropriate these parts of the globe as an extension of their homeland.[566] The Phoenicians manufactured and hawked luxurious items, pieces of glass or jewellery, fabrics, and so on. The Phoenicians felt united to their god by a particularly close bond. The Lord of their city, Baal Melqart not only exercised his authority over the community grouped around his temple, but he extended his protection to their maritime businesses, and settled with them in foreign lands.[567] As a sea-god, the god Melqart "was the boss of shipping and trade."[568] The Phoenician settlers were under his tutelage; his worship was in the religious and economic life of the local and indigenous people.[569]

---

[564] AUBET, 1993, p. 130.
[565] AUBET, 1993, p. 155.
[566] BERCHEM, 1967, p. 76.
[567] AUBET, 1993, p. 131; BERCHEM, 1967, p. 75.
[568] BONNET, 1992, p. 176; AUBET, 1993, p. 128.
[569] BERCHEM, 1967, p. 330.

In their economic geo-strategy with regard to the supply of raw materials for their industries, the Phoenicians preferred to settle in places where they could get metals for their industry, such as gold, silver, copper, or tin, in exchange for manufactured goods.[570] Clearly, these Phoenicians were well aware of the presence of the mineral resources in the Mediterranean basin. They were interested in Sardinia, the south of Spain, the Macedonian coast of Cyprus, and so on.[571] These overseas territories, colonized by the Phoenicians, were given a form of administration through their places of Melqart worship. Thus, the Phoenician administration in places like Rome, Gades, and Thasos was in the form of a sanctuary run by priests.

The cult was officiated over by professional clergy, often organized by colleagues, and exclusively devoted to the service of Melqart. Also, when this god was immigrating to some distant country, it was also required that a priest should be accompanied by his associates, for the strict observance of rituals in the new sanctuary, and to educate future priests of Melqart.[572] In addition, Berchem[573] states:

> "Tyre's merchants were not navigating blindly along the Mediterranean coasts; they were able to recognize the sites where they could exchange the products of their industry against food or raw materials. Phoenicians attempted no settlement where this condition was not fulfilled. Finally, it was also through their trade that the Phoenicians had an influence over the people with whom they traded".

---

[570] BERCHEM, 1967, p. 76.
[571] BERCHEM, 1967, p. 327.
[572] BERCHEM, 1967, p. 77.
[573] BERCHEM, 1967, p. 335.

6.2. Nature and iconography of Melqart

Aramaic stele discovered in the village of Breidj north of Aleppo. It is carved in basalt with a height of 1m 50 and width of 43 cm. It is now at the museum of Aleppo.[574] It was dedicated to Melqart by King Ben-Adad II of Damacus between IXth and VIIIth centuries BC.[575] The stele has a standing picture, face, legs, and head in profile. He is wearing a conical helmet, whose contours are rounded. The god wears a Syrian kilt fashion and covers his left shoulder a fenestrated axe.[576] This character (person) has no ornament. There is a slight relief of the stone that serves as entry fields at the bottom of his feet. The feet are bare and we see the right leg brought forward. In his right hand, he seems to hold the *ankh* (the cross). The *ankh* is a divine attribute, and a hieroglyphic sign, the symbol of life. This symbol is particularly suitable for a god who dies and rises again.[577] According to Mettinger,[578] the object held by Melqart in his right hand is not clearly visible, but it is possible to be interpreted as an *'nḫ* which could be "the hieroglyph for life" or it is a lotus, a symbol of death and life."[579] The axe on this stele is the mark of a divine scepter.[580] This is the anthropomorphic god Melqart. However, the axe is not exclusive to the gods, but it is part of the arms of the kings and men as well as the bow and the dagger.[581]

---

[574] DUNAND, 1939, p. 65.
[575] AUBET, 1993, p. 40.
[576] LIPINSKI, 1970a, p. 39.
[577] LIPINSKI, 1970a, p. 39.
[578] METTINGER, 2001, p. 98.
[579] METTINGER, 2001, p. 95.
[580] DUNAND, 1939, p. 74.
[581] DUNAND, 1939, p. 75.

Illus. 33. Stele of Melqart of the village of Breij from Aleppo Museum, (Dunand, 1939:67), Pl.XIII; see also ANEP, 1969, n°499.

נ צבא ׀ ז י ׀ש סברה ?
ד ד ׀ ב ר ט א ב · פ ש ׀ . . ב ?
מ ל ךא ר סל מ ר א הל מ ל ק ן ר
ת וז ינ ז רל הו ש מ צל ק ן ל
ה

On the bottom of the stele, an inscription of four (4) lines gives us the identity of the person who is the god to whom the Melqart stele was dedicated.[582] Below is the transcription and translation of this epigraphical inscription.[583]

---

[582] DUNAND, 1939, p. 68.
[583] DUNAND, 1939, p. 73.

Translation
L. 1 The stele erected by Bar-Adad (?)
L. 2 son of...a ...,
L. 3 kings of Aram, for his lord Melqart
L. 4 who protected him and heard his voice.

Although the stele dedicated to Melqart is the reason for the answer and the protection of a dedicant, the questions asked are not mentioned. It is certain that Bar-Adad had told Melqart the precise words. However, the inscriptions show that Melqart was the god that protects his faithful followers and hears their prayers. According to Bonnet,[584] the stele of Aleppo shows that from 800 BC Melqart the god was worshipped outside the borders of Phoenicia. Heracles as shown in this stele below took this anthropomorphic form.

A

---

[584] BONNET, 1992, p. 175, note 36.

B C

Illus. 34. Heracles, Jourdain-Annequin (1992:62-63; Caubet, 1979, fig.67); Pl.VIII-16 from Cyprus (Dhali/Idalion), (Louvre AM 641). Height 55cm. The head height 9cm.

The clothing worn by the god is a short and tight tunic, making a few simple folds on the thighs. Heracles holds the body of a lion by the hind legs with his left arm which was near to the body, and lightly bent above. The left leg is forward and the right arm brandishes the club. Between the head and the club, there is a rectangular stone. The breast is held by a tie belt. The scholar Bonnet,[585] argues that this represents the god Hercules holding a club and holding a lion cub and dates from between the sixth and fifth centuries BC.

---

[585] BONNET, 1992, pp. 175-176.

6.3. Melqart god of good fortune and guarantor of treaties

Melqart was mentioned as being the witness of the treaty imposed by the king of Assyria, Esarhaddon on his counterpart the king of Tyre in 676 BC. In the treaty, there is an oath of vengeance from the gods in case of violation:[586]

> "May Baal Shameme, Baal Malagê and Baal Saphon raise an evil wind against your ships to undo their moorings, tear out their mooring pole, may a strong wave sink them in the sea, a violent tide [...] against you. May Melqart and Eshmun deliver your land to destruction, your people to be deported from your land [...]. May they make food for your mouth; clothes for your body, oil for your ointment disappear. May Astarte break your bow in the thick of battle; and have you crouch at the feet of your enemy. May a foreign enemy divide your belongings."

The treaty between Esarhaddon, the Assyria king (681-669 BC) and the king of Tyre, the Baal Melqart appears among the gods.[587] That the gods took part in the oath represented a way of rendering efficient the commitment made.[588] Violation of the agreement could bring about the maritime divine punishments (wrecks, defeat before one's enemies...)[589] Garelli,[590] says that the aim of the treaty was to restore the Assyrian order in the regions. The treaty states:[591]

> ..."May Baal-sameme, Baal-malage and Baal-saphon raise an evil wind against your ships, to undo their moorings, tear out their mooring pole, may a strong wave

---

[586] ANET, 1969, p. 534.
[587] SAA II, 2:5 iv: 14; ANET, 1969, pp. 534-535; NOCQUET, 2004, p. 349.
[588] BONNET, 1988, p. 40.
[589] LIPINSKI, 1995, p. 243.
[590] GARELLI, 1974, p. 118.
[591] ANET, 1969, p. 534.

sink them in the sea, a violent tide against you.
May Melqart and Eshmun deliver your land to destruction, your people to be deported, from your land. May they make food for your mouth, clothes for your body, oil for your ointment disappear.
May Astarte break your bow in the thick of battle; and have you crouch at the feet of your enemy. May a foreign enemy divide your belongings."

The meaning of the first paragraph of the treaty shows that the divinities named this way, made use of natural forces, such as lightning and possessed celestial as well as aquatic elements.[592] Melqart is also the god of navigation, fertility, and good fortune.[593] The second paragraph of the treaty talks about the agrarian functions of Melqart and good fortune. In associating Melqart with other Baal gods, Melqart adopts their respective characteristics, which explains why he becomes the god of winter vegetation and the dispenser of fertility as well. Baal Melqart was part of the group of divinities in charge of the well-being of the population. Due to this, the people were required to show loyalty, without which the gods "metamorphose into terrifying divinities bringing ruin and disaster in which they withdraw their protection and abandon their followers."[594] "They" refers to the divinities that took part in the treaty of Esarhaddon, king of Assyria, and the king of Tyre (Baal Shamem, Baal Malagê, Baal Saphon, and then Melqart). Good fortune, protection, and prosperity are nothing but the logical consequence of the loyalty shown by the followers to their gods. In this way, Melqart does not escape the classic pattern of benediction or malediction.

---

[592] LIPINSKI, 1995e, p. 432.
[593] LIPINSKI, 1995e, p. 432
[594] BONNET, 1988, p. 41.

Greek epigraphic evidence tells us concerning the merchants and the Tyrian ship owners installed at Delos that (152/2 BC) their fellowship was devoted to the worship of the 'Tyrian Heracles, who became the author of the great blessings for men and is the founder of the homeland *'Ηρακλέους τοῦ Τυρίου πλείστων ἀγαθῶν παραιτίου γεγονότος τοῖς ἀνθρώποις ἀρηγοῦ δέ τῆς πατρίδροςὑπάρχοντος* [595] It is likely that the people of Tyre personified their god as industrious or even as a merchant, similar to them. We can now better understand the words of Elijah: "Baal is in deep thought" (1 Kgs 18:27) or "he is busy".

A bilingual epigraph (Aramaic and Greek KAI 47) in Malta dating from the second century BC with a title תבעלצר למלך and *Τύριοι 'Ηρακλεῖ ἀρχηγέτει* means: "to Melqart, lord of Tyre". This bilingual inscription was a prayer of thanks and a vow of two sons to someone named *'BD'SR*. Melqart= "He was god of fertility and of the sea. The Tyrians called him "Lord of Tyre", that is, *Ba'al*. His name itself, (Melek-qart)" Melqart for Aubet, (1993:127) "represents the power of the monarchy and also possesses certain human characteristics, since the foundation of cities and colonies is attributed to him."

6.4. Melqart and the rite of egersis

6.4.1. The date of the ceremony of Melqart's egersis

The name of Melqart appears in a list from Niniveh as a feminine anthroponym, recognized by *Qam Mil-qar-te/GAM Mil-qar-te* which means "Melqart is raised."[596] However, "In the city of Tyre, the chief

---

[595] LAUNEY, 1937, n° 1519.
[596] METTINGER, 2001, p. 97; LIPINSKI, 1995d, p. 230; FALES,

divinity was masculine: Melqart, the protector of the city, symbol of the monarch institution and founder of colonies. Astarte, Baal Shamem, and Baal Hammon played a supporting part."[597] He is a deified king, god of his followers and protector.[598] He is also a dying and rising deity.[599] In Ugaritic language, the expression: *mqm 'lm* "raiser of the deity". Therefore, in this title Müller finds a reference, not to the resurrection of a dead god, but to the waking of a deity to take action and save his worshippers.[600]

About the inscription (KAI 77:1) to the god, Sadrapa found in Carthage,[601] explains that the verb יקץ means "to awake, rouse from sleep" a close synonym of *mqm 'lm*. In that case this meaning can be alluded to in 1 Kings 18:27. For יקץ the LXX used ἐγείρω or ἐγείρομαί (Judg 16:14; 1 Kgs 3:15; Psa 76:65).[602] The scholar, Mettinger[603] said: "A verb is used in the title that is otherwise used about resurrection" (Biblical Hebrew), and in a restored passage (KAI 77:1), there is a synonymous expression, "the one who wakes up the god". According to the work of Clermont-Ganneau,[604] the expression: *mqm 'lm ml[qr]t=* ἐγερσείτης τοῦ Ἡρακλέους means: "the one who wakes up the god." Mettinger,[605] argues that the work of Clermont-Ganneau calls "attention to the striking equivalence between the Phoenician-Punic title and the Greek

---

1979, pp. 57; 59, col III: 21.
[597] AUBET, 1993, p. 127.
[598] BONNET, 1992, p. 175.
[599] METTINGER, 2001, p. 83.
[600] METTINGER, 2001, p. 84; BONNET, 1992, p. 179.
[601] METTINGER, 2001, p. 94.
[602] WALLIS, 1990, pp. 275-276.
[603] METTINGER, 2001, p. 95.
[604] CLERMONT-GANNEAU, 1924, p. 164.
[605] METTINGER, 2001, p. 95.

one" and this "title for the cultic agent of the same deity." This evidence shows that the god Melqart is a risen god.

The celebration of the *egersis* or the resurrection of Melqart took place during the month of *Peritios*, (January-February).[606] Josephus:[607] "speaks of the cultic celebration of the resurrection of Hercules of Tyre." He gives a precise date (month of Peritius) as a moment of celebration to the god Melqart *egersis*.[608] Hiram I, the king of Tyre in tenth century, built a temple for all three divinities, that is, Hercules/Melqart and Astarte. It was he who celebrated for the first time the *egersis*. Regarding this date is of a different opinion, preferring February-March.[609] Finally, Flavius Josephus says that according to Menander of Ephesus, Hiram was the first to celebrate the *egersis* in particular during the month of *Peritios*, corresponding approximately to February, indicating the beginning of spring.[610] According to Aubet:[611] "The *egersis* or resurrection of Melqart took place, then, every spring, when the rains stopped, which gives the personality of the god a solar, and specially an agrarian, character." May[612] writes: "Both the death and the resurrection of the god were celebrated at the New Year festival. To symbolize the winter season which passed between the time of the death and the resurrection of the god, it was necessary to provide an interim between the rites dramatizing these events." For Morgenstern:[613] "It was Melqart, the god

---

[606] LIPINSKI, 1995e, p. 233.
[607] Ant. J. VIII. 146; Apn. 1. 119; METTINGER, 2001, p. 90.
[608] Ant. J. VIII. 146; Apn. 1. 119.
[609] BONNET, 1988, p. 104.
[610] De VAUX, 1941, p. 19.
[611] AUBET, 1993, p. 128.
[612] MAY, 1931/2, p. 84.
[613] MORGENSTERN, 1960, pp. 145-146.

of the expanding sun of winter and spring, the heroic deity, worshipped by rites normally paid to the dead, who, waking from the sleep of death, rose from the netherworld, resurrected and rejuvenated, and returned to this upper world of light and life and to his country and his people, to give light and heat and life, to create and bless." As a seasonal deity, Melqart's nature was in rhythm with the vegetation or agriculture cycle. Aubet,[614]argues that: "The agricultural nature of Melqart, a god who dies and is reborn each year is in accordance with the natural cycles..."

Heliodorus brings another testimony about the celebration of Melqart. He says that the Phoenician merchants offered a banquet in honour of their national god Hercules/Melqart. In order to celebrate the victory of a young man who had won the prize in the battle contest in Delphi, and also to benefit from favourable conditions for their maritime travel, a banquet was celebrated in honour of Melqart, (Heliodorus, The Ethiopians, IV, 16: 6; 8). [615] It was not the ceremony of egersis, but it was a banquet in honour of the god Melqart. Following this testimony from Heliodorus, we conclude that it is also possible that there were other particular celebrations of Melqart. But in that case no date can be fixed.

---

[614] AUBET, 1993, p. 128.
[615] HELIODORUS, The Ethiopians, IV, 16:6;8. „Ils me dirent alors qu'ils étaient des commerçants phéniciens de Tyr, qu'ils étaient en route vers Carthage, avec un gros bateau chargé de marchandises indiennes, éthiopiennes et phéniciennes. Pour le moment ils offrirent ce banquet à Héraclès Tyrien, pour célébrer la victoire du jeune homme (ils me le montrèrent assis en face de moi). Qui a avait remporté le prix au concours de lutte à Delphes même et avait fait triompher chez les Grecs sa ville de Tyr...Et il célèbre cette fête en l'honneur du dieu qui l'avait prévenu en songe, pour le remercier de sa victoire, et en même temps pour obtenir une heureuse traversée."

According to Lucian De Samosate[616] (AD 125), concerning the temple of Hercules of Tyr, he said: "And there exists in Syria temples of a date not much later than those in Egypt, many of which I have seen myself, for instance, the temple of Hercules in Tyre. This is not the temple of the Hercules of Greek legend; but a Tyrian hero of much greater antiquity than he." Concerning *The Syrian Goddess, "De Dea Syria"* compare the translation of Lightfoot:[617] "In Syria, too, there are temples which are almost as old as the Egyptian, most of which I have seen, (including) the temple of Heracles in Tyre not the same Heracles as the one celebrated by the Geeks; the one I mean is much older and a Tyrian hero." We found the same idea in the Greek historian Herodotus (484/2-420 BC). He investigated further about the god Hercules and his origin.

Herodotus II: 44

"I moreover, desiring to know something certain of these matters so far as might be, made a voyage also to Tyre of Phoenicia, hearing that in that place there was a holy temple of Heracles; and I saw that it was richly furnished with many votive offerings besides, and especially there were in it two pillars, the one of pure gold and the other of an emerald stone of such size as to shine by night: and having come to speech with the priests of the god, I asked them how long time it was since their temple had been set up: and these also I found to be at variance with the Hellenes, for they said that at the same time when Tyre was founded, the temple of the god also had been set up, and that it was a period of two thousand three hundred years since their people began to dwell at Tyre. I saw also at Tyre another temple of Heracles, with the surname

---

[616] De Dea Syria, III; see also STRONG and GARSTANG, 2007, p. 29.
[617] LIGHTFOOT, 2003, p. 243, section III.

Thasian; and I came to Thasos also and there I found a temple of Heracles set up by the Phoenicians..."⁶¹⁸

In the city of Tyre there were then two temples built for Hercules, but he (Herodotus) does not give any particular information concerning the celebration of the *egersis* of Melqart.

6.4.2. The ceremony

Three stages had to be accomplished in the ceremony of Melqart.[619] The *egersis* of Baal Melqart would last three days. The first day, after sundown, the god would be burnt on a pyre. The next day in the presence of a sacerdotal picture, he would be buried, when the king and a feminine figure, representing perhaps Astarte, carried out the funeral ritual. Then there would follow the sacred union. The sacred marriage between the king, the resurrector of Melqart, and the goddess would take place in-between the funeral and the resurrection.[620] This marriage was a marriage by proxy. The king, the officiator, represented Melqart, the man divinity. The queen represented Astarte, as well as the priestess.[621] She (Astarte) is the spouse of Melqart. Seyrig,[622] takes Melqart to be the son of Astarte, but Lipinski[623] explains that Melqart is the spouse of Astarte.

---

[618] http://www.sacred-texts.com/cla/hh/2040.htm Consulted: 12 may 2011.
[619] LIPINSKI, 1970a, p. 38.
[620] LIPINSKI, 1970a, pp. 45-46.
[621] METTINGER, 2001, p. 96; De Vaux, 1941, p. 18; LIPINSKI, 1970a, p. 48.
[622] SEYRIG, 1963, p. 28.
[623] LIPINSKI, 1970a, p. 36 note 3; METTINGER, 2001, p. 96 notes 88; 90.

In England, there are confirmations of this divine couple Hercules/Melqart and Astarte. At Corbridge near Newpalace, two dedications were devoted to the Tyrian Hercules and his consort Astarte: 'Αστάρτης βωμόν μ' ἐσορᾷς· ποῦλχέρ μ' ἀνέθηχεν "Of Astarte the Altar me you see. Pulcher I dedicated."[624] On the second altar dedicated to Hercules, we find this inscription:[625] Ηραχλει Τυριω Διοδωρα Αρχιερεια "To Hercules the Tyrian Diodora the high priestess." Aubet (1993:128) says:

> "In the annual awakening of the god, the king of Tyre seems to have played a very active role. The monarch not only took part in the ceremonies, but intervened directly in the festival through a ritual marriage with a priestess or queen herself, as was customary in oriental religions'. This *hieros gamos* had the royal couple playing the role of stand-in for the divine couple, Melqart and Astarte".

We can make a connection between Melqart's egersis and the Egyptian god Osiris, whose resurrection was celebrated in the same time frame. Lipinski,[626] quoting Plutarch, asserts that the death of the god Osiris fell on the 17 of Athyrand and his resurrection was celebrated on the 19 of Athyr, three days after his death. Therefore "in the spring festival of Cybele and Attis at Rome the resurrection occurred on the fourth day."[627] Lipinski,[628] explains that this bridal union between a god and a goddess is a concept venerated by the Semites within the image of a human couple; it makes us think of a divine couple. In the case of Melqart and Astarte we are dealing with a fertility god

---

[624] LIPINSKI, 1970a, p. 38.
[625] IG, XIV: 2553; COLLINGWOOD, 1863, p. 340.
[626] LIPINSKI, 1970a, p. 47.
[627] MAY, 1931/2, p. 84; FRAZER, 2009, pp. 820-821; 825.
[628] LIPINSKI, 1995, p. 65.

and fecundity, and the goddess of love and sensuality. If we attribute the power over rain, springs, germination and growth of cereals to the god, then the power to breed cattle and the power to raise a family are attributed to the goddess.

On the third day, the *egersis,* "rise" or his "resurrection", would take place.[629] The fact that in the iconography, Melqart is represented with an *ankh* in his right hand is a symbol of life, referring to the god dying and rising even though this element refers to the Egyptian divinities.[630] Lipinski[631] adds that it is very possiblity that during ancient times, a human substitute was burnt. This means that a man would have to be burnt alive during the annual sacrifice. It is possible that, during the ceremony, the followers of Melqart danced. Heliodorus described this ceremony in honour of Melqart as follows: "When I left they were still at dancing with music. It was an Assyrian dance, accompanied by flutes that would play in the air with lively rhythm. As lightly as they jumped in the air, as quickly they crouched down and turned to each other as if being possessed", (Heliodorus, The Ethiopians, IV, 17). Regarding the god Attis, the twenty-fifth day (the fourth day) of celebration, Frazer[632] says: "the resurrection of the god was hailed by his disciples as a promise that they too issue triumphant from the corruption of the grave... The divine resurrection was celebrated with a wild outburst of glee."

According to Lipinski:[633]

> "Un témoignage plus ancien encore sur la personnalité de Melqart, dieu mourant et ressuscitant, nous est probablement fourni par le récit biblique du sacrifice du

---

[629] BONNET, 1988, pp. 104-105.
[630] LIPINSKI, 1970a, p. 39.
[631] LIPINSKI, 1970a, p. 45.
[632] FRAZER, 2009, p. 825.
[633] LIPINSKI, 1970a, p. 39; 40; MAY, 1931/2, p. 78.

Carmel (I Rois, XVIII), au temps du prophète Elie, c'est-à-dire au IXᵉ siècle. D'après Rois XVIII, 27, Elie s'adressa aux prophètes de Baal en des termes : Criez plus fort, car c'est un dieu : ...peut-être il dort et doit se réveiller !...Ces paroles ironiques attribuées au prophète peuvent donc faire allusion à la mort et à la résurrection du Baal en question (c'est-à-dire Melqart)".

Prophet Hosea in the eighth century (Hos 6:2) used the terminology of elements probably from the worship of the Tyrian god and certainly the ritual of death and resurrection of Melqart.[634] Come, and let us return to the Lord; For He has torn, but He will heal us; He has stricken, but He will bind us up. *After two days, He will revive us*; [יְחַיֵּנוּ מִיֹּמָיִם] *and on the third day, He will raise us up*, [בַּיּוֹם הַשְּׁלִישִׁי יְקִמֵנוּ] *that we may live in His sight*' (Hos 6:1-2, NKJ). Ephraim goes to Assyria for healing (Hos 5:13-6:3), to be cured by the gods and demons of Assyria as: Ea, Ištar and demons.[635] The prophet used the symbolism of dying and rising of the deity, (the deity of fertility or the fertility cult). May[636] points out that the prophet used parallelism, when he argues that: "which centred on the worship of the vegetation deity who died in the autumn and was resurrected in the spring." This symbolic analysis of prophet Hosea can be connected to the ritual of Melqart who died in autumn and rose in spring through the *egersis* ritual. Another element of this connection is 'the third day' used by the prophet Hosea to talk about the resurrection "He [Yahweh] will raise us up". Yahweh in the prophecy of Hosea played the role of "resurrector" as in the Melqart/Heracles *egersis*.[637] Following an understanding of Melqart's nature, we can examine his functions.

---

[634] LIPINSKI, 1970a, p. 42.
[635] MAY, 1931/2, p. 75.
[636] MAY, 1931/2, p. 73; see Hos. 13:1.
[637] ABEL, 1908, p. 573; METTINGER, 2001, p. 90; BONNET, 1988, p. 146; 1992, p. 178; LIPINSKI, 1970a, p. 31.

6.4.3. The material evidence of Melqart's resurrection

Illus. 35. Vase from Sidon=Bonnet 1988:Pl. 1 fig.1; Mettinger, 2001:fig.3.1.

This vase from Sidon:[638] "has been taken to depict the burning of Melqart and his subsequent resurrection." This marble vase dates from the fourth century BC.[639] This vase had four series of pictures which illustrated the burning of Melqart and his

---

[638] METTINGER, 2001, p. 98.
[639] LIPINSKI, 1970a, p. 43.

resurrection. Barnett,[640] reads the images differently from left to right following his photographs 1, 2, 3 and 4, contrary to Lipinski,[641] who proposes the reading following this order 3, 2, 1 and 4.

Scene 1: In this scene, the god is dressed on a sort of Pyre or flaming altar. To the right and the left sides of this pyre we find respectively a goddess holding the sceptre with a horned cap, Astarte, and the 'consort' of Melqart wearing a cloth of mourning similar to that of mourners of the Ahiram sarcophagus.[642] On the left, there is a male, also holding the sceptre and wearing a "long tunic and a veiled head piece". Probably this person is the king, says Lipinski,[643] he is the: "resuscitator of the divinity", and "consort of Astarte".

Scene 2: This one represents the tomb of the god. According to the scholar Mettinger:[644] "In the panel we find under a winged sun disk a pyramid shaped object, probably a tomb", see the same analysis in the work of Lipinski.[645] This tomb is flanked by two persons holding sceptres in their hands on the right and the left of the pyramid-shaped object. This scene evokes as Mettinger,[646] argues: "the burial day" which is also "The day of mourning which must relate to the third scene."

Scene 3: The pyre. Mettinger[647] says: "In the centre a draped figure appears, apparently bathing in

---

[640] BARNETT, 1969, pp. 9-11.
[641] LIPINSKI, 1970a, pp. 43-46; see also METTINGER, 2001, p. 99.
[642] ANEP, 1969, n°459; METTINGER, 2001, p. 99; LIPINSKI, 1970a, p. 45.
[643] LIPINSKI, 1970a, p. 45.
[644] METTINGER, 2001, p. 99.
[645] LIPINSKI, 1970a, p. 45.
[646] METTINGER, 2001, p. 99.
[647] METTINGER, 2001, p. 99.

flames...Below the panel there is a pair of volutes and an anchor (?), surrounded by what is either ears of grain or, more likely, palm branches."

Scene 4: The epiphany of the god. This scene represents the epiphany of the risen deity who appears at the entrance of the temple. The morning star, appearing twice in symmetry, indicates that the event took place at sunrise.[648]

In conclusion of the study of the god depicted on the Sidon vase, Mettinger,[649] says:

> "The god depicted on the Sidon vase could be Eshmun, but is more likely to be Melqart. The vase provides us with what seems to be iconographical corollary of the textual reminiscences of the death and resurrection of Melqart. If this is right, the vase shows the sequence of rituals celebrating these events in a cultic context (note the temple façade). The ritual procedures comprise at least two different days, perhaps three. The 'epic' order of events is worthwhile: from death to resurrection."

6.4.4. The Ceremony of the egersis: A Palliative to the Weaknesses of Melqart

The ceremony of the death and resurrection of Melqart is nothing but a way to compensate the absence of a god, who disappeared during the dreadful heat of summer, as it was during spring that his power, his benediction over nature, vegetation, men, and animals was expected. Melqart's egersis, celebrated in Tyre in the honour of Tyre's patron, has the sole purpose of "palliating the failure of the god."[650] This way of celebrating their god, shows that the people were full of imagination, but also had a certain intuition. If death was common to all, then their

---

[648] LIPINSKI, 1970a, p. 46; METTINGER, 2001, pp. 100-103.
[649] METTINGER, 2001, pp. 102-103.
[650] DUSSAUD, 1948, p. 207.

god who was their protector had to be able to escape it and show his supremacy. If the god died without coming back to life he would not deserve to be called "god". Since the dawn of time, death has been dreaded by man. The great Gilgamesh, wanted to escape from it as well. Therefore, the gods that protected humans, were regarded as having supernatural powers, as being the creators of the world, nothing could subdue them. The people needed a way to show that summer, with its killing drought, compromised the power of Melqart to bring rain for the fertility of land, and that it was also ephemeral. It was a digression made by the god, who could come back with force, vanquish death that had subjugated him all this time, and prove his power with the returning of spring, source of blessings for all vegetal, animal, human life and the earth.

6.4.5. The Resurrector of Melqart

The king had an important role to play in the resurrection of the god Melqart. This ritual would take place in a bridal room with a priestess, surely with the queen herself, at the time when the people celebrated the *egersis* of Baal Melqart in Tyre, symbolized by a number of rites.[651] Bonnet explains that if the king of Tyre had an important role in the ceremony it was undoubtedly because he was the descendant of Melqart, the king archetype. In this ceremony of Melqart's *egersis* the delegation from Cartagena was present. Lipinski,[652] explains that royalty was sacred in Phoenicia. For this reason, the king and the queen were called to exercise their ritual functions. The king was pontiff and thus had to assume political and

---

[651] BONNET, 1983, p. 196.
[652] LIPINSKI, 1995e, p. 452.

religious functions; Ethobaal was also a priest of Astarte, which could very well be similar to the god Melqart. The terrestrial king was his archetype and his successor, and therefore occupied the privileged role of interlocutor of the god's followers. An important magistrate would take part actively as the resurrector of the divinity.

At this ceremony, a form of communication would be established between the king from above and the king from below. Melqart, the founder of the city and the officiator, appears as the protector.[653] (Bonnet, 1983:195). The king was pontiff, and therefore had a political and religious role. The god Melqart was the guarantor of the perpetuity of the things of this world by the natural cycle that would come to life in spring. Without his power, the people could not hope for anything. His life and death experience was founded on the human condition, the seasonal rhythm, and shows his superiority as god by his immortality.[654] The priestly title of Melqart and Astarte was connected to the Phoenician kingship.

KAI 13

1 אנך תבנת כהן עשתרת מלך צדנםבן
2 אשמנעזר כהן עשתרת מלך שכבבארן

L.1 "I Tabnit, priest of Astarte, king of the Sidonians, son
L.2 of Eshmounazor, priest of Astarte, king of the Sidonians, I am lying in this sarcophagus".

This inscription of Tabnit king of Sidon is dated from the sixth century BC. This inscription on the sarcophagus of the king suggests that the priesthood

---

[653] BONNET, 1983, p. 175.
[654] BONNET, 1988, p. 437.

of Astarte was linked to royalty.[655] We can add this information of Menander of Ephesus cited by Josephus saying that Ethobaal, Jezebel's father, was a king of the Sidonians and a priest of Astarte.[656] The king, however, was not the only resurrector of Melqart. We find other inscriptions indicating other personalities as resurrector. An epitaph (KAI 93:3-4) of someone named *ṢPNB'L* shows that he is "son of 'Abdi-Melqart" בן עבדמלקרת which means "servant of Melqart". We can add another inscription from Carthage (KAI 70:3-4) in which we find בן עבדמלקרת "son of 'Abdi-Melqart". These theophorics with Melqart's name worn by these persons show some devotion to the god Melqart.[657] (Lipinski, 1970b:77). We also find inscriptions which mentioned the title of 'resurrector' מקם אלם literally "festsetzer der Gottheit" from Cyprus dating from the fourth century BC.[658] On an inscription in North Africa, precisely at Carthage, appears the title "Resurrector of blessed divinity."[659] This title of "blessed divinity" was an epithet attributed to Melqart.[660] In the Greco-Roman period, a Greek inscription speaks about a feast at Philadelphia, in modern day Amman (Jordan), of which the Tyrian Hercules (Melqart) was the principal deity.[661] One Gymnasiarch named Maphtan son of Diogenes who exercised the function of "resurrector" in the temple dedicated to Hercules.[662]

---

[655] LIPINSKI, 1970a, p. 52.
[656] Apn. 1. 18:123.
[657] LIPINSKI, 1970b, p. 77.
[658] KAI 44: L. 2.
[659] CIS I, 4872: 4.
[660] LIPINSKI, 1970a, p. 33; CIS I, 4894: I'.
[661] LIPNSKI, p.1970a:31; BONNET, 1992, p. 178.
[662] ABEL, 1908, p. 573; METTINGER, 2001, p. 90; LIPINSKI, 1970a: 31; BONNET, 1988, p.146; 1992, p. 178).

6.5. The ritual of deity Baal Melqart

6.5.1. The animals of the Melqart's ritual

The festive and ordinary rituals of sanctuaries in the Phoenician and Punic areas did not differ at all from the sacrifices of the Old Testament, as they offered the divine sacrifices in blood and vegetal offerings, together with other different gifts.[663] In their blood sacrifices, they used animals like birds, adult cattle, calves, goats, rams, horses, and fawns.[664] The scholar Lipinski,[665] also adds to this enumeration expiatory sacrifices, peaceful sacrifices to win the benevolence of gods. The Holocaust had also a passage of fire for the victim. In these Phoenician sanctuaries, there were cattle and birds ready to be offered as sacrifice. This was done under the command of a group of clergy or priests, who were the ministers of temples or sanctuaries. Certain sacrifices were costly, and only the rich in their opulence could afford them.

The sacrifices consisted of the heads of big adult cattle and the erection of memorial steles. In one relief votive of the fourth century BC, perhaps from Kynosarges, (located outside of Ancient Athens), we can see a bull or cow fed to the god by a priest, followed by a bearded man, a woman, a child and a girl carrying a basket on her head. This suggests a family offering such a sacrifice to the god Hercules.[666] According to Berchem,[667] the Roman Hercules is a barely disguised Melqart. "Hercules was the Greek

---

[663] LIPINSKI, 1995e, p. 465.
[664] KAI 43.
[665] LIPINSKI, 1995e, p. 467.
[666] GEORGOUDI, 1998, p. 303; VAN STRATEN, 1995, p. 88, fig. 93, BERCHEM, 1967, p. 326.
[667] BERCHEM, 1967, p. 326.

name for Melqart."⁶⁶⁸ It can be found in Philo of Byblos in a statement quoted by Eusebius.⁶⁶⁹ Read also KAI 47, an epigraphic bilingual from Malta Ἡραχλεῖ of Tyre. It's interesting to see that he was sacrificing to Hercules a bull or heifer that had never known the yoke.⁶⁷⁰ In the sacrificial practices of the Heraclean cities, Georgoudi,⁶⁷¹ lists the following animals: beef, bull, goat, sheep, pig and ram. The victims could be roasted on the altar fire.

The sacrificial meat was consumed by the people of the city in a friendly atmosphere. The ceremony of Hercules began in the morning, killing the victims, and a first snack in the middle of the day marked a break, but in the evening the banquet began again, while the share belonging to the god was burned on the altar. They were accompanied by singing and dancing. This sacrifice was connected to the sacrifice of Mount Carmel.⁶⁷²

6.5.2. A Substitute in Melqart's Place

According to Pliny the Elder, an annual human sacrifice was offered in honour of Hercules/Melqart in his temple at Carthage:⁶⁷³ *Inhonorus est nec in templo ullo Hercules, Ad quem Poeni omnibus annis humana sacrificaverant victima* "A deed that is without honour and stands in no Hercules' temple before the Carthaginians, were to perform a human sacrifice every year." Tertullian claimed to be an eyewitness to a substitute Melqart representative burned alive in his

---

⁶⁶⁸ SEYRIG, 1944/1945, pp. 62-80; pl. I-IV.
⁶⁶⁹ EUSEBIUS, P. Ev. I.10.27.
⁶⁷⁰ BERCHEM, 1967, p. 320.
⁶⁷¹ GEORGOUDI, 1998, pp. 302-317.
⁶⁷² BERCHEM, 1967, p. 321.
⁶⁷³ EICHHOLZ, 1962, pp. 30-31.

place:[674] *et qui vivus ardebat, Herculem induerat,* "and another who takes the place of Hercules had been burned alive." These two testimonies of Pliny the Elder and Tertullian attest to the death of an appropriate substitute for an early period of the Melqart's egersis.[675] It is unclear when the practice began, and also when it was abandoned. Lipinski,[676] refers to the mythological tradition of the god of death itself, whose remains were to be buried in a tomb. This describes the cremation of the god Melqart.

6.5.3. The God of the Fire

The different Melqart: traditions talk about the death of Melqart in fire on a pyre.[677] Some testimonies of the death in fire of Melqart can be cited. One came from Silius Italicus (ca. 26-101 CE) in his Punica (III, 32-44). He writes that Hercules' death in flames was depicted on the doors of the temple at Gades.[678] Secondly, one comes from Pseudo-Clementine. He speaks of the tomb of Melqart, which is placed in Tyre where the god was cremated: *Herculis apud Tyrum, ubi igni crematus est.*[679] The third testimony comes from Baccos-Dionysos. On his visit to Tyre, he recites a hymn to the deity Melqart. In this hymn he speaks of Melqart as "lord of fire" $ἄναξ$ $πυρός$ [680] In his research on Hercules, Calame,[681] said: "The legendary death of Heracles on the pyre and the ritual celebration of its grand finale on Mount

---

[674] WALTZING and SEVERYNS, 1929, pp. 36-37.
[675] LIPINSKI, 1970a, p. 44.
[676] LIPINSKI, 1970a, p. 45.
[677] METTINGER, 2001, P. 86; LIPINSKI, 1970a, pp. 43-44.
[678] METTINGER, 2001, p. 85; BONNET, 1988, pp. 216-219.
[679] PSEUDO-CLEM., RECOGN.X:24; METTINGER, 2001, P. 87.
[680] NONNOS DIONYS, XL: 368-369; METTINGER, 2001, P. 87.
[681] CALAME, 1998, p. 203.

Oita share at least this in common: the victim is placed, probably living, on the pyre, and his body is entirely consumed by fire".

All these references contributed to proving that the deity Melqart was a god who was cremated in fire or died in fire. We can add the message of the prophet Ezekiel "to the deity-king of Tyre". "So I made a fire come out of you, and it consumed you" (Ezek 28:18). It seems to make an allusion to Melqart who is both deity and king of Tyre.[682]

---

[682] De VAUX, 1967, p. 492.

SYNTHESIS

Having examined the various the hypotheses about god Baal Shamin being associated to the Biblical Mount Carmel, this synthesis attempts to evaluate the strengths and weaknesses of these hypotheses.

To clarify the hypotheses about the Baal of the Biblical Mount Carmel, we must first examine the nature and functions of each god studied in this research, and secondly, the epigraphic and iconographic studies will be compared to the exegetical and critical analysis work of the biblical text of 1 Kings 18. This method will lead us to summarize this research and finally to proceed to the conclusion. In the conclusion, we will be able to respond to this question: among the three Baals (Baal Hadad, Baal Melqart, and Baal Shamin) which one, along with his prophets, were the challengers to YHWH and his prophet Elijah in the ordeal of the Biblical Mount Carmel (1Kgs 18:1-46)?

The third hypothesis supported by some scholars[683] identifies the Baal of Biblical Mount Carmel with Baal Melqart, the patron of Tyre, for five (5) reasons:

I: the diplomatic marriage between Ahab and Jezebel the daughter of the Sidonian king Ethobaal, (1 Kings 16:31).[684]

II: the first lady Jezebel introduced the cult of Baal of Melqart in Israel. The king, Ahab her husband, adopted this divinity and built a temple to it.[685]

III: the ritual dance[686] performed by the prophets of

---

[683] BONNET, 1988, PP. 136-144; DUSSAUD, 1948, PP. 205-230; DE VAUX, 1941, PP. 7-20; RICHIBINI, 1999, PP. 563-565.
[684] BONNET, 1988, p. 137; De VAUX, 1941, p. 8.
[685] BONNET, 1988, p. 137; DUSSAUD, 1948, p. 209.
[686] BONNET, 1988, p. 141; LAFORGUE, 1956, p. 27; HELIODORUS, IV, 17:1.

Baal (1 Kings 18:26) was linked to the dance of the devotees of Melqart, the king of Tyre. About the ritual dance of the prophets of Baal on the Biblical Mount Carmel (1Kings 18:26), (see pages (61-65). "The sacred dance of the prophets of Baal".

IV: this has to do with the mockery of Elijah saying that "Surely he is a god! Perhaps he is deep in thought, busy, or travelling. Maybe he is sleeping and must be awakened" (see 1 Kgs 18:27) a reference to Melqart as the deity of the Phoenician merchants and sailors, according to "the religious ideology of the commercial expansion role played by the deity Melqart in the life of his devotees and worshippers to guarantee them protection in crossing the seas throughout the Mediterranean world, and that his cult was very popular in all Phoenician colonies, from Cyprus to Malta, from Carthage to the whole of north Africa, from Sardinia to Iberia."[687]

The Phoenicians had dominion over the sea known as (the Thalassocracy). Homer in (Iliad, XXIII, 743-745)[688], describes the Sidonians and Phoenicians as craftsmen and navigators. According to Aubet, the father of Jezebel, Ethobaal was an important king of Sidon and Tyre and the king who is the first to develop business activities. About Ethobaal, Aubet,[689] affirms he "first he will call himself king of Sidonians and re-establish his domination over all the southern territory of Phoenicia. Under his kingship both Sidon and Tyre became one state. A single policy will be developed under the sovereignty of a single monarch residing in Tyre. It's he who promoted the commercial sphere in Asia."[690] The scholar De Vaux said that: "the Tyrians

---

[687] RIBICHINI, 1999, p. 564.
[688] GRAS, ROUILLARD AND TEIXIDOR, 1995, p. 33.
[689] AUBET, 1993, pp. 37-38.
[690] AUBET, 1993, pp. 37-38.

had given to their god some features of their own character. They had imagined him industrious and a trader like themselves, and that is enough to explain the word of Elijah" (1 Kgs 18:27).[691]

And finally,

V: the last reason concerns the expression: "he must be awakened," (1Kgs 18: 27d). It was referring to the rising or to the ἔγεροις (the resurrection) of Melqart, and the "fire"[692] in (1Kgs 18:23-25) which was to come to consume the pieces of bull put on the altar, was compared to the burning on the pyre in the ceremony of the *egersis* of Melqart.

All these five arguments lead the proponents of this first view[693] to support the claim that the Baal Melqart is the Baal in the Biblical text (1 Kgs 18). In the ordeal of Biblical Mount Carmel YHWH was represented by the prophet Elijah, and the divine couple Baal and Asherah (1Kgs18:19),[694] were represented by their prophets. In another piece of evidence in the Phoenician epic dating from the fifteenth century BC found at Ras Shamra, the goddess Asherah was given the title "the Lady Asherah of Sea," cf. (Virolleaud):[695]

...Comme Aleïn (fils de) (14) Baal était mort; comme avait péri le *Zbl* du

Baal (15) de la Terre, El cria (16) à la Maîtresse, Ashérat de la Mer: « Écoute,

(17) Maîtresse, Ashérat de la Mer! Donne (-moi) (18) l'un de tes [fils ?] que

je (le) fasse régner. », (19) La Maîtresse, Ashérat de la Mer, répondit: (20) « Non!...

---

[691] De VAUX, 1941, p. 15.
[692] DUSSAUD, 1948, p. 209.
693 BONNET, 1988, pp. 136-144; DUSSAUD, 1948, pp. 205-230; RIBICHINI, 1999, pp. 563-565; DE VAUX, 1941, pp. 7-20.
[694] DHORME, 1928, pp. 178-179; DUSSAUD, 1931, p. 369, note 4.
[695] VIROLLEAUD, 1931, p. 195; PATAI, 1990, p. 37.

As Aleïn (son of) Baal was dead; as had perished the *Zbl* of Baal of the Earth, El cried (16) to the Lady, Ashérat of the Sea. "Listen, Lady Ashérat of the Sea! Give (me) (18) one of your (sons) so that I can make him reign", (19) The Lady, Ashérat of the Sea, replied: (20) No!..."

Probably the title Ashérat de la Mer, (the Lady Asherah of the Sea) associated with this goddess is descriptive of her domain of power. This goddess was also connected to fertility,[696] and was a goddess in Israel during the Iron Age.[697] The term Asherah can designate both the goddess and the sacred tree planted beside an altar.[698] For more information about "Asherah."[699] In the context of 1Kings 18, there is a dual legitimate standing between Baal and YHWH over who has the right to be worshipped as God and Lord of Israel. The central point of this ordeal is: אֲשֶׁר־יַעֲנֶה בָאֵשׁ הָאֱלֹהִים "The god who answers by fire", (1Kgs 18:24). The dilemma must by solved by YHWH and Baal. Now, what are the strengths and the weaknesses of this first view? Our observation, in this part of our research is this: the celebration of the resurrection of Baal-Melqart and the ordeal of the Biblical Mount of Carmel were celebrated in two different contexts. The ἔγερσίς was the annual ritual, but the sacrifice on Mount Carmel was exceptional.[700] The comparison in this part of our research has the aim of seeing if there are some elements in the two cases that can lead us to support this view.

---

[696] WALTON, 2009, p. 339.
[697] SMITH, 1994, p. 206; HADLEY, 2006, p. 6.
[698] DAY, 1986, p. 401; LEMAIRE, 1977, p. 605.
[699] HADLEY, 2000.
[700] NOCQUET, 2004, p. 292.

Synthesis 1

The strengths and weaknesses of the first hypothesis

According to Katzenstein[701] the god that dwells on Mount Carmel is the lord of the skies", or "the master of heavens" namely, Baal Shamin. For him, the Baal whose altar was established in Samaria (1 Kings 16:32-33), is in fact, and for certain, the god Baal Melqart, and the ordeal in 1 Kings 18:20-28) evokes Baal Shamin. For him, the use of בְּעָלִים (v. 18) explains the existence of these two different divinities. The deity Baal Melqart had his cult in Samaria and Baal Shamin on Mount Carmel. Saying this, Katzenstein,[702] did not explain to us why Baal Melqart was chosen for Samaria and Baal Shamin for Mount Carmel. For Keel and Uehlinger,[703] the Baal against whom the prophet Elijah fought on Mount Carmel in 1Kings 18:17-40 was not the Storm-god of MB II.B period (1800-1550 BC), but was the Baal Shamin, the "lord of heveans." What in our research into the nature and functions of Baal Shamin can enlighten us about the third hypothesis concerning the Baal of Mount Carmel?

We recognize that among the three deities of our study, the god Baal Shamin has been difficult to study. This god does not have mythology like Baal Hadad, Tammuz... The only material is found in epigraphic studies. It is in these epigraphs concerning

---

[701] KATZENSTEIN, 1991, pp. 187-191.
[702] KATZENSTEIN, 1991, pp. 187-191.
[703] KEEL and UEHLINGER, 2001, p. 257.

Baal Shamin that we must seek information about his nature and functions. The Baal Shamin was worshipped during the tenth century BC to the third century AD period.[704] The inscription of the king Yehimilk, king of Byblos dating from the tenth century BC,[705] showed that the deity Baal Shamem was probably the supreme god of Byblos. He was not the representative god of the Phoenician kingdom like Baal Melqart of Tyre, and present in Phoenician colonies.[706] It may be said that Baal Melqart had been the diplomatic deity of Phoenician kingdom. The god was exported by traders and navigators, and was established, and worshipped in the different Phoenician colonies. He presided over all colonial business, and the religion was used for political ends.[707] As far as the epigraphs and the thunder or the ear of grain, the lightning or bunch of spikes, bunches of ears of corn and fruit are concerned, this material proves that Baal Shamin, the lord of heavens was the deity of fertility and provider of rain. In Psalm 104:2-19, the God YHWH has the same function. He played role of protector.[708] The god Baal Shamin, was also at the top of the list of Phoenician deities who were witnesses and guarantors of the alliance between kings (Esarhaddon, Assyria king and the king Baal of Tyre).[709] All the deities in this topic in our study have been a divine couple. All of them have a consort: Baal Melqart with Astarte,[710] the Baal in the

---

[704] NOCQUET, 2004, p. 347.
[705] KAI 4:3; COLLART AND VICARI, 1969, p. 201.
[706] BONNET, 1988, p. 141; GRAY, 1970, p. 397.
[707] AUBET, 1993, p. 130.
[708] KAI 4:3; 202: 2-14; 259:3.
[709] KAI 26; ANET, 1969:533-534; NOCQUET, 2004, p. 349; GRELOT, 1972, pp. 363-365.
[710] LIPINSKI, 1970a, p. 36 note 3; METTINGER, 2001, p. 96 notes 88 and 90.

Biblical text has his consort Asherah, (1Kgs 18:19) and the god Baal Shamin with his consort Astarte, (KAI 266:2):

(L 1-3): "The Lord of kings, Pharaoh, your slave Adon, the king of ... May Astarte, the mistress of heaven and earth, and the god Baal Shamin always seek salvation for the Lord of kings, Pharaoh and they consolidate the throne of the Lord of kings, the pharaoh as long as heaven lasts! ..."

According to Nocquet,[711] the deity Baal Shamin and the goddess Astarte would be invoked together as a divine couple.

---

[711] NOCQUET, 2004, p. 351.

Synthesis 2

The Strengths and weaknesses of the Second hypothesis

The second hypothesis is supported by scholars[712] who believe that the god of Mount Carmel is the Storm-god, Baal Adad. We must ask whether the real deity of Mount Carmel was the Storm-god, Baal Hadad and test the strength and weakness of this second hypothesis. In the Carmel ordeal, the sacrifice is a holocaust, because the whole bull was consumed. The ritual was performed to bring back rain and stop the drought. The 'fire' which was to fall from heaven and the sacrifice on Mount Carmel had the aim of causing it to rain and bring fertility. The choice of place (Mount Carmel) is the traditional cultic location of the Storm-god.[713] A Greek inscription discovered in 1952 by archaeologist Avi-Yonah, dating from the second - third century AD, dedicated to Zeus, confirms that the Baal worship at Mount Carmel was the Storm-god.[714] The theophany of Zeus describing a Storm-god known as "Lord of rain and thunder, was located on prominent mountains."[715] He concluded:[716]

> "For without the evidence of our inscription, there are many indications that the Ba'al of the Carmel was Adad: the sacrifice of bull, the invocation הַבַּעַל עֲנֵנוּ ; with the article, that is, addressed to the Ba'al par

---

[712] AVI-YONAH, 1952, pp. 118-124; BRIQUEL-CHATONNET, 1992, pp. 303-313; LIPINSKI, 1995, pp. 284-288.
[713] BRIQUEL-CHATONNET, 1992, pp. 311-312.
[714] AVI-YONAH, 1952, pp. 118-124.
[715] AVI-YONAH, 1952, p. 121.
[716] AVI-YONAH, 1952, p. 124.

excellence; the fact that the whole proceedings were arranged on a mountain; the purpose, namely prayer for rain, which was to restore the fertility of the barren land; the fire (lightning), which fell from heaven... We have therefore to deal with a god of fertility, bulls, mountain, and rain, and lightning in short, with Adad. We conclude therefore that the Ba'al of the Carmel was identical with Adad, the 'Lord of Heaven', the great god of the Syrian and the Phoenicians, whose all-embracing worship was, in the ninth century BC, a serious menace to the God of Israel."

This Greek inscription shows the correlation between Baal-Hadad and Zeus. This evidence and the similarity between these gods (Storm-god and Zeus) make us think that it could be the deity Baal-Hadad who was worshipped on Mount Carmel. The god Zeus was worshipped by the Greeks as god of fertility, of sky, lightining, and storm.[717]

The Storm-god is the Clouds Rider and god of meteorological elements (KTU 1.3IV:6-11). Some iconographies show him holding the lightning or the thunderbolt (cf. illus. 6, 7 and 8). The Baal lightning is the sign of his power and symbolizes rain. According to Greenfield:[718] "Hadad in all likelihood means thunderer and as the Storm-god, he brings both blessings, fertility through abundant rains, and destruction, through fierce winds and storms. His voice (*rigmu*) can be a sign of both blessing and curse". Then, Baal-Hadad or the Storm-god is the deity of fecundity and fertility. In this challenge on Mount Carmel, the context of drought and rain seems to favour the Storm-god. He is the deity known in the Sumerian texts as kù.gal[6] and in Akkadian as *Adad gugallu,* which means the "Adad the canal inspector."[719] Having this epithet *gugallu*, the Storm-

---

[717] HERODOTUS I, 131:1.
[718] GREENFIELD, 1999, p. 382.
[719] CAD/g-*gugallu,* 1a:121; LIPINSKI, 1994, p. 35.

god Baal Hadad is able to prove his power to flash with thunder or "strike with lightning" (CAD/b-barāqum, 1a:104) and send fire.The lightning and thunder are the symbols of the Storm-god. When the prophets call him: הַבַּעַל עֲנֵנוּ, Baal answer us " (v. 26) in this situation, the call of his devotees, he must be able to answer them and send fire to consume the holocaust. Greenfield[720] states, the deity Baal Hadad functions as "a god of oracles and judgement (bēl terēte, bēl purussé)." He did not come to this challenge, in which his devotees called him to respond and prove his power. However, "Baal, the god of thunder and lightning, fails his test. He is unable to set fire to the sacrifice. He is, in fact, no god at all!"[721]

We can add this affirmation of the scholar Parker:[722] "They assume that the Storm-god has gone away on a journey, and perhaps fallen asleep - both are reported in the Hittite absent god myth, and Elijah mockingly suggests one or the other as the explanation for Baal's failure to respond to the rites and appeals of his human functionaries facing the drought in 1Kings." The prophets of Baal and Asherah hoped the voice and fire would come from the god Baal, but no voice, no thunder came from their powerful Baal, the Storm-god. In the tale of Aqhat C i: 40-46, or (CAT 1. 19 II: 40-46) in the Ancient West Semitic it was probably concerned with the cause of annual summer drought, in which the disappearance of Baal causes no rain, no dew, and no voice of Baal:[723] "Seven years shall Baal fail, Eight the Rider of the Clouds. No dew, no rain; no welling up of the deep, no sweetness of Baal's voice."

---

[720] GREENFIELD, 1999, p. 378.
[721] LONG, 2002, p. 216.
[722] PARKER, 1989, p. 296.
[723] ANET, 1969, pp. 149-155, NATAN-YULZARY, 2010, p. 436.

For Briquel-Chatonnet,[724] the pyre on Mount Carmel was not the pyre of Melqart. It is evident that in the case of these two ceremonies, (*egersis* of Melqart, and the ordeal of Mount Carmel), the contexts were totally opposite. The ritual perfomed with the aim of bringing rain and fertility cannot be switched in the context of religious festivity of Baal-Melqart; but it was for Baal Hadad.[725] It is possible to give some clarification to the statement of Briquel-Chatonnet. Of course, the context of the ordeal of Mount Carmel was about the drought and the return of rain (1Kgs 18:1-3; 41-46). However, the aim of the test on Mount Carmel was not to bring rain and fertility, but to establish between Baal and YHWH who is the true god, and who must be worshipped by the people of ancient Israel.

The choice of Mount Carmel is not accidental. The peaks of mountains are the preferred cultic place of the Storm-god Baal. They are the favourite locations on which the Storm-god manifests his power, much better than elsewhere.[726] The different kinds of the deity Baal were located in Canaanite hill country. For example: Baal Hermon is indentifed with the peak of the Lower Lebanon (Deut 3:8; 4:48; Josh 12:1,5); in the Old Testament, Baal of Peor is associated to the mountain of Peor (Num 23:28); Baal Saphon settled on the Shaphon Mountain (KTU 1.41:33-35; 1.65:10-11). In the Ugaritic text, "KTU 1.101: 1-4, the Storm-god, Baal Hadad who dwells on Mount Saphon, holds in his hands lightning and a bundle of thunder."[727] Then, the test between Elijah and the prophets of Baal and Asherah on the peak of

---

[724] BRIQUEL-CHATONNET, 1992, pp. 308-309; 311-312.
[725] MUDLER, 1999, p. 353; NOCQUET, 2004, p. 292.
[726] LIPINSKI, 1995a, p. 80.
[727] GREENFIELD, 1999, p. 382.

Mount Carmel was the choice of Elijah, to let Baal to prove his power on his favourite place. Regarding this aspect of Baal in connection with mountains, we can say that, the Storm-god Baal Hadad was the Baal in conflict with YHWH on the Mount Carmel.

Can all these reasons or elements pointed out by these scholars make the claim for the Storm-god, Baal Hadad? It is true that all these points plead the case of Baal, the Storm-god; therefore, it is important to consider other aspects of the deity Baal Hadad, the Storm-god.

There are some expressions of the irony לְיַהֲתֵּל (and he mocked) of the prophet Elijah in (1Kgs18:27 NIV) like the words: שִׂיג meaning "matter, pursuit, departure or absence." The LXX translates this χρηματιζειν meaning 'take care of business'; it is also means "to be engaged in business" (Bible Works⁷). But, שִׂיחַ means: "he has attend to business"(Bible Works⁷) or 'meditation, thought or worry.'"[728] According to Hausmann[729] the word שִׂיחַ was "in connection with Elijah's mockery of Baal", שִׂיחַ and in this context the meaning denotes someone being "in thought", meaning in this sense that 'Baal is not present or he is en route.' The LXX translates it by ἀδολεσχία "meditation, talking". Although שִׂיחַ could also be simply a variant שִׂיגנוּ (Bible Works⁷). By the meaning of these two words שִׂיג and שִׂיחַ we believe that Elijah's mockery points to the intrinsic character of the Baal deity himself. The character pointed out in the mockery seems to go with the character or the nature of Baal Melqart. The deity Baal Melqart was known as the god of business. Baal Melqart was the "boss of

---

[728] REYMOND, 1991, p. 366.
[729] HAUSMANN, 2004, p. 87.

shipping and trade."[730] Then, he is the god of journey, travelling with his devotees through the seas and the Phoenician colonies. This derision of Ellijah יָשֵׁן הוּא וְיִקָץ אוּלַי "Maybe he is sleeping and must be awakened " (v. 27d), according to a number of authors,[731] this irony about the god who sleeps, makes reference to the *egersis* of Melqart, the celebration of his death and his resurrection. This derision could also be used for all dying and rising deities corresponding to the agricultural cycles of seasons. There are many examples of the gods going on a journey in the mythology of the Ancient Near East. In addition, this disappearance of the gods has vast consequences for human beings, animals, and vegetation. An example is the myth of Telepinus, the Hittite god of farming, ANET, 1996: 126a:

> "Telepinus walked away and took grain, (fertile) breeze... and satiation to the country, the meadow, the steppes. Telepinus went and lost himself in the steppe, fatigue over came him. So grain (and) spelt thrive no longer. So cattle, sheep and man no longer (IS) breed. And even those with young cannot bring them forth. The vegetation dried up; the trees dried up and would bring forth no fresh shoots. The pastures dried up, the springs dried up. In the land famine arose so that man and gods perished from hunger. The great Sun-god arranged for a feast and invited the thousand gods. They ate... but they did not satisfy their hunger; they drank, but they did not quench their thirst."

This is another proof that in ancient Near Estern culture, the journey of a god has great consequences for the land. The vegetation dried up, and human beings and animals perished. Herrmann:[732] "Baal's rule guarantees the annual return of vegetation; as the god disappears in underworld and retuns in the

---

[730] BONNET, 1992, p. 176; AUBET, 1993, p. 128.
[731] GRAY, 1970, p. 398; BONNET, 1988, p. 141.
[732] HERRMANN, 1999, p. 134.

autumn, so the vegetation dies and resuscitates with him." The Epic of *Krt*, is ancient Ugaritic epic poem dated from the Late Bronze Age (1500-1200 BC). In this epic, the tablet (KTU. 16 III, 5-8),[733] are set out the benefits of the rain of the god Baal:

Spy out Baal's rain for the earth,
The exalted one's rain for the field:
Good is Baal's rain for the earth,
The exalted one's rain for the field

About the celebration of Baal, the Storm-god, we do not have any material or evidence. According to Mettinger,[734] the cult of Baal is modelled on the funeral celebration of Ugaritic kings. In this view, the author's main thesis is based on the liturgy used in royal funerals KTU 1.161 and literary elements in KTU1.5-6. By comparing the liturgies of royal funerals, we can understand the worship of Baal. However, we must recognize that it is a deduction or analogy and not material proof.

The mythological funeral of Baal shows the kind of animals killed or sacrificed: bulls, oxen, sheep, stags, mountain-goats, antelopes, (KTU1.6i. 15-20). Each kind of animal killed during the funeral of Baal is equivalent to the number seventy. On Mount Carmel, only the bull was killed for the holocaust (1 Kgs 18:23-26). Nevertheless, we know that myth is not reality, and there is a big difference between the ordeal on Mount Carmel and the myth of the Cycle of Baal. Nevertheless, in the myth, we do not know where the celebration took place. Perhaps, it was on Mount Shaphon where Baal was buried. The duration of this celebration of Baal's funeral was not mentioned, but

---

[733] PARKER, 1989, p. 284.
[734] METTINGER, 2001, p. 82.

the funeral of royal kings lasted for seven days, and on Mount Carmel one day was used for this exceptional celebration.

In the mythology of the Baal Cycle, Baal doesn't wake from his death, but in his dream the god El reveals to the goddness Anat that Baal, will revive (KTU 1.6ii). However, according to the material evidence reflecting the seasonality of the Baal Hadad dying and raising, it is difficult to integrate these two realities (existing reality and vision). Therefore, we can say that the myth of the Baal Cycle was the religious conception of Ugaritic people, and it reflected natural events or phenomena. If we accept the view of Mettinger,[735] the celebration of Baal was modelled on the perception of the fate of Ugaritic kings, who descended into hell as their destiny; but one thing is clear: the deity Baal revives sometime after his death, but the dead kings of Ugarit did not.

We can summarize that many elements lead to the belief that it could be the Storm-god Baal Hadad in the ordeal of Mount Carmel. The bull used in the sacrifice was the symbol of the Storm-god. Another symbol was the thunder or lightning. So, he had the power to produce fire. In the mockery of Elijah, only "Maybe he is sleeping and must be awakened" (v. 27d) could refer to both Baal Hadad and Baal Melqart, like all others death-rebirth-deities: Tammuz, the Sumerian shepherd-god and god of vegetation; Eshmun, the Phoenician god of healing and the god Adonis, the Greek god of beauty and desire.

The period of the challenge on Mount Carmel was situated during the reign of the king Ahab (874-853 BC). The prophets of Baal and Asherah had the support of the queen Jezebel (1Kgs 18:19), because they "eat at Jezebel's table." The reaction of the first

---

[735] METTINGER, 2001, p. 82.

lady, Jezebel, after the massacre of the prophets of Baal and Asherah (1Kgs 18:40; 19:1-3) showed by her attitude, that the Baal in question on Mount Carmel was the Baal of her country (Tyre). It is obvious that Jezebel had been the promoter of the Tyrian Baal, Melqart, who had been in the conflict with YHWH on Mount Carmel.[736] We can add to this the assumption of Bronner,[737] that the deity Baal: "to which Jezebel was so fanatically attached is generally called Melkart". The queen Jezebel demonstrates by her attitude after the killing of Baal prophets and Asherah that it was she who "propagated the worship" of this deity Baal and Asherah.[738]

---

[736] Ant. J. VIII: 316-318; MULDER, 1975, p. 195; RUSAK, 2008, p. 31.
[737] BRONNER, 1968, p. 11.
[738] BRONNER, 1968, p. 13.

Synthesis 3

The Strengths and the Weaknesses of the third hypothesis

The detail of the fire is important for the Baal-Melqart and the element of challenge in the ordeal of the Mount Carmel. In the ἔγερσίς (the resurrection) of Melqart, the fire plays an important role. It will be used to burn the god Baal-Melqart on the pyre.[739] He is known to be ἄναξ πυρός "the lord of fire."[740] This fact does not prove that the god Baal-Melqart can produce the fire himself, but only affirms that the deity was the god who was cremated or died in fire. Along with his power over rain, if he was the supreme god of Mount Carmel, he would be able send thunder or fire to prove his kingship and his right to be the god of Israel. The rain, the thunder, and fire are linked together. Then, in the context of the drought which had lasted more than three years, (1Kgs 17:1; 18:5), Baal-Melqart should have been able to send rain after this competition. The rain was not mentioned as an element in this conflict between Elijah and the prophets of Baal. It is clear that rain did not come, and the rain had stopped because the people of Israel were "limping in their religion", (see 5.5.1). The God YHWH is also known in the Old Testament as the God of fire אֵשׁ In many and diverse occurrences, the theme of fire appears.
-Gen 19:24:

---

[739] METTINGER, 2001, p. 86; LIPINSKI, 1970a, pp. 43-44.
[740] NONNOS DIONYS, XL: 368-369; METTINGER, 2001, p. 87.

"Then the Lord rained down burning sulfur and fire on Sodom and Gomorrah- from the Lord out of the heavens."

-Ex. 9:23-24:

Verse 23 "When Moses stretched out his staff toward the sky, the LORD sent thunder and hail, and lightning flashed down to the ground. So the LORD rained hail on the land of Egypt;

Verse 24 - hail fell and lightning flashed back and forth. It was the worst storm in all the land of Egypt since it had become a nation."

The ungrateful Israelites were consumed by fire during the journey in the desert (Num 11:1-2):

Verse 1-Now the people complained about their hardships in the hearing of the LORD, and when he heard them, his anger was aroused. Then fire from the LORD burned among them and consumed some of the outskirts of the camp.

Verse 2-When the people cried out to Moses, he prayed to the LORD and the fire died down.

The prophet Elijah called down fire from the heavens to consume soldiers who came to arrest him, (2Kgs 1:10-12):

Verse 10-Elijah answered the captain, "If I am a man of God, may fire come down from heaven and consume you and your fifty men!" Then fire fell from heaven and consumed the captain and his men.

Verse 11- At this view the king sent to Elijah another captain with his fifty men. The captain said to him, "Man of God, this is what the king says, "Come down at once!" Verse 12- "If I am a man of God, Elijah replied, may fire come down from heaven and consume you and your fifty men!"

Then the <u>fire of God fell</u> from <u>heaven</u> and <u>consumed</u> him and his fifty men. The same demands were made to Jesus by his disciples to destroy Samaritans who rejected Him, (Luke, 9:54-56).

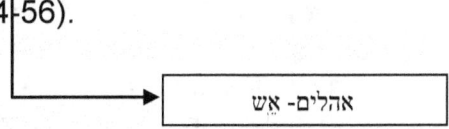

The God YHWH is known as <u>YHWH</u> the "<u>devouring fire</u>" in the Bible

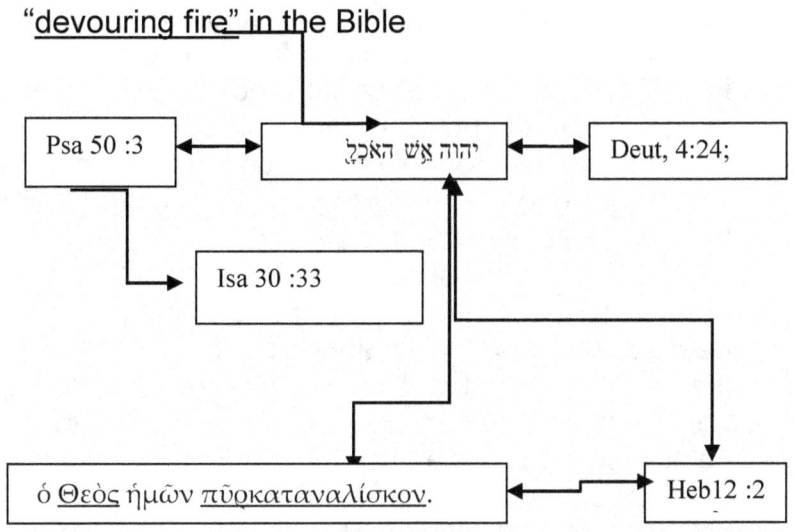

In Psalm 50:3, God is not the devouring fire, but before Him there's devouring fire. In the New Testament, the word καταναλίσκον used in Hebrews 12:29 is the same as הָאֹכֵל which means devouring or consuming. In the two contexts fire is associated with the two deities (YHWH and Baal-Melqart). Therefore, the fire of the holocaust in the episode of Mount Carmel cannot be compared to the fire of the pyre of the ceremony of Melqart. In the Biblical text (1Kgs 18:24) the champion god must be able to create fire or send down fire *ex-nihilo* to consume the holocaust. This god must be the god who is the "<u>master of fire</u>"

and this fire will be the fire which consumes the holocaust.[741]

The prophets are invited to invoke their god. The water-pouring asked for by the prophet Elijah in 1Kings 18:34-34, is "the gesture intended to remove any suspicion" and also to "underline the miracle of the devouring fire" (Tromp, 1975:486). In the context of the ordeal of 1Kings 18, "fire" is the central element of the challenge. The God YHWH and Baal must convince all the people gathered on Mount Carmel by their power to send fire. In this context, the fire of *egersis* in the ordinary ceremony of Baal-Melqart cannot be compared to the fire of this competition. The formula of the competition in 1Kings 18:24 "the god who answers by fire " made by Elijah and the response of all the people:

הדבר טוב "it is well said" (1Kgs 18:24), attest to the agreement of all of them (people and prophets of Baal and Asherah). This approval of the conditions of the challenge fixed by Elijah, is to show that their god will be able to send fire *ex-nihilo* to consume the holocaust. To choose fire in this time of drought is to point to one of the characteristics of this Baal. This part of the text does not make a case for Baal-Melqart.

The two deities have their consort (Baal-Melqart) and Baal in the Biblical text of 1Kings 18. The goddess Astarte is the "consort" or "lady" of Baal-Melqart, and the goddess Asherah is the consort of Baal (1Kgs 18:19). In both cases, it was the divine's consort. The Baal-Melqart has been known to be (the god of fertility) and had agrarian functions. He had power over the rain, spring, germination, and the growth of cereals; Astarte had the power or role to breed cattle and the power to raise the family. There

---

[741] NOCQUET, 2004, p. 104.

are complementary roles for this divine couple (Baal-Melqart and Astarte).

According to scholars Keel and Uehlinger,[742] on the hematite cylinder seal dating from (XVth) century from Megiddo, it was found that the Storm-god was wearing a loin-cloth and pointed head-gear. The Storm-god has in his raised hand the ax, and holds the club in his other hand. At the foot of the god, we can see the bull recumbent. The consort, or the goddess was shown standing, with one of her hands raised in a gesture of greeting, and another removing her clothing. In front of the consort, three bul-heads symbolize the relationship between the goddess and the Storm-god Baal. In the same seal are two persons, one of whom is a prince wearing a coat, and the second holds in one of his hands the Egyptian key of life. For the identical theme, see fig. 31a from Hazor, and see also the two hematite seals, one from Tell el'Ajul and second from Paleo-Babylonian from Beth-Shemesh.[743]

Illus. 36. The Baal and his Consort on the hematite Cylinder Seal from Megiddo dating from the XV[th](?) century. Keel and Uehlinger, 2001:46-47, fig 30.

---

[742] KEEL and UEHLINGER, 2001, pp. 46-49.
[743] PARKER, 1949: n°2 and 8; WINTER, 1983: figs. 269-271, 292. 306; BECK, 1989, pp. 310-312).

In the MT, no Asherah is mentioned in connection with YHWH *as "Yhwh's Asherah"* to mean that YHWH and Asherah are a divine couple. The theology in MT often showed YHWH against *to* other deities and goddesses. Therefore, YHWH's Asherah' was mentioned in the extra-biblical evidence from two sites, *Kuntillet 'Ajrud*[744] and *Khirbet el-Qom*. The fortress *of Kuntillet'Ajrud* had two rooms with various graffiti on the walls and inscriptions on two storages jars (Pithoi A-B). On pithoi A we have this inscription: "YHWH of Samaria and his Asherah" and on pithoi B: "YHWH of Teman and his Asherah." In the inscription from B, YHWH and his Asherah "are invoked for blessing and protection."[745] This archaeological evidence has given rise to much polemic debate among scholars with this intriguing question: was the goddess Asherah the consort of YHWH?[746] If this data causes debate, it must be taken in the context of near eastern religious life and not to impose this evidence on all the theology of MT. In our research on the text of 1Kings 18:19, it's the deity Baal and the goddess Asherah that are presented as a divine couple not YHWH and Asherah.

---

[744] *Kuntillet'Ajurd* is located in the northeast of the Sinai. *Khirbet el-Qom*is in the Biblical kingdom of Judah beween Lakish and Hebron IXth and VIIIth century BC.
[745] KEEL and UEHLINGER, 2001, pp. 224-225; WYATT, 1999, pp. 99-105; DJIKSTRA, 2001, pp. 32-34.
[746] WYATT, 1999, p. 104.

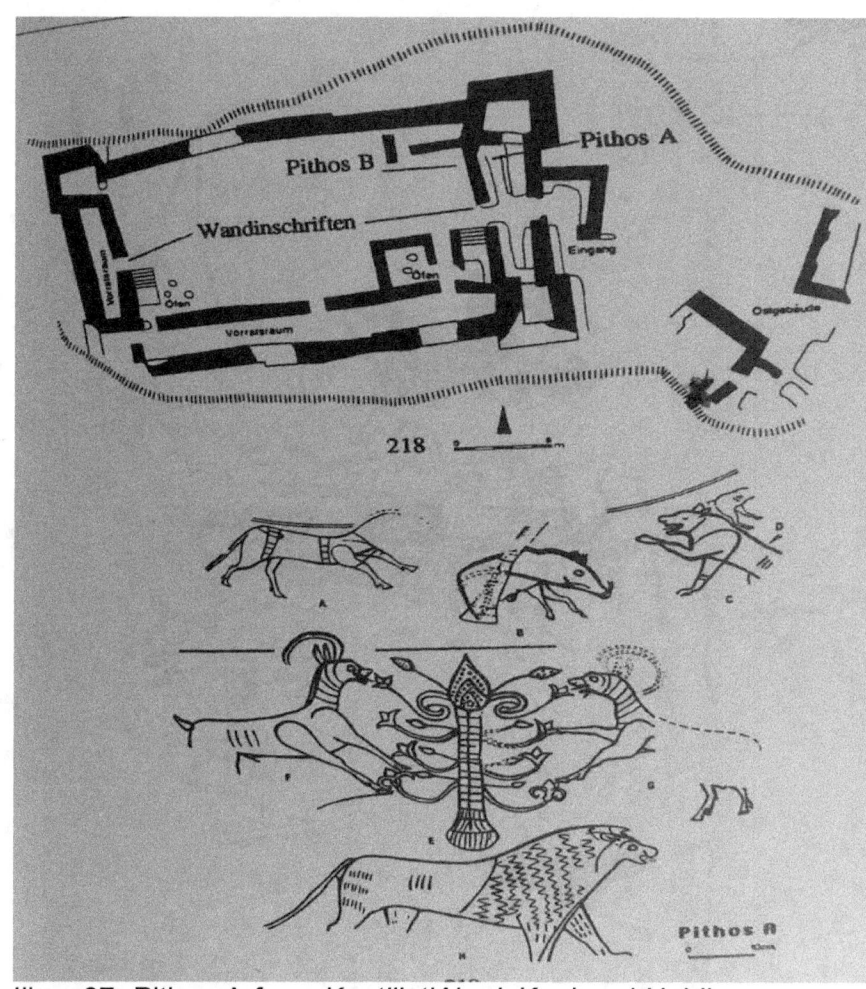

Illus. 37. Pithos A from *Kuntillet'Ajurd,* Keel and Uehlinger, 2001:211, fig. 219.

Illus. 38. Pithos A from *Kuntillet'Ajurd*, Keel and Uehlinger, 2001:212, fig. 220.

Illus. 39. Pithos B from *Kuntillet'Ajurd,* Keel and Uehlinger, 2001:213, fig. 221.

CHAPTER 7

CONCLUSION

Given the different views, assumptions, articles and books written about Baal, our aim is not to write another article or book on Baal's Cycle. This research was undertaken with the aim of establishing which Baal had been worshipped on Biblical Mount Carmel. Who was the Baal par excellence in conflict with YHWH on Mount Carmel in 1 Kings 18? Was it Baal Hadad, the Storm-god, Baal Melqart, or Baal Shamin, the lord of heavens'?. There is no consensus among scholars. Our aim is to know the identity and role of the Biblical Mount Carmel. After this research with the Biblical text (1Kgs 18) and extra-biblical data, we want to present our conclusion concerning our topic: ***The God of Mount Carmel:*** *Contending views about the deity associated with the Biblical Mount Carmel.* Who among the three gods is really the god of Mount Carmel? All the deities dealt with in this research have points in common. They were agrarian deities. They had been worshipped by the people of the old societies of Syro-Palestinian and ancient Near East, according to their role and functions. Therefore, we see the context of the Biblical story of 1Kings 18 during the reign of Ahab and the diplomatic wedding, and diplomatic relationship beween Israel and Tyre or Phoenician kingdom.

7.1. Baal: YHWH'S Competitor in the OT

The thesis set out to provide some clarification about the deity with the common name Baal, before expressing our view. In the Old Testament, the deity Baal occurs 90 times.[747] After YHWH the deity, Baal has the most references. The cult of this deity Baal in the kingdoms of Israel and Judah established the apostasy of people of YHWH. The Old Testament talks abundantly about this god, and his name evokes a deep trauma for the religious identity of Israel.[748] This god, says Herrmann:[749] "...During the early Iron Age the god Baal played a large part in the belief of the Israel population". This deity is the religious competitor god of YHWH in the Old Testament, and was very much detested in the Bible. The adoption by Israel of the cult of Baal, meant that the deity Baal challenged for the worship of Israel. YHWH and Baal are the challengers as masters of weather, rain, atmospheric and natural phenomena, and fertility-gods. They have kingship over the life on earth by the rain they provide. In the Ugaritic texts, Baal has power clouds, storm, and lightning. He manifests himself in his thundering voice (KTU, 1.4 v: 8-9; vii: 29, 31; 1.5 v: 7; 1.101:3-4). He provides dew, rain, and snow, (KTU 1.3 ii: 39-41; 1.4 v: 6-7; 1.5 v: 8; 1.16 iii: 5-7; 1.101:7).[750] In the Codex of Hammurabi, in XXVII. L. 60-67,[751] the king Hammurabi in his imprecation shows the same characterization of god Baal Hadad. This deity Baal Hadad has power over the weather elements. He is the lord of abundance and fertility by providing rain on the land, (KTU1.3 ii: 39; 1.6 iii: 6-7,

---

[747] HERRMANN, 1999, p. 132; NOCQUET, 2004, p. 13.
[748] NOCQUET, 2004, p. 13.
[749] HERRMANN, 1999, p. 137.
[750] HERRMANN, 1999, p. 134.
[751] FINET, 2004, p. 150.

12-13). He is the Storm-god and god of flooding. He is able to stop rain falling on the earth, if the people of the country disobey the laws. The consequences would be the destruction of the life of human beings and animals. The vegetation would dry up, the drought and the famine would affect the country.

Therefore, YHWH in the Old Testament is the creator, and He is master over the waters and the atmospheric elements (Gen 1: 6-10). Other examples in the Bible can be cited, like the crossing of the Red Sea (Exod 14:14-16) and the crossing of the Jordan (Josh 3: 1-4: 1ff) by the intervention of the power of YHWH. Without his power, it would not have been possible for the people of Israel to cross the Red Sea and the Jordan River. The prophet Elijah invoked the name of YHWH, took his mantle and struck the waters and they were divided, (2 Kgs 2: 8, 14, 21ff). YHWH had the extraordinary power to change the waters of Mara to become sweet (Exod 15: 24-26) and the water of the Nile to turn to blood, (Exod 7: 17). In Job 5: 10 YHWH sent rain on the land.

7.2. Which Baal in conflict with YHWH in the Ordeal of Mount Carmel?

In this research, there are two contexts. The context of the nature and functions of these two deities (YHWH and Baal), and the context of the drought, (the life of human beings was critical, and the rain was the symbol of religious and social prosperity). In all the focus on the nature and functions of Baal Melqart, Baal Hadad, Baal Shamin and the Biblical text of 1Kings 18: 1-46, which Baal among the three was in conflict with YHWH on the peak of Mount Carmel? Among the several Baals, the

Biblical text 1Kings 18 mentioned only Baal. If no details about this Baal were given, it was the logical intention of the authors of the Old Testament. For Mulder:[752] "the author of the 1Kings 18 like other authors of the Old Testament, did not intend to give some valuable information about a god, who in his eyes was merely an idol". However, Baal was the chief god in Canaanite and Phoenician life,[753] and he was known in the ancient Near East by the Sumerian and Akkadian societies.

Having completed our synthesis of the three assumptions or contending views associated with the Biblical Mount Carmel in this research, for three reasons we found that either Baal Melqart or Baal Hadad could have been in conflict with YHWH on Mount Carmel. In this final section, I will argue that in the end the cumulative evidence points towards a single deity namely Baal Melqart.

7.2.1. The historical context

The historical context took place under the Omrides (1Kgs 18: 16ff) and in particular during the reign of King Ahab (874-853 BC), who was linked to Phoenicia by a diplomatic-dynastic wedding.[754] Ethobaal the Phoencian king (887-856 BC), was a zealot of his religion, and the priest of Baal-Melqart. He married his daughter Jezebel to the monarch of Israel, Ahab. This marriage might have seemed ordinary and simple, but resulting from this ill-fated liaison, according to the Bible (1Kgs 16:31-32), Baal become Israelite and the people of Israel became profoundly attached to Baal. Historian Josephus

---

[752] MULDER, 1999, p. 185.
[753] BRONNER, 1968, p. 11.
[754] BRIQUEL-CHATONNET, 1992, p. 297.

Flavius brought some clarification about the character of the queen Jezebel, and the king Ahab, the royal couple, and the religious life of Israel. If the introduction of the cult of Baal in Samaria had been instigated by the first lady, then, the king Ahab, to be appreciated by his stepfather Ithobaal, erected a sanctuary for Baal in Samaria and adored it with a full cult.[755] For the love of the queen Jezebel, as well as for diplomatic reasons, the heart of the king Ahab had gone astray in his religious affiliation.

7.2.2. The Ordeal elements

The ordeal elements of the Biblical Mount Carmel (1Kgs18:1-46) and the mockery of Elijah support the case of Baal Melqart. In this connection, we need only to bring out some details of the Biblical text which connect to the Baal Melqart. Fire is important for the Baal-Melqart in his ἔγερσίς, and it is the element of challenge in the ordeal of Mount Carmel. He (Melqart) was known to be ἄναξ πυρός "the lord of fire", (Nonnos Dionys, XL: 368-369; Mettinger, 2001:87). Some expressions of the irony לְיהוה (and the mockery) of the prophet Elijah in 1Kings18:27 NIV like the words: שִׂיג mean "matter, pursuit, departure or absence." The LXX translates this χρηματιζειν meaning "take care of business"; it is also means "to be engaged in business" (Bible Works[7]). The Baal Melqart was known as the god of business. Baal Melqart was the "boss of shipping and trade."[756] Then Melqart was the god of journey, travelling with his devotees through the seas and the Phoenician colonies. This derision of Elijah יֵשׁ הוּא וְיִקֶץ אוּלַי "Maybe he is sleeping and must be awakened " (v.

---

[755] Ant. J.VIII: 316-318; IX: 138; RUSAK, 2008, p. 31.
[756] BONNET, 1992, p. 176; AUBET, 193, p. 128; RICHIBINI, 1999, p. 564.

27d), are elements which make reference to the *egersis* of Melqart, the celebration of his death and his resurrection. Before the Ordeal (1Kgs 18:4) and after, the reaction of the queen Jezebel to the prophets of YHWH, (1Kgs 19:1-2) proves that she defended the Baal Melqart from Tyre, her country.

For the Baal Shamin, we do not have material or details of this deity in connection with the Biblical text (1Kgs 18). The mockery of the prophet Elijah (1Kgs 18:26-27) does not seem to be connected to the character and functions of the deity Baal Shamin. The scholars promoting this assumption did not have any evidence, but only suppositions. It is clear that during Hellenic times, Baal Shamin was worshipped as weather-god, and the people invoked him because of drought.

> The cosmogony and the theology of Sanchuniaton, translated by Philo of Byblos (trough Eusebius of Caesarea), mentions that previous generations in the times of extreme drought entreated the sun for help, whom they take for the single god, the lord of the heaven named Beelsamen...[757]

We can concur with the view of Röllig,[758] that: "Since Baal Shamem appears relatively late in the vicinity of Palestine, it is no surprise that there are no references to him in the classical books of the Old Testament. Mere allusions such as Psalm104:1-4 or Hosea 6:3 to a kind of weather-god cannot prove any argument regarding this god." It is hard to see how this deity can be the god in conflict with YHWH on Mount Carmel.

It is uncertain whether Baal Melqart can be identified as Baal in 1Kings 18, and Baal of Mount Carmel was never identified as Baal Melqart. However, certain elements or details of the scene of biblical Mount

---

[757] RÖLLIG, 1999, p. 150; P. Ev., I. 10.7.
[758] RÖLLIG, 1999, p. 151.

Carmel would seem to correspond to the ceremony of Melqart.[759] Moreover, some details in the biblical text (1Kgs 18) make the case for the Baal Hadad. According to Mulder, (1999:184): "The identity, character, and role of the deity of Mount Carmel as described in Kings 18 are those of a fertility and vegetation god. This fits precisely with the image of Baal obtained from the Ugaritic and other extra-biblical texts." It is clear that among the three Baals (Melqart, Hadad, and Shamin), only Baal Melqart, or Baal Hadad seem to be the Baal of Mount Carmel.

The text of 1Kings 18: 26-28 shows this, the invocation of the prophets of Baal: "Baal answer us" and their dance around beside the altar, after they had set up, particular the mockery of Elijah, (NIV):

Verse 27 "Shout louder!" he said. "Surely he is a god! Perhaps he is deep in thought, or busy, or travelling. Maybe he is sleeping and must be awakened."

Verse 28 So they shouted louder and slashed themselves with swords and spears, as was their custom, until their blood flowed.

According to Mulder,[760] the mockery of Elijah or "the characterization of this Baal is not peculiar to Melqart". In addition, "the cult-cry" is found in the Ugaritic texts: "where is the mightiest Baal, where is the prince lord of earth?" (KTU 1.6 iv:4-5). We cannot agree with Mulder, about this text (KTU 1.6 iv: 4-5) concerning the death of Baal. It is not a cult-cry, but a lamentation. There is no cult in the Cycle of Baal. So this text (KTU 1.6 iv: 4-5) cannot have parallels with 1Kings 18:26-27.

---

[759] MULDER, 1975, p. 195; 1999, p. 184.
[760] MUDLER, 1999, p. 184.

7.3. Final view

We are now able to conclude this research about the god of the Mount Carmel. According to external evidences, the historical context, (7.2.1.) and internal evidences, the Ordeal elements of the Biblical Mount Carmel, (1 Kgs 18:1-46), (see 7.2.2., the first paragraph), we can say that the Baal Melqart was the competitor of YHWH on the peak of the Biblical Mount Carmel. They have (two deities) their consort (Baal-Melqart) and Baal in the Biblical text of 1 Kings 18. The goddess Astarte is the "consort" or "lady" of Baal-Melqart, and the goddess Asherah is the consort of Baal (1 Kgs 18:19). Asharte and Asherah were the divine's consorts. The Baal-Melqart was the deity of fertility and had agriculture functions. This divine couple (Baal-Melqart and Asharte) had the complementary roles.

The story of prophet Elijah and the prophets of Baal and Asherah began in 1 Kgs 17:1 by: "...there will no dew or rain during the next few years..." and after YHWH won this ordeal and Baal was recognized as the impostor god, the return of rain in 1 Kgs 18:45 " Soon the sky was black with clouds. A heavy wind brought a terrific rainstorm...". The god Baal-Melqart was called "lord of fire" $\check{\alpha}\nu\alpha\xi$ $\pi\upsilon\rho\acute{o}\varsigma$.[761] In the context of this ordeal of Mount Carmel, the fire was the central element and the rain was the result of the compition of the peak of this Mount Carmel. The actions and reactions of the queen Jezebel to support the prophets of Baal and Asherah (1 Kgs 18:19, 40; 19:1-3) seem proving that she had the religious affiliation with the god Baal, and that Baal was the Tyrian Baal (Melqart), the national god of her country. All this evidences prove that the Baal of Mount Carmel was the Baal-Melqart.

---

[761] NONNOS DIONYS, XL: 368-369; METTINGER, 2001, p. 87.

Index

Abraham, 178
Adiyaman, 78
Adonis, 89, 106, 238
Aglibôl, 66, 72, 73
agrarian, 11, 75, 99, 188, 203, 206, 244, 249
Ahab, 21, 22, 24, 40, 41, 146, 148, 149, 150, 151, 152, 153, 154, 155, 156, 157, 158, 159, 160, 161, 162, 163, 164, 165, 166, 167, 180, 223, 238, 249, 252
Akko, 23, 37
Akko-Ptomais, 23
Aleppo, 57, 78, 91, 97, 98, 118, 140, 198, 199, 200
Altar, 210
Ammurapi, 112, 115, 122
Anastasi I, 39
Aramaic, 28, 50, 51, 59, 73, 74, 145, 198, 204
Asahel, 155
Asherah, 42, 151, 165, 225, 226, 229, 233, 234, 238, 244, 246, 256
asleep, 146, 190, 233
Aššur, 51, 59
Assyria, 18, 41, 43, 45, 51, 79, 171, 202, 203, 212, 228
Astarte, 40, 58, 142, 190, 202, 203, 205, 206, 209, 210, 214, 217, 218, 228, 229, 244, 256
Attis, 188, 189, 210, 211
awakened, 24, 184, 190, 192, 224, 225, 236, 238, 253, 255
Baal, 11, 19, 20, 21, 23, 24, 25, 26, 27, 28, 29, 30, 39, 40, 42, 43, 49, 51, 52, 53, 54, 55, 56, 57, 58, 59, 60, 61, 62, 63, 64, 65, 66, 67, 68, 69, 70, 71, 72, 73, 74, 75, 76, 78, 79, 81, 82, 83, 84, 85, 86, 87, 88, 89, 90, 92, 93, 94, 95, 96, 97, 98, 99, 100, 101, 102, 103, 104, 105, 106, 107, 108, 109, 110, 112, 115, 116, 117, 119, 120, 121, 122, 123, 124, 126, 129, 130, 134, 135, 142, 143, 146, 147, 148, 149, 150, 152, 162, 163, 165, 166, 167, 168, 170, 171, 172, 175, 176, 180, 181, 182, 183, 184, 185, 186, 187, 189, 190, 191, 192, 194, 195, 196, 202, 203, 204, 205, 209, 212, 216, 219, 223, 224, 225, 226, 227, 229, 231, 232, 233, 234, 235, 236, 237, 238, 241, 243, 244, 245, 246, 249, 250, 251, 252, 253, 254, 255, 256, 261
Baal Adad, 21, 27, 29, 82, 85, 90, 143, 231
Baal Hadad, 11, 63, 64, 87, 98, 223, 227, 231, 233, 234, 235, 238, 249, 250, 251, 252, 255
Baal Malaga, 79
Baal Melqart, 11, 21, 27, 29, 30, 81, 142, 146, 184, 191, 192, 196, 202, 203, 209, 216, 219, 223, 225, 227, 228, 235, 238, 249, 251, 252, 253, 254, 256
Baal Shaphon, 79
Bel, 72, 73
Benê-Maziyân, 54, 56, 75
Bir Wereb, 71, 72
Bull, 68, 82, 129
bunch, 68, 69, 75, 132, 228
Byblos, 22, 59, 60, 73, 220, 228, 254
Canaanite, 46, 51, 150, 181,

257

234, 252
Carmel, 11, 19, 20, 21, 22, 23, 25, 26, 27, 30, 33, 34, 35, 36, 37, 38, 39, 42, 43, 44, 81, 82, 85, 88, 143, 146, 148, 149, 166, 172, 175, 176, 184, 212, 223, 226, 227, 231, 234, 235, 237, 239, 241, 249, 252, 253, 255, 256
Carthage, 24, 52, 61, 64, 76, 205, 207, 218, 220, 224
Celestial, 77, 78
Ceremony, 111, 215
climatic, 104
Cloud, 83
Cloud-Rider, 83
Clouds, 232, 233
cult, 19, 22, 24, 30, 40, 46, 51, 74, 75, 82, 88, 89, 99, 100, 116, 174, 184, 187, 188, 192, 195, 197, 212, 223, 224, 227, 237, 250, 253, 255
Cybele, 188, 210
Cylinder, 245
Cyprus, 24, 197, 201, 218, 224
Dagan, 89, 92, 109, 120, 121
Damascus, 41, 57
Deir-el-Qal'a, 187
deities, 11, 27, 29, 30, 43, 50, 52, 58, 59, 60, 62, 66, 73, 79, 98, 125, 142, 172, 179, 227, 236, 238, 243, 244, 246, 249, 251, 256
deity, 3, 5, 7, 11, 24, 26, 29, 30, 49, 51, 52, 54, 55, 56, 59, 62, 63, 67, 72, 73, 75, 76, 78, 82, 84, 85, 86, 87, 90, 91, 95, 98, 103, 105, 106, 109, 114, 116, 117, 119, 128, 132, 136, 150, 153, 171, 181, 191, 192, 193, 194, 205, 206, 207, 212, 215, 218, 219, 221, 222, 224, 227, 228, 229, 231, 232, 234, 235, 238, 239, 241, 246, 249, 250, 252, 254,

255, 256
disk, 65, 127, 214
divine triad, 71, 72
Eagle, 65
Ears, 132
egersis, 22, 25, 192, 204, 206, 207, 209, 210, 211, 212, 215, 216, 221, 225, 234, 236, 244, 254
Egypt, 39, 45, 58, 127, 192, 208, 242
Elijah, 19, 20, 21, 24, 25, 26, 39, 42, 45, 82, 142, 143, 146, 147, 148, 149, 151, 152, 153, 154, 155, 156, 157, 158, 159, 160, 161, 162, 163, 164, 165, 166, 167, 168, 169, 170, 173, 174, 175, 176, 177, 178, 179, 180, 182, 183, 184, 185, 186, 187, 189, 190, 191, 204, 223, 224, 225, 227, 233, 234, 235, 238, 241, 242, 244, 251, 253, 254, 255, 256
Emperor Hadrian, 53
Epigraphic, 24, 27, 29, 54
Esarhaddon, 51, 61, 79, 202, 203, 228
Ethobaal, 21, 22, 24, 40, 217, 218, 223, 224, 252
fertilizing, 63, 68, 91
Festival, 189
Fire, 82, 189, 221, 253
flowers, 65, 76
fruit, 20, 33, 69, 76, 228
fruits, 34, 75, 89
Gilgamesh, 181, 216
Gönze, 58
Hammurabi, 17, 86, 96, 250
Hazor, 64, 245
Hebron, 35, 246
Heliodorus, 184, 207, 211, 223
Heracles, 145, 190, 193, 195, 200, 201, 204, 208, 212, 221
Hercules, 145, 184, 193, 201,

258

206, 207, 208, 209, 210, 218, 219, 220, 221
Herodotus, 208, 209, 232
Hiram, 37, 73, 206
Hittite, 57, 117, 233, 236
Hosea, 47, 167, 212, 254
Iamblichus, 43
Iconography, 62
Israel, 17, 20, 21, 22, 23, 24, 26, 27, 34, 37, 39, 40, 41, 44, 47, 52, 62, 150, 152, 153, 155, 157, 158, 161, 163, 164, 165, 167, 168, 172, 173, 174, 175, 177, 178, 179, 180, 183, 185, 189, 223, 226, 232, 234, 241, 249, 250, 251, 252
Jekke, 78
Jericho, 164
Jezebel, 21, 24, 40, 41, 146, 148, 157, 161, 218, 223, 224, 238, 252, 254, 256
Jonathan, 164, 179
Josephus, 17, 40, 43, 151, 190, 206, 218, 252
Jupiter, 23, 88
Karatepe, 60, 77
lord of fire, 221, 241, 253, 256
Lucian De Samosate, 208
Luwian, 77
Malakbel, 66, 72
Mari, 92, 97, 98, 118, 131
Master of Heaven, 57, 62, 63, 75, 79
master of the world, 74, 77
Megiddo, 245
Melqart, 11, 12, 21, 22, 24, 27, 81, 142, 143, 145, 146, 147, 184, 190, 191, 192, 193, 194, 195, 196, 197, 198, 199, 200, 202, 203, 204, 206, 207, 209, 210, 211, 212, 213, 214, 215, 216, 217, 218, 219, 220, 221, 222, 223, 224, 225, 226, 227, 228, 234, 235, 239, 241, 243, 244, 252, 253, 254, 255, 256
Menander of Ephesus, 190, 206, 218
Mot, 87, 100, 101, 102, 105, 106, 107, 108, 124
Mount Carmel, 3, 5, 7, 11, 19, 20, 21, 22, 24, 25, 26, 27, 28, 29, 30, 31, 34, 35, 37, 38, 39, 40, 42, 43, 44, 81, 82, 84, 87, 88, 142, 143, 146, 147, 148, 149, 151, 162, 165, 166, 169, 171, 172, 174, 176, 180, 184, 191, 220, 223, 224, 225, 226, 227, 231, 232, 234, 237, 238, 241, 243, 244, 249, 251, 252, 253, 254, 256
Myth, 18, 99, 119
Negev, 35
Niqmadu III, 113, 114, 115
Obadiah, 148, 154, 155, 156, 157, 158, 159, 161, 163
Palmyrene, 49, 73
Papyrus, 39
Pharaoh, 39, 58, 82, 229
Phoenicia, 27, 30, 37, 38, 40, 42, 200, 208, 216, 224, 252
Phoenician, 20, 21, 24, 27, 37, 40, 43, 50, 51, 61, 62, 73, 76, 87, 94, 191, 193, 196, 197, 205, 207, 217, 219, 224, 225, 228, 236, 238, 249, 252, 253
Phoenicians, 22, 23, 37, 39, 41, 52, 76, 184, 191, 196, 197, 209, 224, 232
Prophet, 118, 151, 179, 184, 212
Pyre, 214
Pythagoras, 43
Qedeš/Kadasa, 51
Qumran, 28, 157
Ramses II, 39, 82
Ras Shamra, 83, 86, 87, 94, 135, 225
Resurrector, 216, 218

Ritual, 110, 121
Safaitic, 50, 51, 52, 76, 79
Salmanazar III, 149
Sanchuniaton, 254
sanctuary, 40, 46, 52, 53, 54, 65, 73, 75, 172, 187, 197, 253
Saul, 35, 155, 164
Seal, 63, 64, 126, 129, 245
Shalmaneser III, 43
Sidon, 22, 40, 41, 43, 213, 215, 217, 224
Sidonian, 24, 223
Sidonians, 217, 218, 224
Stele, 67, 78, 133, 136, 137, 199
Storm-God, 97, 128, 131, 133, 134
Syria, 68, 141
Talmud of Jerusalem, 179
Tammuz, 227, 238
Tarhunza, 77, 78, 117
Tell Sfir, 67, 68
Temple, 60, 65
throne, 40, 58, 69, 94, 95, 102, 109, 111, 119, 121, 122, 229
Tiglath-Pilazer III, 39
Tishbite, 151
Tyre, 12, 21, 22, 24, 37, 40, 41, 43, 44, 61, 73, 79, 142, 145, 146, 147, 184, 192, 195, 196, 197, 202, 203, 204, 206, 208, 209, 210, 215, 216, 220, 221, 222, 223, 224, 228, 239, 249, 254
Tyrian, 192, 196, 204, 208, 210, 212, 218, 239, 256
Tyrians, 24, 43, 195, 204, 224
Ugaritic, 18, 29, 31, 45, 83, 84, 90, 93, 94, 96, 100, 101, 104, 110, 112, 115, 117, 119, 124, 129, 142, 205, 234, 237, 238, 250, 255
underworld, 105, 112, 114, 120, 122, 236
Ur, 125, 126
Weat, 132
Yahimilku, 59, 60
Yam, 90, 91, 94, 95, 96, 101, 102, 103, 119
Yamm, 103
Yehimilk, 60, 228
Yhwh, 246
YHWH, 11, 19, 39, 40, 41, 42, 62, 84, 85, 147, 148, 149, 150, 151, 152, 153, 154, 155, 157, 158, 159, 160, 162, 163, 164, 165, 166, 167, 171, 172, 173, 174, 175, 176, 178, 179, 180, 181, 182, 183, 185, 186, 187, 189, 194, 223, 225, 226, 228, 234, 235, 239, 241, 243, 244, 246, 249, 250, 251, 252, 254, 256
Zakkur, 57, 74
Zeus, 19, 22, 23, 43, 51, 76, 82, 87, 88, 231, 232
Zeus of Baalbeck, 23
Zincirli, 94, 113, 136

TABLE OF ILLUSTRATIONS

N°	List of the figures	page
1	Geographical position of Carmel of Judah which belongs to the tribe of Caleb (Aharoni and Avi-Yonah, 1991:50, fig. 68).	36
2	Geographical position of Mount Carmel in the 12th century BC. At this time, Carmel belongs to Phoenicia (Aharoni and Avi-Yonah, 1991:50, fig. 68).	38
3	The Seal from Judah, Keel and Uehlinger, 2001:247, fig. 241a.	63
4	The Seal from Judah, Keel and Uehlinger, 2001:247, fig. 241b	63
5	The Seal from Judah, Keel and Uehlinger, 2001:247, fig. 241c	63
6	The engraving from Gezer, Keel and Uehlinger, 2001:196, no.210.	64
7	An Ivory from Samaria, Keel and Uehlinger, 2001:197-198, no.212a.	64
8	The Seal from Tell el-Fara, Keel and Uehlinger, 2001:198-199, no.213.	64
9	Illus. 28: Seal from Tell el-Fara, Keel and Uehlinger, 2001:198-199, no.213.	64
10	Illus. 10. The lintel of eagles, from the temple of Baal Shamin, Palmyra, Collart and Vicari, 1969: pl. XCVII, 1; Du Mesnil, 1962:317, fig. 185.	66
11	The tiara of Baal Shamin form Copenhagen Glyptotheque, Seyrig, 1953:37, fig. 5.	67
12	The Bull carved on a stele of Tell Sfir, north of Syria, Seyrig, 1946:24, fig. 12; Collart and Vicari, 1969, pl. CIII, 3; Du Mesnil, 1962:328, fig. 5.	68
13	Baal Shamin represented in human form, see Collart and Vicari, 1969, pl.CIII 2; Du Mesnil, 1962:306, fig. 180.	69
14	The votive offering from Pamyra dedicated	71

15	to Baal Shamin. The god holds three ears of corn. The divine triad: the relief from Bir Wereb, Starcky, 1949:35-41; Collart and Vicari, 1969: pl. CV, 2; Dentzer-Freydy and Teixidor, 1993:144-145.	72
16	The stele from Jekke, Bunnens, 2006:119; 162, fig. 78; 1.62 m x 0.70 m. cf. also Dunand, 1940:85-92.	78
17	Cylinder Seal of Ur, Vanel, 1965:173, fig. 9. See Legrain, 1951, Pl. 31, 473(U 3080).	126
18	Storm-god standing on the back of the bull, front (side A) of Ahmar/Qubbah stele, Bunnens, 2006, figs. 7 and 8.	128
19	The thunder on the Back of the bull, (the seal), Vanel, 1965:40, fig. 19. See De Clercq, I, Pl. XVIII, 169.	129
20	The Storm-god, stele B, from Tell Ahmar, Bunnens, 2006:156,fig. 56.	131
21	The Storm-god, stele B, from Tell Ahmar,Bunnens, 2006:157,fig. 58	131
22	The stele of the Storm-god Adad from Tyana, Vanel, 1965:183, fig. 69.	132
23	The Stele of the Storm-god from Niğde, Bunnens, 2006:163, fig.87.	133
24	The Storm-god and the small genie, Vanel, 1965, fig.16.	134
25	The Baal stele from Ugarit, Bunnens, 2006:67, fig. 31. The lightning held by the Storm-god terminates as spear.	134
26	The Storm-god, Stele from Babylon. Date: late 10th – early 9th century. Bunnens, 2006:113; 159, fig. 64.	136
27	The Storm-god. Orthostat from Zincirli. Date: 10th century. (Bunnens, 2006:115; 160, fig. 68).	136
28	Stele from Arslan Tash. Bunnens, 2006:116-117; 161, fig. 73.	137
29	Relief K from the Lion Gate at Arslantepe/Malatya, (Southeastern of Turkey). Bunnens, 2006:128; 166, fig. 102.	138

30a-b	A. Stone block from Tell Ashara. Storm-god figure. H.: 0.90 m. Bunnens, 2006:129; 167, fig. 104.	139
31	Orthostat from the Aleppo Citadel. Storm-god facing a king. Bunnens, 2006:130; 168, fig. 106.	140
32	The eagle-headed-lion. King palace G of Ebla around 2400 BC. From Idlib Museum, Syria.	141
33	Stele of Melqart of the village of Breij from Aleppo Museum, (Dunand, 1939:67), Pl.XIII; see ANEP n°499.	199
34	Heracles: Jourdain-Annequin, (1992:62-63;Caubet, 1979, fig.67); pl.VIII-16 from Cyprus (Dhali/Idalion), (Louvre AM 641). H. 55 cm, the head height is: 9 cm.	200-201
35	Vase from Sidon, Bonnet, 1988, pl.1 fig. 1; Mettinger, 2001, fig.3.1.	213
36	The Baal and his Consort on the hematite Cylinder Seal from Megiddo dating from (XVth?) century. Keel and Uehlinger, 2001:46-47, fig. 30.	245
37	The Pithos A from *Kuntillet 'Ajurd*, Keel and Uehlinger, 2001:211, fig. 219.	247
38.	The Pithos A from *Kuntillet 'Ajurd*, Keel and Uehlinger, 2001:212, fig. 220.	248
39	The Pithos B from *Kuntillet 'Ajurd*, Keel and Uehlinger, 2001:213, fig. 221.	248

Chronological Division for the Ancient Near East

(Hess, 2007:13)

Early Bronze Age (EB)	c. 3300-2000 BC
Middle Bronze Age(MB)	c. 2000-1500 BC
Middle Bronze Age IIA	c. 1850-1750BC
Middle Bronze Age IIB	c. 1750-1650 BC
Middle Bronze Age IIC	c. 1650-1550 BC
Late Bronze Age	1550-1200 BC
Late Bronze Age IA	1550-1450 BC
Late Bronze IB	c. 1450-1400 BC
Late Bronze IIA	c. 1400-1300 BC
Late Bronze IIB	c. 1300-1200 BC
Iron Age	c. 1200-586 BC
Iron Age IA	c. 1200-1100 BC
Iron Age IB	c. 1100-1000 BC
Iron Age IIA	c. 1000-900 BC
Iron Age IIB	c. 900-700BC
Iron Age IIC	c. 700-586 BC
Neo-Babylonian	586-539 BC
Persian	539-332 BC
Hellenistic	332-53 BC

BIBLIOGRAPHY

- ABEL, F., 1908. Inscriptions de la Transjordanie et de Haute Galilée, in RB, n°5, pp. 567-578.
- AHARONI, Y., 1962. *The Land of Israel in Biblical times, a geography history.* Jerusalem, Bialik Institute.
- AHLSTRÖM W.G., 1992. *The Early History of Ancient Palestine from the Paleolithic to Alexander's Conquest.* Sheffield, England, JSOT Press.
- AHLSTRÖM, W.G., 1982. Royal administration and national religion in ancient Palestine, Leiden, Holland, Brill.
- ALAN, J.H and RUSSELL, G., 1990. From Carmel to Horeb : Elijah in crisis, edited by Alan J. Hauser, and Russell Gregory, Sheffield, Shffield Academic Press.
- ALAN, E. B et al., 1930. The Old Testament in Greek. According to the text of Codex Vaticanus, Supplemented from other uncial Manuscripts, with a critical apparatus containing the variants of the chief ancient authorities for the text of the Septuagint. Volume I and II Kings, The University Press, Cambridge.
- ALBRIGHT, W.F. 1942. Archaeology and the religion of Israel. Baltimore, USA, The Johns Hopkins Press.
- ALLAN, R.P., 1998. The Royal God: Enthronement Festivals in Ancient Israel and Ugaritic? *JSOT Sup, 259.* Sheffield, Sheffield Academic Press.
- ALT, A., 1935. "Das Gottesurteil auf dem Karmel' in *Kleine Schriften zur Geschiche Israel II,* Mohr,

- Tübigen, 1953, pp. 135-149.
- ALTER, R. 1981. *The Art of Biblical Narrative.* Edited by Alter R. New-York.
- ATTRIDE, A. et al., 1996. *Qumran cave 4, Discoveries in the Judean Desert XIII, Parabiblical texts, part 1,* Clarendon Press, and Oxford.
- ATTRIDGE, H. W. and Oden R. A. 1976. The Syrian Goddess (De Dea Syria), *Society of Biblical Literature Texts and Translations, no. 9*, Missoula, Mont, Scholars Press.
- AVI-YONAH, M. 1952. 'Mount Carmel and the Baalbek" in *I.E.J,* vol.II, pp.118-124.
- BAR EFRAT, S. 1997. *Narrative Art in the Bible. Bible and literature Series* (vol.17) (3th éd.), *JSOTS*, vol. 70. Shieffield, England, Shieffield academic Press.
- BARROIS, A.G., 1953. *Manuel d'Archéologie Tome II*, Paris, éditions J. Picard et Cie.
- BARTH, C., 1991. *God with us a Theological introduction of the Old Testament.* London, editions Grand Rapids.
- BARUQ, A. et al. 1986. *Ecrits de l'Orient Ancient et Sources, Petite Bibliothèque, Ancien Testament* (vol.2), Paris, éditions Desclée.
- BAUGARTEN, A.I., 1981. *The Phoenician History of Philo of Byblos, A Commentary.* Leiden, Holland, Ej. Brill.
- BAURAIN, C. and BONNET,C.,1992. *Les Phéniciens, marins des trois continents.* Paris, éditions Armand Colin.
- BECK, P., 1989. "Cylinder Seals from the Temple of Area H,' in YADIN, pp. 310-321.
- BERCHEM, V.D., 1967. Sanctuaires d'Héracule-Melqart, Contibution à l'étude de l'expansion Phénicienne en Méditérranée, in *Syria* vol. 44,

pp. 73-79 et 307-338.
- BERNADETTE, S., 1999. *Nonnos de Panopolis, les Dionysiaques,* tome XIV, chants XXXVIII-XL, éditions Les Belles Lettres, Paris.
- BLENKINSOPP, J. 1993. *Une Histoire de la Prophétie en Israël, Lectio Divina* 152, Paris, Cerf.
- BONNET, C. 1988. 'Melqart" in BONNE C. *Melqart Cultes et mythes de l'Héraclès Tyrien en Méditerranée,* Studia Phoenicia VIII, Leuven, Belgium, Press Universitaires de Namur, pp .136-144.
- BONNET, C. 1988. *Melqart, Cultes et mythes de l'Héraclès Tyrien en Méditerranée.* Leuven éditions Peeters. Bibliothèque de la Faculté de philosophie et lettres de Namur, 69 Studia Phoenicia, 8.
- BONNET, C. 1995. 'Melqart est-il vraiment le Baal de Tyr ?" in *UF,* 27, pp. 695-701.
- BONNET, C., 1992. Héraclès en Orient: Interprétatons et syncrétismes in *Héraclès d'une rive à l'autre : bilan et perspectives,* Actes de la table ronde de Rome, Academie Belgica-Ecole française de Rome 15-16 septembre 1989, Bonnet et Jourdain-Annequin (éd.), Bruxelle-Rome, pp. 165-198.
- BORDREUIL, P. 1982. Epigraphie phénicienne sur bronze, sur pierre et sur céramique. In *Archéologie du Levant.* Lyon, France, Recueil R. Saïdah.
- BORDREUIL, P. and PARDEE, D., 1982. 'Le rituel funéraire ougaritique. RS 34. 126 ' in *Syria,* vol. 59, pp. 121-128.
- BORDREUIL, P., 1993. Le combat de BA'LU avec YAMMU d'après les textes ougaritiques in *MARI,* vol. 7, pp. 63-70.

- BOTTERO, J., 1987. *Mésopotamie, L'Ecriture, la raison et les dieux, Bibliothèque des Histoires,* editions Gallimard, Paris, pp. 281-282.
- BRIEND, J. 1989. Montagne sacrée. Lieu sacré depuis l'Antiquité, où furent vénérés Baal et Zeus, *Monde de la Bible,* vol. 58, pp. 3-25.
- BRIEND, J. 1992. Elie et l'expérience de Dieu in *Dieu dans l'Ecriture, Lectio Divina* 150, Paris, Cerf, pp. 13-39,
- BRIEND, J., 1992. Israël et Juda vus par les textes du Proche Orient Ancien in *CahEvSup* 34, Cerf, Paris.
- BRIQUEL-CHATONNET, F. 1992. *Relations entre de la Côté Phénicienne, et les royaumes d'Israël et de Juda, OLA 46,* Studia Phoenicia, XII, Peeters Publshing, Leuven, Belgium, pp. 303-313.
- BRIQUEL-CHATONNET, F., 1992. *Hébreu du Nord et phénicien : étude comparée de deux dialectes cananéens. OLP* 23.
- BRON, F., 1979. *Recherches sur les inscriptions phéniciennes de Karatepe.* Publications du Centre de recherches d'histoire et de philologie de la IVQ Section de l'École pratique des hautes études; Hautes études orientales (vol. 2 et 11*),* Paris-Genève.
- BRONNER, L., 1968. *The stories of Elijah and Elisha as Polimics against Baal worship, Pretoria Oriental Studies* 6, Leiden, Holland, editions, Ej Brill.
- BROOKS, B.A., 1941. 'Fertility Cult Functionaries in the Old Testament' in *JBL, vol. 60,* pp. 227-253.
- Broreuil and Pardee, 1993. 'Le combat de *Ba'lu* avec *Yammu* d'après les texts ougaritiques' *MARI,* vol. 7, pp. 63-70.

- BUIS, P. 1997. *Le livre des Rois, Sources bibliques.* Paris, editions J. Gabalda.
- BUISSON, D.M., 1970. *Etudes sur les Dieux Phéniciens, hérités par l'empire romain.* Leiden, Holland, Ej Brill.
- BUNNENS, G., 1979. *L'Expansion Phénicienne en Méditerranée, essai d'interprétation fondé sur une analyse des traditions littéraires*, Institut Historique Belge de Rome.
- BUNNENS, G., 2006. A *New Luwian Stele and the Cult of the Storm-god at Til Barsib-Masuwari*, A.P.H.A, Peeters, Louvain, Dudley (MA).
- BUREN, VAN, E.D., 1946. The Dragon in the Ancient Mesopotamia, in *Orientalia XV*, p. 45.
- CALAME, C., 1998. Héraclès, victime sacrificielle ? in *Le bestiaire d'Héracules IIIè Rencontre héracléenne,* éditions Centre International d'Etude de la Religion Grecque Antique, Liège.
- CAQUOT, A. and SZNYCER., M., 1980. *Iconography of Religion XV, Ugaritic Religion*, Leiden, Holland, editions Ej. Brill.
- CAQUOT, A. et al., 1974. *Textes Ougaritiques, Tome I:, Mythes et Légendes, Introduction, traduction, commentaire, LAPO 7*, Paris, éditions Cerf.
- CAQUOT, A. et al., 1989. *Textes Ougaritiques. Tome II, Textes et rituels. Correspondances. Introduction, traduction, commentaire, LAPO 14*, Paris, éditions Cerf.
- CAQUOT, A., 1963. Les danses sacrées en Israël et à l'alentour. *In Les danses sacrées, collections Sources Orientales*, (éd.) Paris.
- CARTINI, R., 2003. *Vespasien, Le bon empereur.* Neuily-sur-Seine, France, Michel Lafon.
- CAZELLES, H., 1982. *Histoire politique d'Israël,*

Ancien Testament, (vol.1), Paris, Desclée.
- CAZELLES, H., 1984. Baal et Astarté. In *Dictionnaire des Religions*. Presse Universitaire de France, Paris.
- CLIFORD, R. J., 1990. 'Phoenician Religion' in *BASOR* 279.
- CLIFORD, R.J., 1972. *The cosmic Mountain in Canaan and in the Old Testament*. Harvard, USA, Harvard University Press.
- COLLARD, P. and Vicari J., 1969. *Le sanctuaire de Baal Shamin à Palmyre*, vol. I, topographie et architecture, texte, Neuchâtel, Switzerland, éditions Paul Attinger.
- COLLINGWOOD, J.B., (ed.). 1863. *Roman Wall: a description of the mural barrier of the north of England,* Longmans, Green, Reader and Dyer, London.
- CONROY, C., 1996. Hiel between Ahab and Elijah-Elisha: 1kgs16, 34 and its immediate Literary Context, *Bib 77/2*.
- CORNELIUS, I., 1994. *The Iconographie of the Canaanite Gods Resehef and Baal, Late Bronze Iron Age I, Periods (1250-1000), OBO 140*. Freiburg-Göttingen. Deutschland, Univesitätsverlage Vandenhoeck &Rupreecht.
- DAY, J., 2002. *Yahweh and the Gods and goddesses of Canaan, Journal for the study of the Old Testament, supplement series, 265*, Sheffield, England. Sheffield Academic press.
- De CLERCQ, 1888-1890. *Collection De Clercq, Catatologue métodique et raisonné, I et II, Cynlindre orientaux*, Paris.
- De MOOR, J.C, 1971. The Seasonal Pattern in the Ugaritic Myth of Ba'lu According to the Version of Ilimilku, AOAT, 16.
- De MOOR, JC, 1976, Rāpi'ūma-Rephaim, in *ZAW*

88, pp. 330-333.
- De VAUX, R., 1941. 'Les prophètes de Baal sur le mont Carmel" in *BMB5* : 7-20.
- De VAUX, R., 1967. *Bible et Orient*. Paris, Cerf.
- De VAUX, R., 1971. *Histoire Ancienne d'Israël, des origines à l'installation en Canaan*. Paris, éditions J. Galbada et Cie.
- De VRIES, F., 1992. Carmel (place) in *Achor Bible Dictionary*, vol. 1,A-D, p. 873.
- De VRIES, S.J., 1985. *1 Kings, W BC* (vol.12), Waco, USA, Word Books Publisher.
- DEGEORGE, G., 2001. *Palmyre métropole caravanière*, Imprimerie nationale, Paris.
- DENTZER-FREYDY, J., andTEIXIDOR, J., 1993. *Les antiquités de Palmyre au Musée du Louvre*, Réunion des musées nationales, Paris.
- DHORME, E., 1949. *Les Religionsde Babylonie et d'Assyrie, 'Mana", Les Anciennes religions orientales*, Paris.
- DJIKSTRA, M., 2001. *I have blessed you by Yhwh of Smaraia and his Asherah: The text with Religious Elements from the Soil Archive of Ancient Israel*, in Bob Becking (ed), "Only one God? Monotheism in Ancient Israel and veneration of goddess Ashera', Sheffield, Academic Press, pp. 32-34.
- DOSSIN, G., 1938. Les Archives Epistolaires du Palais de MARI, in *Syria*, vol. XIX.
- DU MESNIL, D.B., 1962. *Les tessères et les monnaies de Palmyre, un art, une culture et une philosophie grecs dans les moules d'une citéet d'une religion sémitiques*, édittions E. de Boccard, Paris.
- DUFF, J.D., 1961. *Silius Italicus Punica, with an English translation,* Havard University Press, London.

- DUNAND, 1939, *Bulettin du Musée de Beyrouth*, vol. 3, p.74.
- DURAND, J-M., 1988. "Les textes propétiques" in *Archives épistolaires de Mari I/1*, éditions Recherche sur les Civilisations, Paris, pp. 377-452.
- DURAND, J-M., 1993. *MARI 7*, 'Le Mythologème du Combat entre le dieu de l'Orage et la Mer en Mésopotamie" *in Annales de Recherche Interdisciplinaires*, éditions Recherche sur les Civilisations, Paris: 44-45.
- DURAND, J-M., 2002. Le culte d'Adad d'Alep et l'affaire d'Alahtum in *Mémoires de N.A.B.U. 8*, Paris, SEPOA, pp. 14-15.
- DUSSAUD, R., 1931. 'La mythologie Phénicienne d'après les tablettes de Ras Shamra" in *RHR*, vol. 104/II, pp. 353-408.
- DUSSAUD, R., 1932. 'Le sanctuaire et les Dieux Phéniciens de Ras Shamra" in *RHR*, vol. 105/ I, pp. 298-300.
- DUSSAUD, R., 1935. "Le Mythe de Ba'al et Aliyan d'après des documents nouveaux", in *RHR*, vol, 111/ I, pp. 5-65.
- DUSSAUD, R., 1936. " Le vrai nom de Baal" in *RHR*, vol, 113/ I, pp. 5-20.
- DUSSAUD, R., 1937. "Aliyan Ba'al et ses messages d'outre=tombe" in *RHR*, vol. 115/II, pp. 121-135.
- DUSSAUD, R., 1938. "Les combats sanglants de 'Anat et le pouvoir universel de El (V AB et VIAB)" in *RHR*, vol.118/ I, pp. 133-169.
- DUSSAUD, R., 1946. Précisions épigraphiques touchant les sacrifices Puniques d'enfants, in *CRAIBL*, pp. 371-387.
- DUSSAUD, R., 1948. "Melqart", in *Syria*, vol. 25, pp. 205-230.

- EDGERTON, W.F. and WILSON, J.A., 1936. *Historical Records of Ramses III. The texts in Medinet Habu, volumes I and II,* The University Press, Chicago.
- EICHHOLZ, D.E., 1962. Natural *History: Libri XXXVI-XXXVII* with English translation by EICHHOLZ, D.E, vol 10, Havard University Press, Lodon.
- EISSFELD, O., 1939. Ba 'alshmen und Jahwe *ZAW* 57.
- FABRY, Heinz-Josef, 2001. נָעֵן *ThDOT,* vol. XI, pp. 253-254.
- FALES, M., 1979. A List of Assyrians and West Semitic Women's names, in *Iraq,* vol. 41, pp. 55-73.
- FELLMANN, R. and DUNANT,C., 1975. *Le sanctuaire de Baal Shamin à Palmyre,* vol. 6, Neuchâtel, Switzerland, éditions Paul Attinger.
- FENSHAM, F.C., 1980. ZAW9. A few Observation on the Polarisation between Yahweh and Baal in 1K gs 17-19, pp. 2227-236.
- FLEMING, D.E., 1992. *The Installation of Baal's High Priestess at Emar, A Window on Ancient Syrian Religion,* Havard Semitic Studies, 42, Atlanta:50.
- FRANKFORT, H., 1939, *Cylinder Seals, A documentary essay on the art and Religion of the Near East,* MacMillan and Co, London.
- FRANKFORT, H., 1955. *The Strasified Cylinder Seals from the Diyala Region,* volumes LXXII. The University of Chicago Press, Chicago.
- FRAZER, J.G., 2009. *The Golden Bough, A Study of Magic and Religion,* 2nd ed., The Floating Press, London.
- FREEDMAN, W., 2001. "Theophany" in *ThDOT,* vol. XI, pp. 254-256.

- FRONZAROLI, P., 1997. 'Les combats de Haddad dans les texts d'Ebla', in *MARI*, vol. 8, pp. 284-285.
- GARDINER, A., 1960. *The Kadesh Inscriptions of Ramsesses II*, published by Oxford University Press.
- GARELLI, P., and NIKIPROWETZKY, V., 1974. La Dynastie d'Omri et l'introduction du culte de Baal: Elie et Elisée in *Le Proche Orient Asiatique, les empires Mésopotamiens d'Israël, l'histoire et ses problèmes.* Paris, Presses Universitaire de France.
- GEORGOUDI, S., 1988. Héraclès dans les pratiques sacrificielles des cités in *Le bestiaire d'Héracules IIIè Rencontre héracléenne,* éditions Centre International d'Etude de la Religion Grecque Antique, Liège.
- GRAS, M., ROUILLARD, P., and TEIXIDOR J., 1995². *L'Univers phénicien*, Collection Pluriel Histoire, éditions Hachette Littérarures, Paris.
- GRAY, J., 1970 ². *I and II Kings.* Old Testament Library, London, SCM Press, LTD.
- GREEN, A.R.W., 2003. The Storm-god in the Ancient Near East, Biblical and Judaic Studies from the University of California, San 8; Winona Lake, IN: Eisenbrauns, p. 195.
- GREEN, A.R.W.,1983. Regnal Formulas. In the Hebrew and Greek Texts of the Books of Kings, *JNES* vol. 42, pp. 167-180.
- HADLEY, J., 2000. The Cult of Asherah in Ancient Israel and Judah: Evidence for Hebrew Goddess, Cambridge, Cambridge University Press.
- HARRINGTON, D.J., and SALDARINI, A., 1987. *The Aramaic Bible, vol. 10, Targum Jonathan of the Former Prophets,* Introduction, Translation

and Notes, T.&T. Clark Ltd, Edinburgh.
- HAUSER, A.J., 1990. *From Carmel to Horeb, Elijah in crisis.* Sheffield, England, editions Almond.
- HAUSMANN, J., 2004. שיח In *ThDOT*, vol. 14, pp. 85-89.
- HAYMAN, L., 1951. A note on 1Kgs 18:27, *JNES*, vol. 10, pp. 57-58.
- HOFTIJZER, J. and Jongeling K., 1995. *Dictionary of the North-West Semitic inscriptions, Part one*, E.J. Brill, Leiden New-York Köln.
- HOMER, *Iliad* XXIII, 740-745. Translation by MURRAY, A.T., and WYATT, W.F., 1999. Homer : *Iliad* II, Cambridge, Mass., p.549.
- HUGH, E.A., 1951. *Où est l'Eternel, le Dieu d'Elie?* Genève, Switzerland, éditions Maison de la Bible, p.108.
- HUGO, P., 2006. *Les deux visages d'Elie, Textes massorétique et Septante dans l'histoire la plus ancienne, du texte de 1Rois 17-18.* Fribourg, Deutscland, Fribourg Academic Press.
- HUSSER, J-M., 1995. Culte des ancêtres ou rites funéraires, Catalogue du devoirs du fils (KTU 1. 17 :I-II) in *UF* vol. 27, pp. 115-127.
- HVIDBERG, F.F., 1962. *Weeping and Laughter in the OT*, Leiden: E.J. Brill.
- JAMES, E .O.,no. d., *The Ancient Gods, The History and diffusion of Religion in the Ancient Near East and Eastern Mediterranean.* London, éditions Weidenfeld and Nicolson.
- JESSE, L., 2002. *1 and 2 Kings.* The College Press, NIV Commentary. Old Testament series, editions College Press Publishing.
- JONES, G. H., 1984. *1 and 2 Kings. NCBC 2*, Grand Rapids, London.
- KASSING, P.J.,1996. *Reliable characters in the*

primary history: profiles of Mose, Joshua, Elijah and Elisha, Sheffield, England, Sheffield Academic Press.
- KATZENSTEIN, H.J., 1965. 'Is there any Synchronism between the Reigns of Hiram and Salomon? *JNES,* vol. 24, pp. 116-117.
- KATZENSTEIN, H.J., 1973. *The History of Tire. From the Beginning of the Second Millennium B.C. until the Fall of the Neo-Babylonian Empire in 538 B.C.,* Jerusalem.
- KATZENSTEIN, H.J., 1991. Phoenicia deities worshiped in Israel and Judah during the time of the first temple in Lipinski E. (ed.). *Phoenicia and Bible.* Studia Phonicia XI OLA 44,Departement Orientalistiek, Peeters Publishing, pp. 187-191.
- KEEL, O. and UEHLINGER, C., 2001. *Dieux, Déesses et figures divines, les sources iconographiques de l'histoire de la religion d'Israël.* Paris, Cerf.
- KEEL, O., 1998. *Goddess and tress new moon and Yahweh: ancient Near Eastern art and the Hebrew Bible.* Schelfield, England, Academic Press Schelfield.
- KENNICOTT, B., no. d. *Vetus Testamentum Hebraicum cum variis lectionibus,* 2vols., Oxford, pp. 1776-1780.
- KETTERER, E. and POIROT, E., 1997. Les figures d'Elie le prophète. *CahEvSup* 100, Cerf, Paris.
- KILLIAN, H. J., 2006, *Elie prophète de feu.* Parole et silence. Paris, Publié par le Centre d'études d'histoire de la spiritualité.
- KOCH, K., 1994. 'Baal Sapon, Ba 'al Shamem and the critique of Israel's prophets" in George J. Brooke, Adrian H.W. Curtis, J. F. Healey (ed.),

Ugarit and Bible. Proceedings of the International Symposium on Ugariti and Bible. Manchester September 1992, Ugaritische Bibleische Literatur 11, Ugarit Verlag, Münster, 1994, pp. 159-174.
- LANCE, H.D., 1990. *Archéologie et Ancien Testament, Le Monde de la Bible.* Genève, Switzerland, Labor et Fides.
- LAUNEY, P.R-M., 1937. *Inscription de Délos. Décrets postérieurs à 166 av. J.C*, Paris, n° 1519.
- LAURENS A.-F., and LISSARRAGUE 1989. Le bûcher d'Héraclès: l'empreinte du dieu in Laurens, A.-F, (ed.), *Entre les hommes et les dieux*, Paris, pp. 81-98.
- LEEMING, H. and LEEMING, K., 2003. *Josephus Jewish War and its Slavonic version*, Leiden Boston, Brill.
- LEGRAIN, L., 1925. *Ur Excavations,* X, 1951, pl. 31, 473 (U 3080*).*
- LEMAIRE, A., Les inscriptions de Khirbet el-Qom et l'Asherah, de Yhwh, *RB, vol.* 84, pp. 595-608.
- LIGHTFOOT, J.L., 2003. *Lucian on the Syrian Goddess, Edited with Introduction, Translation, and Commentary* by J.L. LIGHTFOOT, Oxford University Press, New-York.
- LIPINSKI, E., 1970a. "La fête de l'ensevelissement et de la résurrection de Melqart" in *RAI,* (XVII^è), pp. 31-58.
- LIPINSKI, E., 1970b. "Banquet en honneur de Baal", in *UF* 2, pp. 75-88.
- LIPINSKI, E., 1987. "Le sommeil" in *Dictionnaire Encyclopédique de la Bible*, Paris, Brepols.
- LIPINSKI, E., 1994. *Studies in Aramaic Inscriptions and Onomastic*, II, OLA, 57, Leuven, Belgium, Peeters Publishers, pp. 35-38;

196.
- LIPINSKI, E., 1995a. "Baal" in Lipinski E. (ed.), *Dieux et Déesses de l'univers punique,* OLA, 64, Studia Phoenicia XIV, Leuven, Belgium, Peeters Publisers, pp. 79-89.
- LIPINSKI, E., 1995b. "Baal du Carmel" in Lipinski E. (ed.), *Dieux et Déesses de l'univers punique* OLA, 64, Studia Phoenicia XIV, Leuven, Belgium, Peeters Publishers, pp. 284-288.
- LIPINSKI, E., 1995c. "Baal Marod", in Lipinski E., (ed.), *Dieux et Déesses de l'univers punique* OLA, 64, Studia Phoenicia XIV, Leuven, Belgium, Peeters Publishers, pp. 115-116.
- LIPINSKI, E., 1995d. "Baal Melqart" in Lipinski E. (ed.), *Dieux et Déesses de l'univers punique* OLA, 64, Studia Phoenicia XIV, Leuven, Belgium, Peeters Publishers, pp. 227-243.
- LIPINSKI, E., 1995e. "Service des dieux" in Lipinski E. (ed.), *Dieux et Déesses de l'univers punique* OLA, 64, Studia Phoenicia XIV, Leuven, Belgium, Peeters Publishers, pp. 417-470.
- LIPINSKI, E. 1991. *Phoenicia and Bible, OLA 44.* Edited by E. Lipiński, Leuven, Bruxelles, Peeters Publishers.
- LIPINSKI, E., 2002. "Haut-Lieu" in Dictionnaire *Dictionnaire encyclopédique de la Bible*, Brepols, sl., p. 576.
- Lipinski, E., 2004. *Itineraria Phoenica, OLA, 127.* Studia Phoenicia, XVIII, Uitgerij Peeters en Departement Oosterse Studies, Leuven-Paris-Dubley, MA, pp. 268-289.
- LONG, C. J. Jr., 2002. *1 and 2 Kings, The College Press NIV commentary. Old Testament seiries* V, Copyright © 2002, College Press Publishing Co. All Rights Reserved. Copyright © 1973, 1978, 1984 by International Bible Society. Used by

permission of Zondervan Publishing House. All Rights Reserved.
- MACDONALD, J., 1969. *The Samaritan Chronicle N° II*, (or: Sepher Ha-Yamim). From Joshua to Nebuchadnezzar, edition Walter de Gruyter and Co, Berlin.
- MANN, T., 1971. "The Pillar of Cloud in the Reed Sea Narrative", in *JBL*, vol. 90, pp. 19-24.
- MARGALIT, B., 1980. *A Matter of Life and Death, a Study of the Baal-Mot Epic, (CTA 4-5-6), AOAT,* 206.
- MASSON, M., 1992. *Elie ou l'appel du silence,* Paris, éditions Cerf.
- METINGER, N.D. 2001. *The Riddle of Resurrection. 'Dying and Rising Gods' in the Ancient Near East.* Coniectanea Biblica Old Testament, Series 50, Stockholm, Sweden.
- MICHALOWSKI, K., SUDURSKA, A., GAWLIKOWSKI, M., 1960ss, *Palmyre, fouilles polonaises, I-VIII,* Varsovie.
- MONTGOMERY, J.A., 1951. *A critical and exegetical commentary on Books of Kings.* In Henry Snyder Gehman (ed.) The ICC, Edinburg, Scotland, T. & T. Clark.
- MORGENSTERN, J., 1960. The King-God among the Western Semites and the meaning of Epiphanes in *VestusTestamentum,* vol. 10, pp. 138-197.
- MÜLDER, M.J., 1999. Carmel, in *DDD*, pp. 182-185.
- MÜLDER, M.J., 1975. Ba'al in *ThDOT*, pp. 181-200.
- MÜLDER, J. M., 1999. Carmel in *D .D. D* (2nd éd.), pp. 182-184.
- NIEHR, H., 2014. *The Aramaeans in the Ancient Syria,* Brill, Leiden.

- NOCQUET, D., 2004. *Le livret noir de Baal, la polémique contre le Dieu Baal dans la Bible hébraïque et l'ancien Israël*, Genève, Switzerland, éditions Labor et Fides.
- NORMAN, C.H., (éd.)., 1964. *Yahweh versus Baal: a conflict of religious cultures: a study in the relevance of Ugaritic materials for the early faith of Israel.* St. Louis, New-York. Published for the School for Graduate Studies, Concordia Seminary.
- OBERMANN, 1947:195-208. How Baal destroyed his rival: A Mythological incantation scene. *Journal of the American Oriental Society* 67 (3).
- OLMSTEAD, A.T., 1921. Shalmaneser III and the Establisment of the Assyrian Power, in *JOAS*, vol. 41, pp. 345-382.
- PARKER, B., 1949. Cylinder Seals form Palestine, *Iraq* n°11, pp.1-42.
- PARKER, S.B., 1989. KTU.1.16III, the Myth of Absent God and 1Kings 18, in *UF 21*, pp. 283-296.
- PATAI, R., 1990. *The Hebrew Goddess*, Wayne University Press, Detroit, Michigan.
- PROVAN, I.W., 1997. *1 and 2 Kings, Old Testament Guide*. Sheffield, England, Sheffield Academic Press.
- REHM, B., 1965. *Pseudoklementinen*, vol. 2, *Rekognitionen in Rufins Übersetzung*. Berlin, pp. 343.
- RENDSBURG, G.A., 1988. The *Mock of Baal in 1 Kings 18:27.* CBQ 50/3.
- RIBICHINI, S., 1999, 'Melqart' in D.D.D, *(*2nd éd.), pp. 563-565.
- RINGGREN, H. and STRÖM, A.V., 1960. *Les Religions du Monde*. Paris, Payot.
- RUSAK, T., 2008. The Clash of cults on Mount

- Carmel in *SJOT*, vol. 22, n° 1, pp. 29-46.
- RYCMANS, G., no. d., Baalsamin 'le maître des cieux' in *Le ciel et la terre dans les inscriptions Safaitiques*, éditions Desclée et Cie, Paris.
- RYHMER, J., 1985. Panorama du Monde Biblique Cerf, Paris.
- SCHWAB, Moïse, 1960. *Le Talmud de Jérusalem*, Traduit pour première fois en Français par Schwab Moïse, éditions G.-P. Maisonneuve, Paris, pp. 243; 257.
- SEBASTI, M.A. and VERNET, J., 2004. *Ougarit la terre et le Ciel*. Bordeaux, France, éditions La part des Ages.
- SEYRIG, H., 1934. Le culte de Bêl et de Baal Shamin à Palmyre in *Antiquités Syriennes,* 1ère Série, Librairie Orientaliste Paul Geuthner, Paris, pp. 87-125.
- SEYRIG, H., 1946. *Antiquités Syriennes,* 3è Série, Librairie Orientaliste Paul Geuthner, Paris.
- SEYRIG, H., 1953. Les monuments palmyréens de Baal Shamin à Palmyre in *Antiquités Syriennes,* 4è Série, Librairie Orientaliste Paul Geuthner, Paris, pp. 31-37.
- SMITH, S.M., 1986. Interpreting of Baal Cycle, in *UF*, 18, pp. 313-339.
- SMITH, S.M., 1990. The Early History of God: Yahweh and the other Deities in *Ancient Israel*. San Francisco, USA, Harper & Row.
- SMITH, S.M., 1994. *The Ugaritic Baal cycle, Volume I, Introduction with text, translation and commentary of KTU1.1-1.2,* Leiden/New-York/Köln, editions Ej. Brill.
- SMITH, SM and PITARD, WT, 2009. *The Ugaritic Baal Cycle, Volume II, Introduction with Text, Translation and Commentary of KTU/CAT 1.3–1.4.SVT, volume 114,* Leiden-Boston.

- SPERBER, A., 1959.The *Bible in Aramaic II. The former prophet according to Targum Johathan*. Edition E.J. Brill, Leiden.
- SPRONK, K., 1986. *Beatific Afterlife in Ancient Isreal and in the Ancient Near East*, AOAT 219, Kevelaer and Neukirchen-Vluyn.
- STARCKY, J. and GAWLIKOWSKI, M., 1985. *Palmyre,* édition revue et augmentée, des nouvelles découvertes, Librairie d'Amérique et d'Orient, Paris.
- STARCKY, J., 1953, Les proseynèmes du relief de la triade in Seyrig,1953, *A.S, 4è serie*, Librairie Orientaliste Paul Geuthner, Paris, pp. 38-44.
- STRATEN V. F.T.1995. HIERA KALA. *Images of Animal Sacrifice in Archaic and Classical Greece,* Leiden, Brill, p. 88, fig. 93.
- SUTCLIFFE, E.F., 1953. The Clouds as Water-Carriers in Hebrew Thought, in *Vestum Testamentum*, III, pp. 99-103.
- SWINDOLL, R.C., 2001. *Elie un homme humble et héroïque.* Longueuil (Québec), éditions Ministères Multilingues.
- TALON, P., 1993, Prophétie et oracles dans le Proche Orient Ancien. Documents autour de la Bible, *CahEvSup88*, Paris, Cerf.
- TEIXIDOR, J., 1980. Les cultes tribaux à Palmyre, in *Revue de l'Histoire des Religions,* tome 197, n°3, pp. 277-287.
- THOMPSON, O.H., 1992. Carmel (Mount) in Freedman DN, (ed.), A B D, (A-C vol.1), New Haven and London, Yale University Press, pp. 874-875.
- TROMP, N.J., 1975, Water and Fire on Mount Carmel: A Conciliatory Suggestion, *Bib,* vol. 56, pp. 480-502.
- TSUMURA, D. T., 1993. *The Interpretation of the*

Ugaritic Funerary Text KTU 1.161. Papers of the First Colloquium on the Ancient Near East - The City and its Life held at the Middle Eastern Culture Center in Japan (Mitaka, Tokyo) March 20-22, 1992. edited by EIKO MATSUSHIMA THE MIDDLE EASTERN CULTURE CENTER IN JAPAN.

- VANEL, A., 1965. *Iconographie du dieu de l'orage dans le proche orient ancien jusqu'au VII è siècle avant JC.* Paris, éditions, J. Galbada et Cie.
- VERMEYLEN, J. 1972. *Les miracles d'Elie au temps de la sécheresse* (1Rois 17-18).
- VIAN, F., 1995. *Nonnos de Panopolis, les Dionysiaques,* tome V, chants XI-XIII, éditions Les Belles Lettres, Paris.
- VIEYRA, M., 1946. Une stèle Hititte de Malatya, in *CRAIBL,* pp. 130-137.
- VIGOUROUX, F., no. d., Baal in *Dictionnaire de la Bible,* A-B, (2nd éd.), Paris, Lézouzey et Ané.
- VIROLLEAUD, Ch., 1937-38. *Annuaire de l'Ecole Pratique des Hautes Etudes, Section des sciences religieuses.*
- VIROLLEAUD, Ch., 1931. Un poème phénicien de Ras-Shamra. La lutte de Mot, fils des dieux, et d'Aleïn, fils de Baal, in *Syria* Tome XII, fascule 4, pp. 193-224.
- VISCHER, W. 1951. "Elie" in *Les premiers prophètes, L'ancien Testament, témoin du Christ, Collection L'actualité protestante, série biblique,* Neuchâtel, Switzerland, éditions, Delachaux et Niestlé.
- VOELZELV, R.F., 1972. *Elie le prophète: ascète, homme politique,* Paris, éditions, Delachaux.
- WALLIS, G., 1990, קִיץ קוּץ in *Th.DOT,* vol. 6, pp. 274-278.

- WALSH, J.T., 2008. "Elijah" in Freedman DN, (ed.), *A B D, (*D-G vol. 2), New Haven and London, Yale University Press, pp. 463-466.
- Waltzing J.P. and Severyns A.1929. Tertullien Apologeticum, Texte établi et traduit par Waltzing J.P. et Severyns A., éditions Les Belles Lettres, Paris.
- WARD, W.H., 1912. The *seal Cylinders in the Pierpont-Morgan, Collection*, Washington.
- WATERSON, A., 1989. Death and resurrection in the A.B. Cycle, *UF 21*, pp. 425- 434.
- WEVERS, J.W., 1952, A study in the Textual History of Codex Vaticanus in the Books of Kings, *ZAW 64*, pp. 178-189.
- WILFRED, G.L., 1965. "Nebukadnezzar, King of justice", *Iraq, vol. 27.*
- WILLEMS, F.G., 1985. *Elie le prophète, Bible, Tradition, Iconographie.* Leuven, Bruxelles.
- WINTER, U., 1983. *Frau und Göttin. Exegetishe und ikonographishe Studien zun weibbli-Umwelt* (OBO 53), Fribourg, Suisse, Göttingen, (1987²).
- WISEMAN, D.J., 1956. A Fragmentary Inscription of Tiglath-Pileser III from Nimrud in *Iraq,* vol.18, pp.117-129.
- WOLFRAM, V.S., 1994. *The Ancient Orient. An Introduction to the Study of the Ancient Near East,* edition B. Eerdmans Publishing Co, Michigan.
- WYATT, N., 1998. "Arms and the king" in *AOAT,* vol. 250, pp. 833-877.
  WYATT, N., 1998. *Religious texts from Ugarit, the words of Illimilku and his colleagues.* Sheffield, England, Shelffield Academic Press.
- XELLA, P., 1992. "Baal Ṣmd" in *Dictionnaire de la civilisation phénicienne et punique,* LIPINSKI É., (ed.) et al., Turnhout, p. 62.

WEB BIBLIOGRAPHY:

- http://www.alyabbara.com/voyages_personnels/syrie/Ebla/images/museum/element_incrustation/e_incrustation_aigle_leontocephale (Consulted, 09/09/2014 at 11:13 AM).
- http://www.sacred-texts.com/cla/hh/2040.hMT Consulted: 12 may 2011, at 04 h 35 PM